MW00563881

stacked

# stacked

## the art of the perfect sandwich

# owen han

## with rick rodgers

HARVEST
*An Imprint of* WILLIAM MORROW

This book is dedicated to my dad, "Pops."
Thank you for instilling the love of food in me.

FIRST EDITION

Designed by Melissa Lotfy
Photography by Ren Fuller

Library of Congress Cataloging-in-Publication Data
has been applied for.

ISBN 978-0-06-333065-8

24 25 26 27 28 RTLO 10 9 8 7 6 5 4 3 2 1

# Contents

# Introduction

Welcome! Before we get to the good stuff, let's answer the excruciatingly controversial question on everyone's mind: What qualifies as a sandwich? The USDA describes a sandwich as "a meat or poultry filling between two slices of bread, a bun, or a biscuit." No shade, but the USDA dropped the ball a little here. A sandwich can be and is so much more. If the ingredients are stackable with a flour/bread component (yes, including tortillas and cookies), and if it can be eaten out of your hands (or sometimes with a fork and knife), it's a sandwich in my (literal) book.

In July 2021, I posted my first recipe video, shrimp toast, on the social media platform TikTok. The entire world was in a state of lockdown amid a global pandemic nobody saw coming, and I was less than one year out of college, in the midst of transitioning from one entry-level job I didn't care much about to another I cared even less about. Shrimp toast is a recipe that has been published online thousands of times over, but my recipe video was different. It didn't include a laundry list of ingredients or step-by-step instructions. It focused on sound. The chef's knife slicing through and pounding shrimp until it's smushed to paste; the cracking of an eggshell, then the yolk plopping down atop water chestnuts, celery, scallion, and cilantro; the sizzling of shrimp-topped bread in a 375°F/190°C pool of vegetable oil: audible sensations anyone who's ever stepped foot in a kitchen didn't know they could fall in love with, delivered to their smartphones on a social media app best known for preteen dance videos. That video received 250,000 views in two hours.

Since video #1, millions of followers across the internet have listened to me cook and watched me bite into countless "epic" sandwiches across social media. Though, until now, only a select few friends knew food is my culture, heritage, and upbringing.

I have always been incredibly fortunate to be surrounded by delicious food. I was born in Milan, Italy. And for the first six years of my life and every summer thereafter, I spent thousands of hours in my nonna's (grandmother's) kitchen in a little village in Tuscany called Pascoso, where the population was and remains a two-digit number. Thanks to an insatiable appetite and lack of Wi-Fi or video games, entertainment growing up meant watching Nonna prepare enormous meals for our large family and a seemingly never-ending lineup of friends and neighbors from the surrounding area who would come to enjoy her masterful dinners. In Pascoso, I fell in love with cucina povera, or "peasant cooking," which refers to the traditional Italian mentality of using humble ingredients to yield extraordinary meals. This phenomenon is responsible for the inception of many of the greatest Italian dishes in existence: bruschetta, ribollita, panzanella, and biscotti—as well as many staple recipes Nonna would go on to share with me, including sugo di pomodoro (see page 115), pork roast in milk gravy (arrosto di maiale al latte), pastas laden with rich ragù or meaty Bolognese, pork-studded carbonara, turkey legs braised in vegetables and wine, and homemade pizza from her outside oven.

As evidenced by the plump-looking six-year-old Owen Han in childhood photos you won't find publicly available, tasting was where my exploration of the culinary arts started and ended at this point in my life. Tired of watching me grow fat but enthralled by my love of food, Nonna reached out to a local village restaurant owner-chef and asked that she allow her grandson the opportunity to receive some formal training in the kitchen. Chef Daniella owned and operated La Fonte. Considering less than a hundred people live in Pascoso, it's amazing to me that I've yet to taste a better pasta dish in all my years dining out in Los Angeles. I wish I could tell you Chef Daniella was a stern, hard-hitting teacher who would cuss and scream at me like I was a Gordon Ramsay TV show contestant—it would certainly make for a more interesting read. But the truth is, her teaching style emulated the charm of the tiny village: quiet, patient, and caring. Ultimately, I owe my nonna and my dad the world for instilling in me a lifelong passion for food.

I tell the story of having been raised in Italy under the tutelage of a grandmother who frequently catered the entire village's dinners because it paints a picture of half of my culinary upbringing. The other half stems from my Chinese heritage, the Han family. While my mother and her family are from Italy, my father and his family are from Shanghai, China. Italy certainly exposed me to fresh ingredients, early culinary education, and Italian cuisine, though it was really my father who gifted me the passion of sharing and bonding over food. In the years following my family's immigration to the United States, my father would encourage my brothers and me to invite our close friends to our home to enjoy Chinese-inspired feasts.

On the menu? Egg rolls; homemade dumplings; my favorite, "red-cooked" pork hock simmered in soy sauce; and many Chinese dishes my father and his parents would serve that the average American children would turn away from while we enthusiastically dug in. My pops truly had a passion for hosting and instilled in me the value of bonding with people over food throughout my entire life. Sharing home-cooked meals with my friends and father are some of my most cherished memories. Many of the recipes and techniques I draw from in this book stem from my late father and his parents' Chinese culture.

Later in life, I would go on to attend the University of Southern California, where I studied economics, nutrition, and health promotion.

Upon graduation, I landed a job at a hospital in Los Angeles, where I assisted patients with meal ordering and deliveries. I assumed my career would eventually lead me to becoming a dietitian. However, 2020 proved to be a pivotal year for the entire world that would ultimately change many of our lives forever. To date, the novel coronavirus has claimed the lives of millions of loved ones around the world, and on April 8, 2021, my father included. Following my father's passing, returning to work at a hospital where I was constantly surrounded by families undergoing similar hardships and pain was extremely difficult. At that point in time, a typical workday consisted of me crying in the bathroom for hours while neglecting my work. I was in a lot of pain, felt aimless, and knew I needed a change. After leaving my job at the hospital, I committed to starting a new job as an operations associate for a popular restaurant franchise in Los Angeles.

A week or so prior to officially starting my new gig, my roommate H Woo Lee, who had found success posting recipe videos on TikTok, encouraged me to do the same. Remember that shrimp toast? It was a recipe from Ma (Grandma) Han's cookbook that my father gifted to me before his passing. Watching that video go explosively viral brought some much-needed joy to one of the darkest periods in my life. And as a result, in an act of impulsiveness, I let my new employer know I would be withdrawing my acceptance of their position so I could commit my full time and energy to online recipe content creation. The following years' worth of sandwich recipe videos would accumulate billions of views and become the catalyst for a career in food media.

This brings us to today and, more specifically, this book. The recipes here have a marked difference from the ones online, which are more sketches than full-blown formulas and rely on the visual and aural aspects of cooking to make their points.

I have carefully tested these recipes to provide you the details and information you would expect in a cookbook. While I have included some fan favorites from my social media feeds, the majority are brand-new recipes. I offer you tips on how to make that elusive perfect sandwich, give information on ingredients, and tell you about what makes my favorite sandwiches. I share with you some of the behind-the-scenes particulars of how I produce my videos. I tell the fascinating (for fellow sandwich nerds) stories behind iconic sandwiches. Now, put down your phone, grab your knife, get some bread, and LET'S MAKE SOME SANDOS!

Owen Han

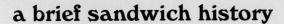

# a brief sandwich history

The average American eats about two hundred sandwiches a year. In a study that ended in 2012 (the last statistics available), 47 percent of adults in the US ate a sandwich that day, usually for lunch, but about 19 percent had one for dinner. Grilled cheese is the favorite sandwich in our country.

The sandwich has been around in some form and by various names ever since humans have baked, but it took a celebrity to give it a name that stuck. That person was the Earl of Sandwich, Montagu, who was a famous London society figure in the late 1700s. The legend says that the Earl, a notorious gambler, did not want to leave the gaming table during a winning streak, so he sustained himself with sliced beef between bread. It gained popularity among the British smart set, and the word finally showed up in the US press in 1816.

It wasn't long before non-meat fillings (like cheese, mushrooms, and eggs) became known. And some combinations became so popular that they are recognized by name. Examples include the Reuben (hot corned beef, sauerkraut, and cheese on rye with Russian dressing), the Club (named for the Saratoga Club House in New York), and the Dagwood (a towering "everything but the kitchen sink" concoction named for the beloved comic strip character of the 1930s and beyond, who loved tall, overstuffed sandwiches). The most recent innovations on sandwich menus include an interest in vegetarian and vegan options, breakfast sandwiches, and international influences.

# 1

# the sandwich kitchen

My kitchen is where the magic happens. I'm going to share my pro tips with you so you can make the best sandwiches you have ever eaten in your life.

# Equipment

When you supply your kitchen with the right tools, you will have fun and success making my recipes—and anytime you cook. Everyone has to make do with what they have, but cooking can be frustrating if you are not equipped to some degree. Most people don't feel that they have enough kitchen space. Although I admit my kitchen is pretty large, even by LA standards, I often feel the same way. So, I look to get multiple applications from the kitchenware that I own.

## Pots and Pans

These are the implements that hold the food while it cooks. If you are purchasing a new pot, pan, or skillet, always get the best you can afford, and it can last a lifetime.

**Cast-iron skillet:** If you have a nonstick skillet, why do you need a cast-iron one, too? The heavy metal construction of an old-fashioned cast-iron pan retains heat extremely well and gives a superior sear to meats. It also does a good job browning burritos and wraps and is an excellent choice for deep-frying.

Cleaning cast-iron pans requires a different approach than other pots and pans. Don't wash cast-iron with soap because it will remove the protective coating that has built up from the cooking. When that coating is gone, the iron will rust. To clean cast-iron skillets, scrub out the skillet with a paste of salt (any kind) and hot water and a sturdy soap-free scouring pad. The scouring will remove the cooked-on food and the salt will kill bacteria. Rinse and dry the skillet well, then put it over high heat for a few minutes to evaporate any remaining moisture. Rub the skillet with a little vegetable oil on a paper towel. Never cover cast iron for storage, and just leave it in the open air.

**Dutch oven:** Usually made of enameled cast iron, this heavy pot is perfect for long-simmered meats and sauces because it holds the heat beautifully. It should have a capacity of 5 to 7 quarts/4.7 to 6.6 L. Oval Dutch ovens are great because they will hold elongated roasts without crowding.

**Grill pan:** This skillet has rows of raised ridges on its surface. I use it to toast bread for sandwiches and make appetizing brown sear marks on meat. (The marks add flavor, too.) Combined with a sandwich press (see below) or a flat pot lid, this is the pan for toasting panini.

**Griddle:** The large surface of a griddle is perfect when you want to cook a few sandwiches at once. Griddles are made in a range of metals and weights. If you are purchasing one, look for models that are flat on one side and ridged on the reverse side to act as a grill pan. While cast-iron griddles are great, they are unwieldy, and I've seen some lighter and thinner versions work just as well. (And when you want to make pancakes, you will be glad you have a griddle.) I recommend buying the size that best fits your storage area. Electric griddles and frying pans are good, too, but you usually get more cooking surface from stovetop models.

## Utensils and Tools

As with my pots and pans, I am very selective about my kitchen tools. I don't collect gadgets or appliances. I like hardworking devices that can do a few different jobs.

**Chopping board:** You want a relatively large, solid chopping board (either wood or hard plastic) for chopping ingredients (of course), but also for cutting finished sandwiches. When slicing freshly roasted meat, it is very helpful to have a carving board, which has a shallow well around the perimeter to catch the carving juices. (Of course, a carving

board can also serve as a chopping board.) I suggest two boards, one for prepping produce and another dedicated to meat products only or one board that can be flipped over to do double duty for both uses.

**Blender:** I love my high-power blender with its big jar and powerful ability to pulverize food. It is much faster than smaller, standard blenders. But the smaller models do a good job, too. I find powerful high-capacity blenders to be worth the investment, especially if you like smoothies. Important tip: If you puree hot food (say, tomato soup) in a blender, drape a kitchen towel over the blender jar instead of covering with the lid while blending so the steam can escape. If you don't, the steam will build up and blow the lid right off, potentially burning you, and definitely making a mess in your kitchen.

**Box grater:** This is the granddaddy of grating tools. As much as I like my Microplane for zesting citrus or finely grating Parmigiano-Reggiano cheese, the clunky, four-sided box grater is still a good tool to own. The large holes will grate onions smaller than you can chop them, which is perfect for some ground meat fillings. There is a slot for slicing cheese, one set of small holes for grating hard cheese, and a set of smaller and sharper holes for miniscule grating of garlic, ginger, and the like.

**Electric meat slicer:** There are various reasonably priced electric meat slicers for home users that passionate sandwich owners will want to have for French dip, Italian beef, and other classics that require thinly sliced meat. Sometimes a high-quality electric knife does an acceptable job, but the slicer will always win out in a showdown.

**Food processor:** For prepping salsas and other chopping, grating, and slicing jobs, this machine is hard to beat. I don't use one a lot, but when I do, I'm glad I have it. One thing to watch out for: Don't use the chopping blade for onions, as the

fast rotation will knock out too much juice, and the onions will be too wet to brown properly. The slicing and grating blades (for thinly slicing cabbage for slaw or prepping potatoes for hash browns or potato pancakes, respectively) do not have the same problem.

**Garlic press:** Some cooks hate garlic presses because they admittedly have only one function. But when you want a garlic puree (as opposed to the tiny nibs of minced-by-hand), it does its job very well. You can also puree the garlic with a chef's knife: Mince the garlic as finely as you can and sprinkle it with some of the salt from the recipe; using the side of the knife, smash and smear the garlic onto a work

surface until it is crushed into a paste. If I am feeling lazy, I will default to the garlic press.

**Half-sheet pan:** A baking sheet is a baking sheet, right? Nope. The half-sheet pan is the king of baking sheets. A full-sheet pan, measuring 18 × 26 inches/45 × 66 cm, is a professional item and only fits into a large commercial oven. A half-sheet can be used in a home oven and measures 18 × 13 inches/45 × 33 cm. Made to hold up under heavy use, it has 1-inch/2.5 cm tall sides to contain liquids. Half-sheet pans are fairly heavy, whereas cookie and baking sheets can be lightweight and flimsy and don't always have four raised sides. Their thinness encourages burned cookie bottoms, and without sides, drips can run into the oven. A half-sheet pan can be useful for much more than just baking cookies, and once you start, you will never go back to Grandma's cookie sheets. The half-sheet can also be pulled into play to become a good-sized tray for holding all the components in your mise en place (see page 6). When size isn't important, I will sometimes call for a generic baking sheet. But a half-sheet is more versatile by far.

**Immersion blender:** This blender looks like a thick plastic-and-metal stick. It can puree hot food right in a pot without transferring to a standing blender. (See the tip in the blender section on page 3 for more details about why hot food isn't ideal in a blender.)

**Kitchen torch:** In my videos, you see me embrace my inner pyromaniac with a propane torch. I like to use the direct flame, as that gives a more appetizing browned surface than a broiler, especially for melted cheese. I admit it is not entirely necessary, but it sure looks cool! There are three main options: The first is a heavy-duty propane tank, which can be fitted with a separately purchased pencil torch, both of which are sold at your local hardware store. (By the way, you don't refill the tank, you just buy a new filled one, retaining the torch.) Next up is the lightweight kitchen torch, specifically for the home kitchen, fueled by butane. Be sure to pick up a refill can of butane, too. I hate it when I run out of fuel in the middle of browning cheese. However, this smaller torch doesn't pack much of a punch, heat-wise. My favorite option is a larger, heavy-duty "trigger" torch attachment for the propane tank, which puts out quite a flame. Be very careful when using this kind of torch, as its output could surprise you.

When using any kitchen torch, the trick is to wave the flame just above the cheese, close enough for melting and browning but not actually touching the food. If the flame gets too close, you could transfer the taste of the fuel to the food.

**Knives:** For all sorts of important kitchen chores, have a good chef's knife that you can sharpen, preferably made from high-carbon stainless steel. Those "never sharpen" knives really mean that you cannot sharpen them! A serrated knife is indispensable for cutting through crusty bread and, conversely, delicate tomatoes. A thin carving knife is great for cutting cooked meat and poultry for your sandwiches. Have a good knife sharpener handy at all times to keep your knives in good order.

If you have an electric knife, try it the next time you need to carve beef into very thin slices, but don't run out and buy one.

**Mandoline:** When thin and even slices are called for, a mandoline is the tool to use. It doesn't have to be one of the big, shiny metal ones. There are inexpensive handheld plastic vegetable slicers that do a great job at a fraction of the price. Remember, these are sharp, and always use the food guard that is included. If you are accident-prone, and even if you are not, purchase protective kitchen gloves to protect your fingertips.

**Meat pounder:** Today's chicken breasts are much larger than in the past, and often a typical half-breast is too large for one serving. Also, they are too thick. Pounding the chicken between plastic wrap or plastic bags to about ½ inch/1.25 cm thickness ensures even cooking. A flat meat pounder does this job admirably, but you can also use a rolling pin or an empty wine bottle. Some meat pounders have a pointed side to use to tenderize tough cuts like round steak, but I don't use that type in this book.

**Mini food processor:** To prepare small quantities of food, especially condiments, this is a very useful little machine. In most cases, you can use a regular food processor, but the little one grinds the reduced ingredient amounts better and is easier to clean.

**Parchment paper:** I don't use this often, but when I do, it is for its nonstick qualities and to help with cleanup of sticky ingredients baked on the half-sheet pan. It is no longer a specialty item, and it is now sold in rolls in most supermarkets. If you buy it rolled up (it is also sold in flat sheets at restaurant suppliers and online), grease the pan first so the paper can adhere and not curl.

**Sandwich press:** A heavy, flat metal rectangle (or square or round) that is stacked on top of the sandwich in a skillet or griddle to weight and compress it, also allowing the heat to pass through the sandwich more easily. You may already own a flat skillet lid that will work well, but the hefty weight of a dedicated sandwich press does the best job.

**Skillets:** Many people have one all-purpose skillet, but a collection of three sizes is better: small (about 8 inches/20 cm in diameter across the top), medium (about 10 inches/25 cm), and large (about 12 inches/30.5 cm). It is also nice to have a very large skillet (around 14 inches/35.5 cm) that will easily hold a few sandwiches for toasting. Nonstick skillets are convenient because they are so easy to clean. Sometimes, when the food in the skillet needs to be browned or melted under a broiler or cooked further in the oven, you will want a heatproof handle. If you have any doubts that the skillet isn't safe for broiler or oven, wrap it in a double thickness of aluminum foil for protection before placing it in the hot zone.

**Squeeze bottle:** Made from soft, flexible plastic, this bottle makes it easier to add squiggles of sauces and condiments to your sandwiches. Adding garnishes with a bottle is especially helpful when the topping is visible, as with Ma's Shrimp Toast (page 90).

**Thermometers:** When deep-frying, a dedicated frying thermometer (sometimes called candy thermometer) is really helpful. An instant-read thermometer is a must-have for roasting meat, and some of them can do double-duty for deep-frying.

# Techniques

There are a few basic cooking techniques that I use over and over to make my sandwiches. Here are the main skills, and they can be applied to all the recipes in your life.

## Mise en Place

I am often asked how I can produce so much content. It boils down to one phrase: "mise en place." This means "set in place" in French, and professional chefs make a big deal about it. I'd like to say it is a chef-y thing and that you can skip it, but I actually agree that it is important. I don't routinely cook "simple" or "fast and easy" sandwiches. I make outrageously mouthwatering sandwiches with multiple layers of flavors and textures. And an organized mise en place is the best way for you to recreate my recipes. I first utilized mise en place when I was organizing and cooking big dinner parties at a USC fraternity, and I have never looked back. Follow the steps below, and when it comes

time to build the sandwiches, you will whip through any recipe, from this cookbook or wherever it may originate.

**Read the recipe:** This sounds basic, and it is. But most of my recipes have a few moving parts, and if you get the sequence in your mind, you will be pumped for success. Read the recipe a couple of times until you can say "I got this." And then read it again.

**Gather your tools:** If a recipe calls for a tool that you have to retrieve from its storage place, say, an immersion blender, get it out before you start cooking. Don't find yourself digging for a tool when you are in the middle of cooking.

**Prep it:** Make the condiments or sauces, chop the herbs, grate the cheese—these little prepping steps will make the difference in your cooking. Do as much prep and measuring as you can before you start cooking.

**Follow the recipe:** When I get questions from followers about a recipe that didn't turn out to their expectations, usually it is because they made substitutions. "I swapped milk for the cream and the sauce was too thin." That kind of thing. Please: Follow the recipe as written the first time. The next time you make it, do the substitutions, if you must. Of course, if you have allergies or other food issues, you will have to adjust the recipe as needed. (By the way, because my followers live around the world, I give both American and metric weights, measurements, and temperatures.)

**Keep hot food hot:** In some recipes, the first batch of cooked food is kept warm in a low oven while you are cooking subsequent batches. You want to serve the hot sandwiches when they are hot (and the cold ones, cold). When making hot sandwiches, get in the habit of setting the oven to 200°F/95°C as a preliminary step, so you are good to go when the time comes to keep the necessary components warm until serving.

**Use assembly-line moves:** When you have to make a few of the same sandwiches, switch over to assembly-line mode. For the sake of convenience, I often give recipe instructions for a single sandwich. But when you are making, say, four sandwiches, use the following process for your final assembly: First, have all the filling ingredients prepped and waiting to go. Clear space on your work area to lay out all 8 slices of bread, spread with the desired condiment(s), divide one-quarter of the ingredients among 4 slices, top with the remaining 4 slices, and cut them up.

## Toasting Bread

I don't toast the bread for every sandwich. When I do, I have my reasons. Toasting adds flavor, as well as crispness, to help keep the bread from getting soggy from moist and saucy toppings. However, sometimes you want an untoasted roll to soak up the cooking liquid like a sponge—I'm thinking of Chicago Italian Beef Sandwich (page 104). You have choices for toasting the rolls, buns, or bread. Exact timing will depend on the heat source and its distance from the bread surface.

When a recipe calls for warmed or lightly toasted bread or rolls, just choose your toasting method, but remove it from the heat before it browns.

For heating tortillas, see pages 11–12.

**Broiler:** A broiler is often the most efficient way to toast bread because you can toast quite a few rolls or slices at once. Position a rack 4 to 6 inches/10 to 15 cm from the source of heat and preheat the broiler on High. Arrange the opened rolls or buns (cut sides up) or bread slices on a broiler rack. Broil until browned, turning once for bread slices, 30 seconds to 1 minute per side.

**Toaster oven:** Everyone knows this kitchen workhorse, but it has its capacity limitations, and most models will hold a maximum of four bread slices. Put the bread slices or rolls (cut sides up) in the toaster and toast until browned, 1 to 2 minutes. If you wish, turn and lightly toast the other sides for another minute or so. Watch thick rolls closely because they will be close to the heat source.

**Skillet:** Rolls, buns, and sliced bread toast best in a skillet if they are weighted down with a sandwich press or a flat skillet lid. Heat a large, empty skillet over high heat. (If you have used the same skillet for cooking the filling, clean and dry the skillet.) Add the rolls (cut sides down) or bread slices and weight with a sandwich press (or a flat lid that is a little smaller than the inside of the skillet). Cook until toasted, 1 to 2 minutes. Flip, weight, and toast the other sides, 1 to 2 minutes longer.

**Grill pan:** The ridges on this pan apply distinctive and flavorful caramelized stripes to the food, be it meat or bread. You can use a sandwich press on top to weight the food and make darker markings. Some grill pans come with a lid that serves as a press. To use, preheat the empty pan over medium heat. Add the rolls (cut sides down) or bread slices and weight the top with a sandwich press, a flat pan lid, or grill pan's dedicated lid/weight. Cook until the underside is toasted with brown stripes, 1 to 2 minutes. Flip, weight, and toast the other side, 1 to 2 minutes longer. Adjust the heat as needed so the bread will heat up without burning.

## Cooking Bacon

Bacon is a popular flavor builder. When it is in a recipe, you have many options to cook it, so choose the method that you prefer. The exact cooking time will depend on whether you use standard or thick-cut bacon.

**Fried:** The secret to skillet-cooked bacon is starting it in a cold skillet. This helps render the fat more slowly for even cooking and browning. Place the sliced bacon in a single layer (it can overlap slightly, as it will shrink) in a cold large skillet, preferably cast-iron. Cook over medium heat, flipping the bacon halfway through cooking, until crisp and browned, 8 to 10 minutes. Transfer to paper towels to drain and cool. Reserve the bacon fat for another use, if desired.

**Baked:** This is a great technique for large batches, as it can cook about a pound at a time. Place the bacon strips in a single layer (they can overlap slightly, as they will shrink) on a half-sheet pan. For easier cleanup, line the pan with parchment paper. Bake in a preheated 400°F/200°C oven until crisp and browned, about 20 minutes. There is no need for turning. Transfer to paper towels to drain. Reserve the bacon fat for another use, if desired.

**Microwaved:** This method calls for a microwave-safe plate. Line the plate with paper towels. Arrange the bacon in a single layer and cover with more paper towels. Microwave on High/100% power until crisp, 3 to 5 minutes. Remove the bacon from the paper towels immediately after cooking, as it tends to stick. You can also use a microwave bacon cooker according to the manufacturer's instructions. If the cooker doesn't have a lid, cover the bacon with paper towels before cooking.

## Slicing Cheese

You can purchase many different kinds of pre-sliced cheese for sandwiches—Cheddar, Swiss, provolone, and Monterey Jack come to mind. But many of my favorite cheeses are sold in chunks and never pre-sliced. These include Gruyère and Fontina. By the way, I usually opt for sliced cheese over grated cheese. Grated cheese melts quickly, but it is hard to keep from rolling off the sandwich filling, whereas sliced cheese stays put. To slice a chunk of cheese at home, there are a few options.

**Box grater:** Many box graters have slits on one side that will slice a chunk of semi-hard cheese.

**Cheese planer:** To use, draw the planer across a flat side of the cheese to create thin slices.

**Cheese slicer:** This tool has a thin wire stretched taut on a handle and cuts right through semi-firm cheese. It isn't meant to be used on hard cheeses, such as Parmigiano-Reggiano.

**Knife:** Of course, a knife works, but it makes thicker slices and is slower than the other methods. If you use a knife, it should have a thin blade.

**Swivel vegetable peeler:** This is my preferred method: Use a swivel vegetable peeler to shave thin slices of cheese from a block. I always have a vegetable peeler handy, whereas cheese slicers can fall into the "one-trick pony" category of kitchen tools that I want you to avoid.

## Deep-Frying

This cooking method gives a crisp coating that cannot be matched by other techniques. Once you know the basics, it is as easy as cooking in boiling water. Sure, you can use an air fryer, but I still prefer the OG method of a pot with hot oil on the stove. The problem with air fryers is that you are restricted by the size limitations of your model.

Here's how deep-frying works: Add the food to hot oil, and the item cooks from the outside to the inside, turning an appetizing and crunchy golden brown in the process. The oil must be hot enough to cook steadily, crisping the surface but heating the interior. If the oil is too hot, the outside will burn by the time the inside is done. If it is too low, the food will soak up the oil and become greasy. That's why a deep-frying thermometer is important when cooking in a large saucepan. When you use a skillet with a shallower amount of oil, there is a visual clue that works (coming up below).

Never skimp on the oil because the food must swim in it to fry. I will often tell you how deep the oil needs to be in the pot or skillet for successful deep-frying. Some people advise cooling, straining, and refrigerating the leftover oil for another deep-frying session. I don't do this because, frankly, very few homes deep-fry often enough to make this practical. The best oils for deep-frying are usually canola, vegetable, and peanut.

The following is a game plan for deep-frying.

**The right pot:** You need a heavy pot, preferably cast iron, for the oil, with about a 5-quart/4.7 L capacity. Sometimes, for thin or wide items, you can use a large skillet with sides about 3 inches/7.5 cm high.

**Temperature control:** A thermometer is a good way to check the oil temperature, but not always. When deep-frying in a skillet, the depth is usually too shallow to get an accurate reading. The classic low-tech way to check oil temperature is to add a cube of bread or a piece of the food to be fried to the oil. If it starts to bubble and brown immediately, the oil is ready. If you are cooking in a skillet, oil heated to the correct temperature for deep-frying will be shimmering. Never heat oil until it is smoking. When it reaches that state, it means the oil is breaking down and it will taste odd.

**Don't crowd:** Add the food in batches to avoid overcrowding. Not only will crowding make the food soggy (from accumulated steam escaping from the food as it cooks), but the oil may bubble over.

When food is added to the hot oil, the temperature will drop. Adjust the heat so the oil stays at its optimum temperature. The oil should be bubbling around the food but not browning too rapidly. When you cook in batches, let the oil return to the frying temperature before adding more food.

**Straining:** A wire spider, wok strainer, or mesh skimmer, all sold at Asian markets and online, are the best tools for removing the food from the oil, although a slotted spoon can stand in.

**Draining:** Most cooks habitually drain fried food on paper towels or brown paper bags, but both are imperfect. When food is drained on paper, steam builds up where the food touches the paper, and before you know it, the nice crunchy coating turns limp. Instead, put the food on a wire rack set over a half-sheet pan, let the oil drip off (blotting off any oil from the top surface with paper towels, if you wish), and then keep it warm in a very low (200°F/95°C) oven.

# Breads for Sandwiches

It is obvious that there is a world of bread out there, but not every bread is sandwich material. Some sourdough breads have too many holes, and the ingredients will fall through. When I make a sandwich, I look for a balance between the ingredients. A soft filling may get squashed by bread that is too firm. A crisp filling may not harmonize with a too-soft bread. So, if you must make a substitution, consider the texture factor. Other breads may be too sweet for the recipe. Even with that being said, my list of bread candidates is pretty long.

## Bagel

The flavor of the bagel is up to you. You just don't want one that is going to fight with the filling. Poppy, sesame, and plain are all neutral options, garlic and onion—not so much.

## Brioche

See Enriched Breads below.

## Buns

These are all about their soft texture and relatively sweet flavor. Round hamburger buns are reliable for burgers, of course, but also some other sandwiches. Cemita is a Mexican-style sesame bun that is sold at panaderías (Mexican bakeries). Hot dog buns are what you need for frankfurters, of course. Brioche dough is now used to make particularly rich hamburger and hot dog buns.

## Challah

See Enriched Breads below.

## Enriched Breads

Bolstered with higher amounts of sugar, fat (butter or oil), and eggs—examples of this category are brioche (sold in loaves and buns), challah (usually sold as braided loaves), Hawaiian sweet (King's is a familiar brand), Texas toast (sometimes sold frozen and pre-sliced), and milk bread (a specialty of Japanese and Chinese bakeries; my recipe is on page 237).

## Focaccia

If you live near an Italian delicatessen, they are likely to sell a version of the thick flatbread focaccia. I offer an easy Tuscan version, schiacciata (page 234), which I developed specifically to split in half for sandwiches.

## Pita

Choose between pocket pita (slice off the top inch or so and open the bread to make space for a filling) or flat pita (without a pocket). Laffa is an oversized Israeli flatbread similar to pita. It is very useful for big wraps with saucy fillings.

## Rolls

There are a couple of considerations to make when choosing sandwich rolls. First is the crust—crisp or soft? Next, the interior crumb—sourdough or not? (The former will often have a lot of holes. The latter, sometimes called "sweet," meaning the opposite of "sour," has a tight or "close" crumb.) Oblong or round? Depending on your location, the soft oblong style can also be called hoagie, submarine, or grinder rolls. French or Italian (including ciabatta) rolls are examples of the crusty variety.

## Rye

I use this on only a few sandwiches, where tradition demands it. Rye bread is characterized by its tanginess. Light rye has the lightest flavor and color. Pumpernickel is very dark brown with a tight crumb and almost sour taste. Marble rye swirls the two types together.

## Sandwich Bread

Firm and slightly sweet, we all know good old sandwich bread. Just don't pick one that is too soft and fluffy. Pepperidge Farm is a solid national brand. If you like whole wheat, use it, but watch out for breads in this category because they tend to be highly sweetened, which can throw off the flavor profile in some recipes.

## Sourdough

When bread dough is fermented over time, lactic acid builds up to give the baked loaf a sour flavor and caramelized, crisp crust. The fermentation also creates carbon dioxide, which creates bubbles in the dough to riddle the bread with many holes. This is called an "open crumb," whereas sandwich breads without any holes are known to have a "tight crumb." All this adds up to a special flavor that most people love. But if the bread has too many holes, the filling will fall through. The problem is accentuated when you cut the loaf crosswise into traditional slices, as the holes are more likely to appear. The better the sourdough, the more holes, so it becomes a catch-22.

There are solutions to get that unique sourdough flavor and chew but avoid the food falling through the holes and into your lap. One is to simply purchase sourdough rolls and use a serrated knife to split them open lengthwise. You can also make your own "rolls" from a sourdough loaf. Start with a large, wide loaf (often called a bâtard, but this also works with a narrow baguette). Cut the loaf crosswise into chunks 4 to 6 inches/10 to 15 cm long. Split each chunk of bread through its middle and . . . voilà! You have a sourdough roll that doesn't look like Swiss cheese. This is especially useful with ciabatta, a bread that is characterized by its weblike interior. The exterior crust keeps the ingredients in place, and you get great flavor.

## Tortillas

Staples in Mexican cooking, the classics are the flour and corn versions, although you will find multigrain and gluten-free variations. I use three basic sizes: street taco (about 4½ inches/11 cm), taco (about 6 inches/15 cm), and burrito (about

10 inches/25 cm). Corn tortillas are only made in smaller sizes because, lacking gluten to hold them together, wider diameters fall apart. Tortillas must be warmed before folding. You can follow the heating instructions on the package, but, basically, you have a few options for warming.

**Microwave:** This is the easiest way. Stack 6 tortillas. Wrap in a swath of paper towels and sprinkle the wrapped stack with water. Microwave on High/100% power until heated through, about 45 seconds.

**Griddle:** A griddle is great for heating up tortillas because it will hold a few at a time, and the light toasting adds flavor. Heat an ungreased griddle over medium heat. Add the tortillas and cook, turning halfway through, until warmed through, about 30 seconds. Don't toast them until they are browned.

**Grill:** If you already have the grill heated for a filling, use it to warm the tortillas, too. This is an especially good method for a lot of tortillas. Adjust the heat to Medium (about 500°F/260°C) on a gas grill. For a charcoal grill, the coals probably will have burned down to the proper moderate temperature by the time the filling has been cooked anyway. Brush the grill grate clean and don't oil it. Lay the tortillas on the grate and cook, turning once, until seared with grill marks and heated through, 15 to 30 seconds. Watch out for overcooking—they should be warmed, not toasted. In many of my recipes, I put the burrito or wrap in a skillet for a final toasting anyway, a step that adds flavor and crunch.

**Skillet:** Because of its diameter, the average skillet works best to warm small amounts of tortillas or for browning a couple of burritos or wraps. Treat it like a griddle.

**Oven:** This is another good method for heating a larger number of tortillas. Place the tortillas directly on the oven rack (a baking sheet is optional) and bake in a preheated 350°F/180°C oven until heated through and pliable, 3 to 5 minutes. To keep the heated tortillas warm, lower the oven temperature to 200°F/95°C, wrap the stack in aluminum foil, and place in the oven for up to 15 minutes.

# Ingredients

I look around the world for inspiration and have learned that great ingredients make great sandwiches. It is that simple. So, the more you know about the groceries you buy, even the commonplace ones, the better your cooking will be.

## Butter

I use unsalted butter in my cooking. That way, I can control the amount of salt. An 8-tablespoon/115 g stick can contain anywhere from ¼ to ½ teaspoon of salt. If you want to use salted butter, just reduce the salt in the recipe and rely entirely on your sense of taste when seasoning.

## Cheese

Most popular American sandwich cheeses are conveniently pre-sliced. But sometimes you want an imported cheese, and you have to do the slicing yourself (see Slicing Cheese, page 8). The following are the cheeses I use in this book.

**American:** Not my favorite cheese because of its blandness, but I have to admit it melts really well and it is a classic for some sandwiches. It is almost always sold sliced.

**Brie:** Sold in wedges, and the rind of this famous French cheese is edible. There are domestic versions, too, but I usually get a French one.

**Blue cheese:** For most purposes, the economical domestic crumbles are fine. If you want to show off, use French Roquefort or Italian Gorgonzola. If you like really sharp and funky blue cheese, use Stilton from the UK.

**Cheddar:** Use mild or sharp, according to your preference. There are a lot of great small-batch versions sold, including the original Cheddar from Britain. American Cheddar is sold both sliced and unsliced.

**Colby:** Colby is a Wisconsin cheese similar to mild Cheddar. Colby Jack is a marbleization of Colby and Monterey Jack.

**Cream cheese:** Use the full-fat version for the best flavor, not light or reduced-fat. I like spreadable whipped cream cheese for some purposes and specify it when needed.

**Feta:** Made from sheep's milk, the best feta is imported from France, Bulgaria, or Greece. The domestic version is just fine, and crumbled feta is very convenient, but for a real taste treat, try a foreign feta. Each one has a distinctive flavor and texture. Feta does not melt well, and Bulgarian is the creamiest.

**Fontina:** The Italian version is more expensive than the Danish, but the former has a richer taste. If you go Italian, look for Fontina d'Aosta, which has an especially creamy texture and rustic flavor.

**Goat cheese:** Any rindless, spreadable cheese will do, but Italian caprino is perfect in panini to give a bit of authenticity.

**Gouda:** For sandwiches, use the semi-hard young version of this Dutch cheese, not the hard aged kind.

**Gruyère:** This semi-firm, nutty cheese is in the Swiss family, but it has smaller holes. Comté is similar and a good substitute.

**Monterey Jack:** This mild, creamy but semi-firm cheese is also sold flavored with jalapeños as pepper Jack. Colby Jack is a marbled cheese that combines Monterey Jack and Colby. Like many American cheeses, it is sold both sliced and in blocks.

**Mozzarella (fresh):** Sold in balls or logs, this retains the liquid from the milk it is made from. I use fresh mozzarella when I want its creaminess to play a role in the sandwich. (See the note on burrata and stracciatella on page 161.)

**Mozzarella (low moisture):** This is the familiar supermarket variety, sold in blocks, that is drier than the fresh kind and melts so beautifully. It excels in hot sandwiches.

**Parmigiano-Reggiano:** For convenience, many people call this Parmesan cheese. However, to good cooks, there is only one kind of "Parm," the authentic Italian Parmigiano-Reggiano, sold in a wedge and freshly grated at home. Domestic Parmesan is nothing like the imported version. One way to tell the difference is that the real Parmigiano is labeled with its hyphenated Italian name, and the lesser versions are just marked "Parmesan." Also, the Italian version has the name repeatedly stamped on its rind. When it comes to this cheese, hold out for the real Italian variety. When grating Parmigiano-Reggiano, use the smallest holes on a box or flat grater. Many people love to use a cheese Microplane. But keep in mind that the Microplane makes fine, fluffy shreds that weigh less than the cheese shredded with other hand graters, so if measuring by volume instead of weight, pack the Microplaned cheese tightly into the cup.

**Provolone:** This sharp cheese is sold in domestic and imported Italian versions. You will find balls of wax-covered, smoked provolone at Italian delis and cheese stores. I use the standard supermarket-variety sliced provolone, and smoked or not—your call.

**Swiss:** Domestic Swiss is fine. For deeper flavor, buy imported Swiss or Emmenthaler, Comté, or Gruyère (see page 13) and slice it yourself.

## Condiments

We all know the Big Three of condiments: mayonnaise, mustard, and ketchup. You probably already have your favorite brands, so I'm not going to get into that argument. I do have a few comments, though. First of all, homemade is not necessarily better because sometimes the handmade versions lack the familiarity or nostalgia of the store-bought types. However, whenever I "show off" my homemade condiments to guests, they appreciate my effort, and I do, too. You will probably be surprised to find how easy the homemade versions are to make.

**Mayonnaise:** When it comes to the homemade versus store-bought condiment conundrum, the exception might be mayonnaise, which is easy to make at home and tastes terrific. (See my recipe on page 218.) Hellmann's, Best Foods, Kewpie, and Duke's all have their fans, and I love them all. Kewpie, made from a Japanese recipe, has the edge in my Asian-inspired recipes. If you want to hold out for the authentic Japanese version (which includes MSG as a flavor booster), buy your Kewpie at an Asian market, where the stock is likely to be imported. The supermarket variety is an American product and is MSG-free.

**Mustard:** I use French Dijon mustard in many recipes. Some brands (such as the French brand Maille) are hotter than others, and some may be made domestically (Grey Poupon) and still are very good. Use the one you like. There are very few times in my life when I would use yellow "ballpark" mustard, and then I would have to be at an actual ballgame.

**Ketchup:** Your pick for this all-American favorite is your call. If you ever have a couple of hours on your hands and want to make it from scratch, be my guest.

**Hot sauce:** This is another item where there is no accounting for personal taste. Some brands (Frank's and Crystal) are milder than others (Tabasco). I often make my own hot sauce (page 226) because it is easy and delicious. Plus, I can control the flavor and heat level, and it keeps well.

**Relish:** Hot dog relish comes in two varieties, sweet pickle and dill. The former (for which I have a homemade version on page 165) is the most familiar. Dill is for people who prefer tart to sweet flavors, and it is especially good in the classic New Orleans sauce remoulade (page 92).

## Flour

I'm not a big baker, and I almost always buy my bread, but there are times when nothing beats home-baked. And that's when it helps to know a little bit about flour. Deciding which flour to bake with comes down to the amount of gluten in the flour, as high gluten content makes for chewier finished baked goods. For everyday cooking, like coatings and batters, I use either bleached or unbleached all-purpose flour without making a distinction between the two. However, for piadine and yeasted doughs, I use unbleached or bread flour for their higher gluten content. For the steamed buns recipe on page 147, I use cake flour, which has a low gluten content and makes a very tender bun.

There is some controversy around how to measure flour. In America, many cooks use measuring cups for flour instead of weighing it. I provide both volume and weight measurements for my non-American followers. Americans should know that I use the "dip-and-sweep" method for measuring flour. Stir the flour in its container to loosen it a bit. Dip the measuring cup into the flour so it overflows the cup. Using a dinner knife, scrape off excess flour so the flour in the cup is even with the cup edge. I allow 140 g for 1 cup of flour, 130 g for 1 cup of cake flour.

## Oils

For most cooking, use an oil with a neutral flavor, such as vegetable, canola, or peanut. As for olive oil, the key is whether it will be used for cooking or not. Extra virgin olive oil (identified visually by its green color and on your palate by its fruity, complex flavor) is a wonderful product, but it will lose its delicacy when heated. That's why it is usually served on salads or drizzled onto sandwiches as a finishing flavor. If you are really into olive oil, buy a boutique brand from an individual estate (similar to having a favorite wine from a special vineyard); France, Italy, Spain, Greece, and California are five top areas with single-estate olive oils. If you are going to be using olive oil mainly for sautéing, you may as well use the standard, golden-hued variety. There is another approach, which is to use mid-range extra virgin oil (name or warehouse store brands) for everything, keeping in mind that it will have less of that fruity flavor when it is heated. It's all up to you. However, avoid cheap pomace olive oil, which means that it has been processed from the leftover pulp and seeds after the good oil has already been extracted from first and second crushes.

When purchasing sesame oil, choose dark toasted oil (which has a fuller flavor and is meant for seasoning) over the pale expeller-pressed kind (which should be reserved for cooking).

I discuss the oils to use for deep-frying on page 9.

## Salt

Regardless of the type, all salts taste pretty much the same. Problems occur when you have to measure the salt, and sometimes you get better results with a measurement instead of the subjective "to taste." You can't go wrong with fine sea salt. It has a clean flavor, and most brands are additive-free. Fine sea salt crystals remain the same from brand to brand, which is not true of kosher salt. There are two main kosher salt brands in the US: Diamond Crystal (in a red and white box) and Morton (in a navy blue box). Diamond Crystal's salt crystals are larger

# sandwiches around the world

Legend says that the OG sandwich was beef and bread, as the British love their red meat. From Britain, the concept evolved throughout the Western world. (It also changed in England to become the much more delicate tea sandwiches on crustless white bread with dainty fillings like egg salad and cucumber or watercress with butter.) Sandwiches are now part of Eastern cuisine, especially Japanese, which has added some pretty unique contributions to the genre (see the fruit and the egg sandwiches on pages 206 and 190, respectively), nicknamed with the cute moniker of "sando." There are entire restaurants devoted to banh mi (see my contribution on page 144) in both Vietnam and the US.

Other countries across the globe are known for their sandwiches, as well, which feature their own ingredients and culinary sensibilities. Here is just a short summary of some of my favorites.

In Mexico, it's all about the torta, always served on a roll with local ingredients like chorizo, beans, avocado, and salsa. And, of course, the taco, burrito, and chimichanga. In Italy, where I spent my early years, there are two entirely different forms. A panino (plural panini) is a closed sandwich that can be toasted on a ridged sandwich pan and pressed to make it more compact and seared with pan marks, but it can also be a cold, untoasted more generic version. Tramezzini ("in-between" in Italian) were originally the Italian answer to English teatime sandwiches when British tourists were making their presence felt in the country and cafés had to answer their request for late afternoon snacks. These are always served on soft white bread and cut diagonally into triangles. The fillings are a bit heartier than the English tea treats and include Italian foods like cold cuts and olives. The French have an open-faced sandwich called the tartine, and, of course, the croque monsieur and its sister, the croque madame, are bistro menu staples. Scandinavia has its own subset of open-faced sandwiches on rye bread, with the Danish smørrebrød the best known.

than Morton's. If you already have kosher salt in your kitchen and want to use it, the measurement conversion is pretty simple. For every teaspoon of fine sea salt, use 1½ teaspoons of Morton or 2 teaspoons of Diamond Crystal, but still taste the food for seasoning whenever you can. Table salt and fine sea salt are similar for measuring purposes and are interchangeable.

# Tech Talk

A lot of my followers ask me about my tech setup.

I have a unique situation where my kitchen is not just for cooking but for shooting video while I'm cooking. I'm lucky that I have the space to leave my equipment in place 24/7. This saves me an incredible amount of time with setup and break-down. Because cooking on camera is no longer a hobby for me, but a profession, I have invested in top-quality gear. I know many influencers who use a smartphone or two, and that works for them. But this is *my* setup. On average, it takes me about twelve hours for each video, from conception to shopping and prepping, shooting the steps, cleaning up the kitchen, postproduction editing, and posting. And since I do a few posts a week for various platforms, it is a full-time job.

## Layout

I have a big sliding glass door that leads to a small outdoor deck, so I have a fair amount of natural light coming in from the left. (A fence stops the light from streaming in, so I still need an additional light source, even though I'm off to a good start. However, because I live near water, I have a fair number of dark and foggy days.)

The kitchen itself is a large room, about 20 by 14 feet. I have a large professional stove with strong gas burners, but that isn't much help for the videos, as I shoot mostly on a kitchen island with a propane-fueled hot plate.

## Cameras

I shoot from two, front and overhead, both at once. With two cameras recording, I can move ahead with the recipe and not worry about resetting with angles.

**Main camera:** Sony FX3 with SIGMA 28–70 lens. This is what I use for my front shots. It's on a tripod secured in place with a sandbag, always ready to be put into use.

**Overhead:** Sony A6400. I can punch in during editing for cooking or chopping closeups.

## Sound

Microphone: RØDE Wireless Go II.

## External Video

Monitor: I run the video from the cameras on the monitor during taping so I can glance over and check that the angles are correct.

## Postproduction

I edit the final piece in good ol' iMovie. It is probably the simplest editing software, but it works for me. Once I've edited the entire video together, I migrate it into the various platforms, add background music, and post.

# 2

# breakfast

# Bacon and Egg Biscuit Sandwich

## with sriracha honey

**Makes 2 sandwiches**

When you are really hungry in the morning, nothing satisfies like a breakfast sandwich. This is a basic version, but you will come up with your own variation. Swap out ham for the bacon? Go for it. Add sautéed red peppers or mushrooms to the eggs? Why not?

### sriracha honey

1 tablespoon unsalted butter

3 tablespoons honey

1 teaspoon sriracha or your favorite hot sauce

Pinch of crushed hot red pepper

### omelet

4 large eggs

¼ teaspoon fine sea salt

A few grinds of black pepper

2 slices thick-cut bacon, cooked (see page 7) and chopped into ½-inch/1.25 cm pieces

1 tablespoon unsalted butter

½ cup/55 g shredded Cheddar cheese

2 Buttermilk Sandwich Biscuits (page 232), split and lightly toasted

**1)** **Make the sriracha honey:** Melt the butter in a small saucepan over medium heat. Stir in the honey, sriracha, and hot red pepper. Bring to a simmer, reduce the heat to low, and simmer until lightly thickened, about 1 minute. Set aside and let cool. (It runs too much when it is hot.)

**2)** **Make the omelet:** Whisk the eggs, salt, and pepper in a medium bowl. Stir in the bacon. Melt the butter in a medium nonstick skillet over medium heat. When the butter subsides, pour in the eggs and cook until the eggs are beginning to set around the edges, about 1 minute. Using a heatproof spatula, lift up the eggs at one edge and tilt the skillet so the uncooked eggs flow underneath. Repeat in a couple of other places around the skillet and let it cook for about 1 minute more, occasionally repeating the tilting, until the eggs gradually build up into an omelet with a shiny top. Sprinkle the cheese over the omelet. Cover and remove from the heat. Let stand for about 1 minute to melt the cheese. Using the spatula, cut the omelet in half.

**3)** For each sandwich, place a biscuit on a plate, cut side up. Generously drizzle with the sriracha honey. Using the spatula, fold a half omelet over on itself into thirds in the skillet, then transfer to the biscuit bottom. Cap with the biscuit top and serve hot.

# Breakfast Burrito

**Makes 2 burritos**

More often than not, I have some kind of burrito
for breakfast, usually incorporating leftovers
from yesterday's shoot or dinner. This is the basic
template. If you want to save time in the morning,
make the hash brown potatoes the night before,
and just heat them up in the microwave when you
are ready to make the burrito. Mix things up by
substituting your favorite cooked pork (such as ham,
Spanish or Mexican chorizo, or breakfast sausage)
for the bacon.

---

1½ pounds/680 g baking
potatoes, such as
russets, peeled or
unpeeled, shredded

Fine sea salt and freshly
ground black pepper

4 tablespoons vegetable
or canola oil

1 tablespoon unsalted
butter

4 large eggs

2 tablespoons whole milk

1 cup/100 g shredded
Monterey Jack or mild
Cheddar cheese

4 slices bacon, cooked
(see page 7) and
coarsely chopped

2 burrito-sized flour
tortillas, warmed

1 ripe Hass avocado,
pitted and sliced

1 scallion, white and
green parts, sliced

Mexican-style hot sauce,
such as Cholula, for
serving

**1)** Put the potatoes in a large bowl and add enough
cold water to cover. Swish the potatoes in the water to
release their starch. Drain. Repeat rinsing the potatoes
a few more times until the water is mostly clear. Drain
well. In batches, wrap the potatoes in a kitchen towel
and wring to remove excess moisture. Transfer the
shredded potatoes to a medium bowl and season with
1 teaspoon salt and ½ teaspoon pepper.

**2)** Preheat the oven to 200°F/95°C.

**3)** Heat 3 tablespoons of the oil in a large nonstick
skillet over medium heat until the oil is shimmering.
Spread the potatoes in the skillet into a thin layer.
Cover and cook until the underside is crisp and golden
brown, about 5 minutes. Uncover and flip the potatoes
over in two or three sections. Increase the heat to
medium-high. Cook, uncovered, until the other side is
browned and the potatoes are tender, about 5 minutes
longer. Transfer to a heatproof plate and keep warm in
the oven. Wipe out the skillet.

**4)** Melt the butter in the skillet over medium heat.
Whisk the eggs, milk, ½ teaspoon salt, and ¼ teaspoon
pepper in a medium bowl. When the butter subsides,
pour the eggs into the skillet and reduce the heat to
medium-low. Cook, stirring constantly, until the eggs
are scrambled into moist curds, about 1½ minutes.
(Do not overcook, as they will cook more from the
residual heat.) Remove from the heat. Sprinkle with
the cheese and bacon and cover with a lid to melt the
cheese, about 1 minute.

*Recipe continues*

5) For each burrito, spoon half of the potatoes in a row in the center of the tortilla. Cover with half of the scrambled eggs, half of the avocado slices, and half of the scallion. Fold the tortilla up from the bottom to cover the filling. Fold the right and left sides 1 to 2 inches/2.5 to 5 cm over the filling. Roll up from the bottom to close the burrito, tucking in the corners as needed. The filling should be entirely enclosed. Transfer to a plate or baking sheet, seam side down.

6) Wipe out the skillet. Add the remaining 1 tablespoon oil and heat over medium heat. Add the burritos, seam side down, and cook until the undersides are toasted, about 1 minute. Turn and toast the other side, about 1 minute more. Transfer to a chopping board. Cut each in half, transfer to plates, and serve immediately with the hot sauce on the side.

## scrambled eggs

You would think that something as commonplace as scrambled eggs wouldn't need much explanation. But there are a few tips that will help keep your eggs bright yellow and fluffy instead of . . . well, not. First, a nonstick skillet is best, mainly for easier cleanup. Second, temperature control is key. Don't rush the eggs—use medium-low heat. High heat will make the eggs tough and rubbery. Third, stir the eggs frequently with a silicone spatula or wooden spoon. Cook the eggs to your liking, but keep in mind that if the eggs are going to be part of a filling and reheated (as with the Breakfast Burrito), cook them only until they are just barely set and have formed moist, not-quite-done curds. If you like especially creamy scrambled eggs, add 2 tablespoons whole milk into the eggs before you whisk them.

# Cemita with Chorizo and Eggs

**Makes 4 sandwiches**

*Cemita* means "sesame" in Spanish. But, in Mexican cooking, it is also the sesame seed buns you'll find in Mexican bakeries (panaderías) as well as the sandwiches made from the rolls. There are as many recipes for cemitas as there are for American sandwiches, but here is one that is perfect for breakfast with chorizo, fried eggs, and cheese. There are two kinds of chorizo, hard Spanish and soft Mexican, so read the Note at the end of the recipe to make sure you use the right version.

---

1½ pounds/680 g soft Mexican-style chorizo (see Note), preferably bulk, or use links with casings removed

4 ounces/115 g low-moisture mozzarella cheese, sliced or shredded

4 large eggs

Fine sea salt and freshly ground black pepper

4 sesame seed buns, preferably Mexican cemitas, split crosswise

½ cup/120 ml Chipotle Mayonnaise (page 219)

16 slices Pickled Jalapeños (page 223) or store-bought nacho slices

½ small red onion, thinly sliced and separated into rings

**1)** Shape the chorizo into 4 patties, each about 4 inches/10 cm in diameter. Heat a large nonstick skillet over medium-high heat. Add the patties and cook, turning halfway through cooking, until cooked through and browned on both sides, about 5 minutes. During the last minute, top each with cheese and cover with the lid to melt the cheese. Transfer the patties to a plate, leaving the fat in the skillet, and tent the patties with aluminum foil to keep warm.

**2)** Crack the eggs into the fat in the skillet and season with salt and pepper. (The whites may run together, but they can be cut apart later.) Cover and cook until the eggs are sunny-side up, with set whites, or to your taste, 2 to 3 minutes. Remove from the heat.

**3)** Meanwhile, for each sandwich, spread a roll with 2 tablespoons of the mayonnaise. On the bottom half, place a chorizo patty, 4 jalapeño slices, a fried egg, and a few onion rings. Cap with the top half. Cut in half and serve immediately.

**note** Mexican-style chorizo has the texture of American breakfast sausage. It is not the same as hard, smoked Spanish-style chorizo, which is sliceable like pepperoni. Soft chorizo is sold in mild or spicy versions, in plump links or in bulk without casing, at Latino grocers and many supermarkets in areas with large Mexican populations. If unavailable, make your own: Mix 1 pound/455 g ground pork, 1 tablespoon chili powder, 1 tablespoon red wine vinegar, 2 cloves garlic (mashed into a paste or crushed through a press), 1 teaspoon fine sea salt, ½ teaspoon freshly ground black pepper, and a large pinch of cayenne pepper with your hands in a medium bowl. Cover and refrigerate for at least 1 hour or overnight before using.

# Corned Beef Hash Sandwich

**Makes 4 sandwiches**

To many people, corned beef hash topped with a fried egg is the ultimate breakfast. Make it into a sandwich on rye toast and it gets even better. If you happen to have freshly braised corned beef after St. Patrick's Day, use it, but I usually can't wait that long and opt for what I can get from the deli.

## corned beef hash

1 large baking potato, about 10 ounces/280 g

1 tablespoon unsalted butter

1 medium yellow onion, chopped

½ red bell pepper, seeded and cut into ¼-inch/6 mm dice

2 tablespoons seeded and minced jalapeño chile

1 clove garlic, minced

Fine sea salt and freshly ground black pepper

10 ounces/280 g cooked corned beef, finely chopped (about 2 cups)

1 large egg, lightly beaten

2 tablespoons plain dried breadcrumbs

3 tablespoons vegetable oil

———

2 tablespoons unsalted butter

4 large eggs

Fine sea salt and freshly ground black pepper

8 rye bread slices, toasted

Russian Dressing (page 219) for serving

**1) Make the corned beef hash:** Put the potato in a medium saucepan and add enough cold salted water to cover by 1 inch/2.5 cm. Bring to a boil over high heat. Reduce the heat to low and simmer, partially covered, until tender when pierced with the tip of a knife, 25 to 30 minutes. Drain and transfer the potato to a bowl of ice water. Let stand until cold, about 10 minutes. Drain and peel the potato. (The potato can also be pierced with a fork and microwaved at High/100% power until tender, turning the potato over halfway through cooking, 9 to 11 minutes. Let cool until easy to handle before peeling.) Cut it into ½-inch/1.25 cm cubes (the exact size is not important). Transfer to a large bowl.

**2)** Melt the 1 tablespoon butter in a medium skillet over medium heat. Add the onion, bell pepper, jalapeño, and garlic and cook, stirring occasionally, until the onion is golden and tender, about 5 minutes. Season with salt and pepper. Add to the potatoes in the bowl. Add the corned beef, egg, and breadcrumbs. Season with ¼ teaspoon salt and ½ teaspoon pepper. Squeeze the mixture between your fingers to smash the potatoes until the ingredients are combined and hold together. Shape into 4 oval patties in the same shape as the bread slices.

**3)** Preheat the oven to 200°F/95°C.

**4)** Heat the oil in a very large nonstick skillet or griddle over medium-high heat. Add the patties and cook, carefully turning once, until crisp and browned on both sides, about 5 minutes. Don't worry if they fall apart when turned. Transfer to a baking sheet and keep warm in the oven.

**5)** Melt the 2 tablespoons butter in the skillet. Crack in the eggs and season with salt and pepper. (The whites may run together, but they can be cut apart later.) Cover and cook until the eggs are sunny-side up, with set whites, or to your taste, 2 to 3 minutes. Remove from the heat.

**6)** For each sandwich, spread the toasted rye with about 2 tablespoons of the Russian dressing. Add a patty to 1 slice and top with a fried egg. Cap with another slice and transfer to a dinner plate. Cut in half and serve hot.

## fried eggs

The best advice I can give you about cooking fried eggs starts with the age of the egg. It should be as fresh as possible because the proteins in the white are still firm, and the egg won't run as much as an older egg, where the white has loosened with age. (Conversely, choose older eggs for hard-boiled eggs because the egg interior pulls away from the shell as the liquid has evaporated over time.) Covering the skillet as the eggs fry helps them cook more evenly. This creates a slight film on the yolk, but that also keeps the yolk from running as you transfer it from the skillet. Like your eggs fried "over"? Flip them with a pancake turner and let them cook for about 10 seconds, to your preferred doneness. In most cases, the fried egg is inside the sandwich and won't be seen, so a broken yolk is not the end of the world.

# Breakfast Croissant

## with tomato jam

**Makes 2 sandwiches**

This breakfast sandwich has everything you want and more. Tomato jam (tomatoes are fruits, after all) is an amazing sweet-and-savory condiment that takes very little effort to pull together, and the payoff is huge. As with scrambled eggs for all sandwiches, cook them on the moist side because by the time you have finished making the sandwich, they will have firmed up more from the skillet's residual heat.

### tomato jam

12 ounces/340 g whole cherry tomatoes (about 2 heaping cups)

3 tablespoons light brown sugar

2 tablespoons fresh lime juice

1 tablespoon finely chopped shallot

2 cloves garlic, minced

½ teaspoon ground cumin

Fine sea salt and freshly ground black pepper

2 tablespoons unsalted butter

4 large eggs

½ teaspoon fine sea salt

¼ teaspoon freshly ground black pepper

2 croissants, halved crosswise and lightly toasted

6 strips bacon, cooked (see page 7)

½ cup/50 g shredded Cheddar cheese

**1)** **Make the tomato jam:** Cook the cherry tomatoes, brown sugar, lime juice, shallot, garlic, cumin, ¼ teaspoon salt, and ⅛ teaspoon pepper in a medium saucepan over medium-high heat until the tomato skins split, about 3 minutes. Reduce the heat to medium-low and simmer, stirring often and breaking up the tomatoes with a wooden spoon, until the juices thicken, 25 to 30 minutes. Season with salt and pepper. Makes about 1 cup/220 g. (The jam can be refrigerated in a covered container for up to 3 weeks.)

**2)** Position a broiler rack about 4 inches/10 cm from the source of heat and preheat the broiler on High.

**3)** Melt the butter in a medium nonstick saucepan over medium heat. Whisk the eggs, salt, and pepper together in a medium bowl. When the butter subsides, add the eggs and cook, stirring constantly, until the eggs are scrambled into moist curds, about 1½ minutes. (Do not overcook.) Remove from the heat.

**4)** For each sandwich, spread about 2 tablespoons tomato jam on the bottom half of the croissant. Top with half of the bacon, half of the eggs, and half of the cheese. Arrange all the croissant halves, cut sides up, on a broiler pan. Broil to melt the cheese and lightly toast the croissant bottoms, about 1 minute (remove the tops first, if necessary). Sandwich the halves together. Cut in half and serve immediately, with the remaining tomato jam on the side.

# Croque Madame

**Makes 4 sandwiches**

We Americans love grilled ham and cheese, and
the French have their version, smothered with rich
cheese sauce (of course). It's called croque monsieur,
but if you put a fried egg on top, the name changes to
croque madame. In one form or another, it is on the
menu of almost every casual French restaurant from
corner bistro to roadside gas station. Why? It's bomb.
Serve it with a small green salad for the perfect
lunch or supper. Try it another time with sliced
turkey standing in for the ham.

## sauce

3 tablespoons unsalted
 butter

3 tablespoons all-
 purpose flour

2 cups/480 ml whole
 milk, warmed
 to steaming in
 a microwave or
 saucepan

½ cup/50 g shredded
 Gruyère cheese

¼ cup/25 g freshly
 grated Parmigiano-
 Reggiano cheese

Fine sea salt and freshly
 ground black pepper

Pinch of freshly grated
 nutmeg

Cooking oil spray, if
 needed

¼ cup/60 ml stone-
 ground Dijon mustard

1¼ pounds/570 g ham
 steak with bone, cut
 into 4 portions to fit
 the bread

8 slices white sandwich
 bread, very lightly
 toasted

8 ounces/225 Gruyère
 cheese, half thinly
 sliced and half
 shredded

2 tablespoons unsalted
 butter

4 large eggs

Fine sea salt and freshly
 ground black pepper

Finely chopped fresh
 chives for garnish
 (optional)

**1)** **Make the sauce:** Melt the butter in a medium
saucepan over medium heat. Whisk in the flour. Let
bubble without browning for 1 minute. Whisk in the
warm milk and bring to a boil, whisking often. Reduce
the heat to low and cook until smooth, whisking often,
about 2 minutes. Remove from the heat and whisk in
the Gruyère and Parmigiano cheeses until smooth.
Season with the salt, pepper, and nutmeg. Transfer
to a bowl and cover with plastic wrap pressed on the
surface to discourage a skin forming on the sauce.
(The sauce can be refrigerated for up to 1 day. Reheat
in a microwave oven or in a small saucepan, whisking
often, until warm and spreadable.)

**2)** Position a rack in the upper third of the oven and
preheat to 450°F/230°C. Line a half-sheet pan with
parchment paper or aluminum foil sprayed with
cooking spray.

**3)** Mix ¼ cup/60 ml of the sauce with the mustard in a
small bowl.

**4)** Heat a large nonstick skillet over medium-high heat. Add the ham and cook, turning halfway through cooking, until lightly browned and heated through, about 3 minutes. Transfer the ham to a plate. Set the skillet aside.

**5)** Spread each bread slice on one side with about 1 tablespoon of the mustard sauce. Place 4 bread slices, sauced sides up, on the prepared half-sheet pan. Divide the ham and the sliced Gruyère cheese equally among the slices on the pan. Cap with the remaining bread slices, sauce side down. Arrange the sandwiches well apart on the pan. Divide the remaining warm, plain cheese sauce equally over the sandwiches, spreading with a spatula so the sauce runs down the sides. Sprinkle the shredded Gruyère cheese equally over the tops. Bake until the cheese is melted and browned, about 10 minutes.

**6)** Just before the sandwiches are done, fry the eggs. Melt the butter in a very large nonstick skillet over medium-high heat. Crack the eggs into the fat in the skillet and season with salt and pepper. (The whites may run together, but they can be cut apart later.) Cover and cook until the eggs are sunny-side up, with set whites, or to your taste, 2 to 3 minutes. Remove from the heat.

**7)** Transfer each sandwich to a plate, top with a fried egg, and sprinkle with the chives, if using. Serve hot, with a fork and knife.

# Hawaiian Breakfast Sliders

**Makes 8 sliders**

Ever since World War II, when US Army PXs swarmed the islands, Hawaiians have loved Spam. You'll find it in lots of Hawaiian recipes, but this is one of my favorite ways to enjoy it—glazed with teriyaki sauce and served on a sweet bun with a fried egg. Because it is quite rich, sliders are the way to go for smaller portions. The only way to make this more Hawaiian is to put pineapple on it, which I am not necessarily recommending, but a fresh fruit side salad would be a nice go-with. And you will love the method of baking a large batch of "fried" eggs on a sheet pan.

## spam

One 12-ounce/340 g can original Spam

¼ cup/60 ml reduced-sodium soy sauce

2 tablespoons mirin, sake, or dry sherry

2 tablespoons light brown sugar

2 tablespoons unsalted butter, cut up

2 tablespoons vegetable oil

8 large eggs, as fresh as possible

Fine sea salt and freshly ground black pepper

About 8 tablespoons Sriracha Mayonnaise (page 219)

8 Hawaiian-style sweet dinner rolls, such as King's, sliced crosswise into halves

1 scallion, white and green parts, thinly sliced

1) Preheat the oven to 425°F/220°C. While the oven is preheating, place a half-sheet pan in the oven to heat at the same time.

2) **Meanwhile, cook the Spam:** Cut the Spam crosswise, then horizontally to make sixteen ¼-inch/8 mm slices. Heat a large nonstick skillet over medium-high heat. Add the sliced Spam and cook, flipping halfway through cooking, until browned, 2 to 3 minutes. Mix the soy sauce, mirin, and brown sugar in a small bowl to dissolve the sugar and pour over the Spam. Bring to a boil and reduce the heat to low. Simmer, uncovered, flipping halfway through cooking, until the liquid is reduced by about half and the Spam is glazed, about 1½ minutes. Do not reduce the liquid too much or it will harden when cooled. Remove from the heat and cover the skillet to keep the Spam warm.

3) Carefully remove the hot half-sheet pan from the oven and place on a heatproof surface. Add the butter and oil, return to the oven, and let the butter melt, 1 to 2 minutes. Remove the pan from the oven again and tilt it to coat the bottom with the hot fat. Place on the heatproof surface. One at a time, crack the eggs, spacing them as evenly apart as possible, into the hot pan. Don't worry if the whites run together, as they can be cut apart later. Return the pan to the oven and bake until the egg whites are set but the yolks are still runny, about 5 minutes. During the last few minutes, place the cut rolls on another sheet pan and bake to warm them, about 3 minutes.

4) Season the eggs with salt and pepper. For each sandwich, spread a roll on both sides with about 1 tablespoon mayonnaise. Top the bottom half with 2 slices of Spam. Use a spatula to cut out and transfer 1 fried egg to top the Spam, folding the white over as needed to fit. Sprinkle with some of the scallion and cap with the top of the roll. Serve immediately.

# Lox 'n' Egg Open-Faced Sandwich

**Makes 4 sandwiches**

Perfect your weekend morning meal with this open-faced sandwich with three Jewish delicatessen classics (bagel, smoked salmon, and latkes, aka potato pancakes), stacked into a towering masterpiece. One tip: The secret to crispy latkes is plenty of hot oil to give them their essential golden exteriors. They should fry in a nice pool of oil—do not skimp on the oil!

### herbed cream cheese

½ cup/90 g whipped cream cheese

2 tablespoons finely chopped fresh chives, dill, or a combination

### latkes

1¼ pounds/570 g baking potatoes, peeled

1 small onion, peeled

1 large egg, beaten

2 tablespoons matzo meal or plain dried breadcrumbs

¾ teaspoon fine sea salt

¼ teaspoon freshly ground black pepper

Vegetable or canola oil for frying

4 large eggs

Fine sea salt and freshly ground black pepper

2 bagels (your favorite kind), split and toasted

6 ounces/170 g sliced lox or smoked salmon

Pickled Red Onions (page 222)

**1) Make the herbed cream cheese:** Mix the whipped cream cheese and herbs in a small bowl. Set aside at room temperature.

**2) Make the latkes:** Shred the potatoes and onion on the large holes of a box grater (or use the coarse shredding disk of a food processor). A handful at a time, working over the sink or a bowl, squeeze the excess juices from the vegetables and transfer them to a large bowl, discarding the juices. (Or, in batches, wrap the vegetables in a kitchen towel and wring to remove excess moisture.) Transfer to a medium bowl. Add the egg, matzo meal, salt, and pepper and mix well.

**3)** Preheat the oven to 200°F/95°C. Line a half-sheet pan with a wire cooling rack.

**4)** Pour enough oil to come about ¼ inch/6 mm up the sides of a large skillet and heat over medium-high heat until shimmering. Using about ⅓ cup/75 ml for each latke, transfer portions of the potato mixture to the oil and spread each into a cake about 3½ inches/9 cm in diameter. Fry until the underside is crisp and golden brown, about 3 minutes. Flip the latkes and cook to brown the other sides, about 3 minutes more. Do not undercook—the outsides should be nice and crunchy. Transfer the latkes to the rack and keep warm in the oven. Repeat to make 8 latkes total.

**5)** Pour out all but 2 tablespoons of the oil from the skillet and return to medium heat. Crack the eggs into the skillet and season with salt and pepper. (The whites may run together, but they can be cut apart later.) Cover and cook until the eggs are sunny-side up, with set whites, or to your taste, 2 to 3 minutes. Remove from the heat.

**6)** For each sandwich, spread a bagel half with about 2 tablespoons of the herbed cream cheese. Place the open bagel on a dinner plate. Top with a latke, one-quarter of the lox, 1 fried egg, a second latke, and a few onion rings. Serve open-faced, with a fork and knife.

# bagels

The bagel, while it can be found anywhere in America (and, possibly, the world) these days, used to be the culinary symbol of New York City, specifically that of Jewish Polish immigrants. The Lower East Side was home to many small bagel shops, where the bagels were rolled by hand, simmered in treated water, then baked by the thousands. The prebaking water bath is what gives the bagels their characteristic thin and shiny crust, and high-gluten flour provides their chewiness. Although today's bagels are likely to be more industrial than artisan, if you have access to "the real deal," buy a dozen at a time and freeze what you don't eat right away.

# Chicken and Waffles

## with hot maple syrup

**Makes 4 servings**
**Special equipment: Waffle iron with quadrants about 4 × 5 inches/10 × 12.5 cm (see Note)**

Chicken and waffles is the most sinful and delicious pairing since hot fudge and ice cream. I love it so much that sometimes I have been known to hack mine with frozen waffles. But honestly, my buttermilk batter is so easy that the only reason not to make them from scratch is the lack of a waffle iron. And this recipe is a great reason for buying one. I prefer the standard iron that makes four squares, and not the model for deep Belgian waffles. One other suggestion: Use smaller-than-average chicken breast halves because the dish is too rich for the typical larger size.

**note** If you use a Belgian-style waffle maker, double the batter.

### waffles

1 cup/140 g all-purpose flour

1 tablespoon sugar

1 teaspoon baking powder

½ teaspoon baking soda

¼ teaspoon fine sea salt

1 cup/240 ml buttermilk, plus more as needed

4 tablespoons/56 g (½ stick) unsalted butter, melted and cooled until tepid

1 large egg, lightly beaten

Vegetable oil for the waffle iron

### chicken

Two 6- to 8-ounce/ 170 to 225 g skinless, boneless chicken breast halves

1 cup/240 ml buttermilk

1 cup/140 g all-purpose flour

½ teaspoon fine sea salt

¼ teaspoon freshly ground black pepper

Vegetable or canola oil for frying

### hot maple syrup

1 cup/240 ml pure maple syrup or honey, such as clover blossom

3 tablespoons your favorite mild hot sauce, or more to taste

Unsalted butter, at room temperature, for serving

**1) Make the waffles:** Whisk the flour, sugar, baking powder, baking soda, and salt in a large bowl. Whisk the buttermilk, melted butter, and egg in another bowl. Pour over the dry ingredients and stir with a wooden spoon just until combined. Do not overmix—it can be a little lumpy. It should be thick but flowable. If it's too thick, add more buttermilk.

**2)** Preheat the oven to 200°F/95°C.

**3)** Heat the waffle iron according to the manufacturer's directions. Lightly oil the grid with a wad of paper towels dipped in oil or a heatproof silicone brush. (Do not use cooking oil spray with lecithin.) Pour enough batter (usually about 1 cup/240 ml) into the iron to almost fill the grids.

*Recipe continues*

Close the lid and cook according to the manufacturer's instructions until golden brown. Transfer the first batch of cooked waffles directly to the oven racks. Continue until all the batter has been used. Makes about twelve 4-inch/10 cm waffles, depending on the waffle iron. (The waffles can also be cooked, cooled on wire cooling racks, and stored uncovered at room temperature for up to 4 hours. Reheat directly on the oven racks of a preheated 350°F/180°C oven for 5 to 10 minutes. Leftover waffles can be cooled and frozen. To reheat, wrap each loosely in aluminum foil and bake in a preheated 400°F/200°C for 5 to 10 minutes.)

**4)** **Make the chicken:** One at a time, place a chicken breast half between sheets of plastic wrap and pound with the flat side of a meat pounder until it is about ½ inch/1.25 cm thick. Cut each in half crosswise to make 4 portions total.

**5)** Pour the buttermilk into a wide shallow bowl or pie pan. Whisk the flour, salt, and pepper together in a second bowl or pie pan. One at a time, dip the chicken into the buttermilk to coat on both sides, then transfer to the flour to coat. Shake off excess flour and place on a half-sheet pan.

**6)** Line a second half-sheet pan with a wire cooling rack and place near the stove. Pour enough oil to come about 1 inch/2.5 cm up the sides of a large heavy skillet (preferably cast iron) and heat over high heat until the oil is shimmering and reads 350°F/180°C on an instant-read thermometer.

**7)** Working with two pieces at a time, add the chicken to the oil and fry until the underside is golden brown, about 3 minutes. Flip the chicken and cook until the other side is golden brown, about 3 minutes more. Using a slotted spatula, transfer to the cooling rack. (If you pierce the chicken in its thickest part, there should be no sign of pink. If there is, cook longer.) Keep warm in the oven with the waffles until all the chicken is fried.

**8)** **Make the hot maple syrup and serve:** Stir the syrup and hot sauce in a small saucepan over medium heat until beginning to simmer (or microwave on High/100% power in a microwave-safe bowl). Pour into a syrup dispenser or sauceboat. For each serving, stack a waffle, a chicken breast portion, and a second waffle on a plate. Top with a dollop of softened butter. Serve immediately with a fork and knife and the warm syrup.

# Spanish Potato Omelet (Tortilla) Sandwich

**Makes 4 sandwiches**
**Special equipment: Mandoline or plastic slicer (optional)**

In Spain, a tortilla is an egg-based dish similar to a potato frittata, and like a frittata, it can be varied almost endlessly. If you are a "pork for breakfast" person, add ½ cup/55 g chopped (¼-inch/6 mm dice) Serrano ham or prosciutto to the eggs. Spanish tortilla is a great lunch or breakfast dish on its own, especially served at room temperature. Get to know it if you haven't already. And the same can be said for the terrific Iberian condiment romesco.

## romesco

3 Roma (plum) tomatoes, halved lengthwise

1 medium red bell pepper, halved lengthwise and seeded

3 cloves garlic, unpeeled

½ cup/40 g sliced blanched almonds

¼ cup/10 g plain soft breadcrumbs, from crusty stale bread (see page 58)

2 tablespoons sherry vinegar or red wine vinegar

½ teaspoon smoked paprika

¼ teaspoon cayenne pepper

¼ cup/60 ml extra virgin olive oil, plus more as needed

Fine sea salt and freshly ground black pepper

## spanish tortilla

6 Yukon Gold potatoes (about 1½ pounds/680 g), unpeeled and scrubbed

Fine sea salt and freshly ground black pepper

Extra virgin olive oil

1 small yellow onion, cut into thin half-moons

3 cloves garlic, thinly sliced

6 large eggs

4 crusty French or Italian rolls, split lengthwise and opened like a book

1 cup/30 g mixed baby greens

**1) Make the romesco:** Preheat the oven to 425°F/220°C.

**2)** Line a half-sheet pan with aluminum foil for easy cleanup. Place the tomatoes and bell pepper, skin side up, on the pan. Add the unpeeled garlic and roast until the tomato and bell pepper skins are mostly blackened and split, 20 to 25 minutes. Transfer the vegetables to a bowl, cover with plastic wrap, and let them cool until easy to handle. Remove and discard the skins. Transfer the peeled bell pepper, tomatoes, and garlic to a blender or food processor and add the almonds, breadcrumbs, vinegar, paprika, and cayenne. Blend until smooth. With the machine running, gradually pour in the oil to make a smooth spread. Season with

*Recipe continues*

salt and pepper. Serve at room temperature. Makes about 2 cups/480 ml. (The romesco can be covered and refrigerated for up to 5 days.)

3) **Make the Spanish tortilla:** Slice the potatoes into 1/8-inch/3 mm rounds with a mandoline or chef's knife or in a food processor. (A mandoline or a food processor with the slicing disk do the best job for uniform slices.) Rinse the potatoes well in a colander under cold running water and drain. Spread onto kitchen towels and pat dry. Season with 1 teaspoon salt and 1/2 teaspoon pepper.

4) Pour enough oil into a medium nonstick skillet with a flameproof handle to come 1/8 inch/3 mm up the sides. Heat the oil over medium-high heat until shimmering. Carefully (watch out for hot oil) spread the potatoes in the skillet. The bottom layer of the potatoes should be almost swimming in the bubbling oil. Cover tightly and cook, occasionally flipping the potatoes, until they soften, about 5 minutes. Uncover and continue, occasionally flipping the potatoes, until they are mostly golden brown and tender, about 7 minutes. Move the potatoes to one side of the pan. Add the onion and garlic to the pool of oil on the opposite side and cook, stirring them occasionally, until softened, 2 to 3 minutes. Mix the vegetables together and cook to blend the flavors, 1 minute more. Drain the potato mixture in a colander set over a large heatproof bowl to remove excess oil, reserving the oil.

5) Position a broiler rack in the oven about 4 inches/10 cm from the source of heat and preheat the broiler on High. Whisk the eggs with a pinch of salt and a few grinds of pepper in a large bowl. Stir in the potatoes. Return 2 tablespoons of reserved oil to the skillet and heat over medium heat. Discard the remaining oil. Pour the potato mixture into the skillet, spreading it into a thick cake. Cook until the edges are set, about 1 minute. Using a wooden spatula, lift up the tortilla so the uncooked portion can flow underneath, tilting the pan to help the movement. Cook, occasionally lifting up the tortilla with the spatula so the uncooked eggs can flow underneath, until the eggs on top are almost set, about 1 minute more. Transfer to the broiler and cook until the top is set, about 1 minute. Slide the tortilla from the skillet onto a plate. Leave the broiler on.

6) Lightly toast the open rolls on a broiler pan in the broiler, about 1 minute. For each sandwich, spread about 2 tablespoons of romesco onto both sides of the roll. Cut the tortilla into quarters. Add one-quarter to the roll and top with a sprinkle of greens. Close the roll, cut in half, and serve with the remaining romesco passed on the side.

# Shakshuka Breakfast Sandwich

**Makes 4 sandwiches**

Shakshuka (or one of its derivations) is a popular breakfast throughout northern Africa, Israel, southern Europe, and Turkey, which covers quite a lot of territory. It is quite simple, consisting of eggs poached in a spicy vegetable sauce. Served on a toasted roll, it becomes a more substantial meal.

If you wish, add sliced avocado to your sandwich. Living in California, I put avocado on everything I can!

### spicy tomato sauce

1 tablespoon extra virgin olive oil

1 small yellow onion, chopped

½ large red bell pepper, seeded and cut into ½-inch/1.25 cm dice

3 cloves garlic, minced

½ teaspoon ground cumin

½ teaspoon sweet or smoked paprika

⅛ teaspoon cayenne pepper

One 14.5-ounce/411 g can diced tomatoes

Fine sea salt and freshly ground black pepper

4 large eggs

½ cup/50 g crumbled feta cheese

2 tablespoons finely chopped fresh flat-leaf parsley or cilantro

4 crusty round sandwich rolls, such as kaiser rolls, split, brushed with olive oil, and toasted

**1) Make the spicy tomato sauce:** Heat the oil in a large skillet over medium heat. Add the onion, bell pepper, and garlic and cook, stirring occasionally, until the onion is tender, about 5 minutes. Add the cumin, paprika, and cayenne and stir until fragrant, about 30 seconds. Add the tomatoes with their juices and bring to a boil. Reduce the heat to medium-low and cook at a brisk simmer, stirring often, until the juices thicken, about 10 minutes. Season with salt and pepper.

**2)** Using the back of a large spoon, make 4 evenly spaced wells in the sauce. Crack an egg into each well. Cover the skillet and simmer over medium-low heat until the whites are set but the yolks are still runny, 4 to 5 minutes. Season the eggs with salt and pepper. Sprinkle with the cheese and parsley (feta cheese does not melt). Remove from the heat.

**3)** For each sandwich, place a roll on a dinner plate. Use a large spoon to transfer an egg and a serving of the sauce onto the roll bottom. Cap with the roll top, cut in half, and serve immediately with a fork and knife.

# Steak and Eggs Breakfast Sandwich

**Makes 4 sandwiches**

This breakfast sandwich is based on the popular diner breakfast of steak and eggs, and it is as hearty as they come. Plan on skipping lunch if you eat this in the morning. I serve it with My Hot Sauce (page 226) whenever I can to give it a personal touch.

---

1 pound/455 g top sirloin steak, trimmed

Olive oil

½ teaspoon garlic powder

½ teaspoon onion powder

Fine sea salt and freshly ground black pepper

2 tablespoons unsalted butter

6 large eggs

2 tablespoons whole milk

8 slices unsmoked provolone or low-moisture mozzarella cheese

4 soft oblong rolls, split and opened like a book

Fresh chives, thinly sliced (optional)

My Hot Sauce (page 226) or store-bought hot sauce, for serving

**1)** Brush the steak with about 1 tablespoon oil. Mix the garlic powder, onion powder, ½ teaspoon salt, and ¼ teaspoon pepper in a small bowl and sprinkle all over the steak. Heat a large skillet or grill pan with a flameproof handle over medium-high heat.

**2)** Add the steak to the skillet and cook until the underside is browned, about 4 minutes. Flip the steak and cook until the other side is browned, about 3 minutes for medium-rare. Transfer to a carving board with a well and let stand for 5 minutes. Using a sharp knife, cut the steak into bite-sized cubes.

**3)** Position a broiler rack about 4 inches/10 cm from the source of heat and preheat the broiler on High. Add the butter to the skillet and melt over medium-low heat. Whisk the eggs, milk, ¼ teaspoon salt, and a few grinds of pepper in a medium bowl. When the butter subsides, add the eggs and cook, stirring frequently, until barely set but quite soft, about 1 minute. Stir in the steak cubes (reserve the carving juices from the board) and spread into an even layer. Top with the cheese. Broil until the cheese melts, about 1 minute. Remove from the broiler and leave the broiler on.

**4)** Lightly toast the open rolls on a broiler pan in the broiler, about 1 minute. Divide the egg and steak mixture into 4 portions in the skillet. For each sandwich, use a spatula to transfer one-quarter of the egg mixture to a split roll and sprinkle with some chives, if using. Drizzle the steak juices on the exposed rolls. Close the rolls, cut in half, and serve, with the hot sauce on the side.

# 3

# poultry

# Buffalo Chicken Sandwich

## with blue cheese dressing

**Makes 4 sandwiches**

Who would have thought that fried chicken wings would become the most famous thing about Buffalo, New York? You can even buy the spicy coating sauce at the supermarket, but don't—it is super easy to make at home. If you want to substitute chicken tenders for the sliced chicken, be sure to remove the tendons first. Give the chicken plenty of room in the skillet as it cooks to brown nicely. If you have leftover blue cheese dressing, save it for a salad at another meal.

### blue cheese dressing

½ cup/120 ml mayonnaise

¼ cup/40 g whipped cream cheese or room-temperature block cream cheese

3 tablespoons buttermilk

½ teaspoon Worcestershire sauce

¼ teaspoon garlic powder

¼ teaspoon onion powder

½ cup/56 g crumbled blue cheese, such as Danish, Roquefort, or piccante Gorgonzola

Fine sea salt and freshly ground black pepper

### chicken

Two 10- to 12-ounce/ 280 to 340 g skinless, boneless chicken breast halves

¼ cup/35 g all-purpose flour

1 teaspoon fine sea salt

½ teaspoon freshly ground black pepper

2 tablespoons vegetable or canola oil, plus more as needed

### buffalo sauce

½ cup/115 g (1 stick) unsalted butter

¼ cup/60 ml mild hot sauce, such as Frank's RedHot

1 tablespoon distilled white vinegar

1 teaspoon Worcestershire sauce

½ teaspoon garlic powder

2 large celery ribs, cut crosswise into very thin slices (a mandoline or plastic slicer work best)

4 soft oblong sandwich rolls, lightly toasted

**1) Make the blue cheese dressing:** Combine the mayonnaise, cream cheese, buttermilk, Worcestershire sauce, garlic powder, and onion powder in a medium bowl. Add the blue cheese and process with an immersion blender until the dressing is combined but still chunky. Or mash up most of the cheese with a fork, then stir well to combine. Makes about 1½ cups/360 ml. (The dressing can be refrigerated in a covered container for up to 3 days.)

**2) Make the chicken:** Pound each chicken breast half between sheets of plastic wrap with the flat side of a meat pounder until it is about ½ inch/1.25 cm

*Recipe continues*

thick. Cut across the grain into slices about ½ inch/1.25 cm thick. Cut the longer slices in half to make strips about 2 inches/5 cm long. Transfer to a large bowl. Sprinkle with the flour, salt, and pepper and toss to coat.

3) Heat the oil in a large skillet over medium-high heat until shimmering. In two or three batches, add the chicken, shaking off excess flour, and cook, flipping the chicken halfway through cooking, until golden brown and opaque when pierced in the thickest part with the tip of a small sharp knife, about 5 minutes. Transfer to a medium bowl and tent with aluminum foil to keep warm.

4) **Make the Buffalo sauce:** Melt the butter in a small saucepan over medium heat. Add the hot sauce, vinegar, Worcestershire sauce, and garlic powder. Whisk well and bring to a simmer. Pour over the chicken and toss well to coat.

5) Mix the celery and 2 tablespoons of the blue cheese dressing in a small bowl to make a celery salad. For each sandwich, spread a split roll with 2 tablespoons of the remaining dressing. Add one-quarter of the chicken and top with one-quarter of the celery salad. Close the roll, cut in half, and serve hot.

# Butter Chicken Burrito

**Makes 4 burritos**

Butter chicken is very similar to tikka masala, but no matter what you call it, the dish consists of marinated chicken simmered in a creamy and spicy tomato sauce. Hands down, it is one of the most flavor-packed dishes on the planet, and it is another entrée that also makes a terrific sandwich (in the form of a burrito). Check out the note on Kashmiri chile, which is not your standard-issue ground chile or chili powder.

**note** Kashmiri ground chile (sometimes labeled Kashmiri chili powder) is pulverized sun-dried red chiles originally from Kashmir in the northernmost part of India. It is a staple in Indian markets (and sold online) and has a relatively mild heat level. Do not substitute generic Indian "chili powder," which is typically cayenne or another very hot variety and can ruin your dish with too much heat. Be sure "Kashmiri" is on the label. An acceptable substitute is sweet paprika with a pinch or two of cayenne pepper to bring up the heat to your taste.

## grilled marinated chicken

- ½ cup/120 ml plain yogurt (not Greek yogurt)
- 2¼ teaspoons garam masala
- 2 teaspoons Kashmiri chili powder (see Note)
- Fine sea salt
- 3 cloves garlic, minced
- 1½ pounds/680 g skinless, boneless chicken thighs, trimmed of excess skin and fat
- Vegetable oil for the broiling pan

## sauce

- 4 tablespoons/56 g (½ stick) unsalted butter
- 1 small yellow onion, chopped
- ½ teaspoon ground coriander
- ½ teaspoon ground cumin
- One 14-ounce/390 g can crushed tomatoes
- ¼ cup/35 g unsalted whole cashews
- ⅔ cup/165 ml heavy cream

## spiced rice

- 1 tablespoon vegetable oil
- 2 green cardamom pods, crushed to open the pods
- 1 tablespoon cumin seeds
- One 2-inch/5 cm cinnamon stick
- 2 whole cloves
- ½ medium yellow onion, chopped
- 1 cup/185 g basmati rice
- 3 cups/720 ml reduced-sodium chicken broth
- ½ teaspoon fine sea salt

- 4 burrito-sized flour tortillas, warmed
- ½ small red onion, cut into thin half-moons
- 2 tablespoons seeded and minced jalapeño chile
- 2 tablespoons finely chopped fresh cilantro
- ¾ cup/180 ml plain low-fat yogurt (not Greek yogurt), in a squeeze bottle
- 1 tablespoon vegetable or canola oil, plus more as needed

**1) Marinate the chicken:** Whisk the yogurt, 1½ teaspoons of the garam masala, 1½ teaspoons of the chile powder, ½ teaspoon salt, and 1 clove garlic together in a medium bowl. Add the chicken, turn to coat, and cover with plastic wrap. Refrigerate for at least 30 minutes and up to overnight.

*Recipe continues*

**51**

2) **Grill the marinated chicken:** Position a broiler rack about 4 inches/10 cm from the source of heat and preheat the broiler on High. Lightly oil a broiler pan.

3) Arrange the chicken on the broiler and broil until lightly browned, 4 to 5 minutes. Flip the chicken and continue broiling until browned, 4 to 5 minutes. Transfer to a carving board and let stand while you make the sauce.

4) **Make the sauce:** Melt 2 tablespoons of the butter in a large saucepan over medium heat. Add the onion and cook, stirring occasionally, until softened, about 3 minutes. Stir in the remaining 2 cloves garlic and cook until fragrant, about 1 minute. Add the remaining ¾ teaspoon garam masala and ½ teaspoon chile powder, the coriander, and the cumin and stir until fragrant, about 30 seconds. Stir in the tomatoes, ¼ cup/60 ml water, and the cashews and bring to a boil. Reduce the heat to low and simmer, uncovered, stirring occasionally, until lightly thickened, about 15 minutes. Remove from the heat. Add the heavy cream and the remaining 2 tablespoons butter. Using an immersion blender, puree the sauce. (Or puree in a blender, draping a kitchen towel over the blender jar instead of covering with the lid, and return the sauce to the pot.) The sauce should be quite thick.

5) Cut the chicken into 1-inch/2.5 cm chunks. Do not worry if the chicken is slightly pink inside. Stir in the chicken and its juices and return to medium heat until simmering. Season with salt. Remove from the heat and cover tightly to keep warm.

6) **Meanwhile, make the spiced rice:** Heat the oil in a small saucepan over medium heat. Add the cardamom, cumin, cinnamon, and cloves and stir until the spices are fragrant, about 20 seconds. Add the onion and cook, stirring occasionally, until softened, about 3 minutes. Add the rice and cook, stirring often, until the grains begin to toast, 2 to 3 minutes. Add the broth and salt and bring to a boil. Reduce the heat to very low. Cover tightly and simmer until the rice is tender and has absorbed the liquid, about 20 minutes. Do not stir the rice. Remove from the heat and let stand, covered, for 5 minutes. Fluff the rice. Pick out and discard the cinnamon sticks and any large spices.

7) Preheat the oven to 200°F/95°C.

8) For each burrito, spread ½ cup/90 g of the spiced rice in the center of the tortilla. Top with about one-quarter of the warm butter chicken. Sprinkle with some onion, jalapeño, and cilantro and squeeze on a zigzag of yogurt. Fold the right and left sides 1 to 2 inches/2.5 to 5 cm inward to partially cover the filling, tucking in the corners as needed. Fold up from the bottom to cover the filling, tucking tightly at the top, and then roll to close the burrito. The filling should be entirely enclosed. Set aside on a baking sheet, seam side down.

9) Heat the oil in a large nonstick skillet and over medium heat. Add 2 burritos, seam side down, and cook until the undersides are golden and toasted, about 1 minute. Turn and brown the other side until toasted, about 1 minute more. Transfer to a half-sheet pan and keep warm in the oven while cooking the remaining burritos, adding more oil as needed. Cut each burrito in half and serve warm. (The leftover rice can be cooled, covered, and refrigerated for up to 2 days. Reheat, covered, in a microwave oven on High/100% power for about 3 minutes.)

# Chicken and Bean Chimichanga

**Makes 4 chimichangas**

Chimichanga is the burrito's sassy sibling, and it wears its golden shell with pride. This recipe has the earmarks of the classic version with flavorful chicken and beans to give contrast to the crisp exterior. Shredding the braised chicken filling (tinga) in a heavy-duty mixer is a great hack. You will want to keep this poultry filling in mind for other Mexican tortilla dishes such as tacos, burritos, enchiladas, and more.

### chicken tinga

1½ pounds/680 g skinless, boneless chicken breast halves

3 cups/720 ml reduced-sodium chicken broth or water, plus more as needed

½ medium white onion, cut into thick half-moons

2 cloves garlic, crushed and peeled

½ large jalapeño chile, seeded and coarsely chopped

1½ teaspoons chili powder

½ teaspoon ground cumin

½ teaspoon fine sea salt

¼ teaspoon cayenne pepper

3 tablespoons finely chopped fresh cilantro

4 burrito-sized flour tortillas, warmed

One 16-ounce/455 g can refried beans (no need to heat them)

2 cups/200 g shredded sharp Cheddar or Monterey Jack cheese

Vegetable or canola oil for frying

### garnishes

Sour cream or Mexican crema in a squeeze bottle

Smoky Tomato Salsa (page 221)

Chopped fresh cilantro

**1) Make the chicken tinga:** Bring the chicken, broth, onion, garlic, jalapeño, chili powder, cumin, salt, and cayenne to a boil in a medium saucepan over medium-high heat. Add more broth or water as needed to barely cover the ingredients. Reduce the heat to low and simmer, uncovered, until the chicken looks opaque when pierced with the tip of a sharp knife, about 20 minutes. Transfer the chicken to a bowl and let cool until warm, about 15 minutes. Strain the cooking liquid and reserve ½ cup/120 ml. (The remaining cooking liquid can be strained, cooled, covered, and used as chicken broth.)

**2)** In a heavy-duty mixer fitted with the paddle, mix the chicken with the reserved cooking liquid on medium speed until it is shredded, about 30 seconds.

**54**

(Or shred the chicken by hand with two forks, transfer to a bowl, and stir in enough liquid to moisten.) Stir in the cilantro. Makes about 2 cups/405 g. (The cooled tinga can be refrigerated in a covered container for up 3 days.)

3) Preheat the oven to 200°F/95°C. Place a wire cooling rack over a half-sheet pan.

4) For each chimichanga, place a warm tortilla on your work surface. Spread one-quarter of the beans in a 2-inch/5 cm wide strip running horizontally in the center of the tortilla. Top with one-quarter of the tinga and one-quarter of the cheese. Fold up the bottom of the tortilla to cover the filling, tucking it tightly at the top. Fold the right and left sides 1 to 2 inches/2.5 to 5 cm inward to partially cover the filling. Roll up from the bottom to close the chimichanga, tucking in the corners as needed. The filling should be entirely enclosed. Transfer, seam side down, to a plate or baking sheet.

5) Pour enough oil to come 1 inch/2.5 cm up the sides of a large, deep skillet and heat over high heat until shimmering. Carefully add 2 chimichangas to the hot oil, seam side down, and fry until the underside is golden brown, about 2 minutes. Carefully flip and brown the other side, about 2 minutes more. Transfer to the wire rack and keep warm in the oven while frying the remaining chimichangas.

6) Place each chimichanga on a dinner plate. Garnish each with a zigzag of sour cream from the bottle, add a spoonful of salsa on top, and sprinkle with cilantro. Serve hot, with the remaining salsa on the side.

# Chipotle Chicken Philly

**Makes 2 sandwiches**

Philadelphia is an incredible sandwich town, and while there are those who might disagree, its king of stacked food is the cheesesteak. Most renditions are beef-based, but here is a chicken variation that I have been making for a long time. It's spicy, cheesy, and saucy and brings a lot of unexpected flavors to the familiar chicken on a roll.

### chipotle sauce

¼ cup/60 ml mayonnaise

Grated zest of 1 lime

2 tablespoons fresh lime juice

1 chipotle chile in adobo, minced, or more to taste

1 teaspoon chili powder

1 teaspoon ground cumin

½ teaspoon garlic powder

Fine sea salt

### chicken filling

2 tablespoons olive oil

1 medium yellow onion, cut into thin half-moons

Fine sea salt

2 large poblano chiles, roasted (see Note), seeded, and cut into strips about ½ inch/1.25 cm wide

One 12-ounce/340 g skinless, boneless chicken breast half, cut across the grain into strips about ½ inch/1.25 cm wide

4 ounces/115 g thinly sliced Monterey Jack cheese

2 oblong rolls, split and toasted

### garnishes (optional)

Thinly sliced fresh jalapeño chiles, Pickled Jalapeños (page 223), or nacho slices

Chopped fresh cilantro

Tajín seasoning

**1)** **Make the chipotle sauce:** Process the mayonnaise, lime zest and juice, chipotle, chili powder, cumin, and garlic powder in a small bowl with an immersion blender to puree the chipotle. Season with salt.

**2)** **Make the chicken filling:** Heat 1 tablespoon of the oil in a large skillet over medium-high heat. Add the onion and season with salt. Cook, stirring occasionally, until just translucent, about 3 minutes. Stir in the poblanos. Transfer onion mixture to a bowl.

**3)** Position a broiler rack about 4 inches/10 cm from the source of heat and preheat the broiler on High.

**4)** Heat the remaining 1 tablespoon oil in a large skillet with a flameproof handle over medium heat. Spread out the chicken strips in the skillet and cook until the undersides are browned, about 2 minutes. Flip the chicken and continue cooking just until it shows no sign of pink when cut, about 2 minutes more. Do not overcook. Stir in the reserved onions and poblano. Top with the cheese and broil just until the cheese is melted, about 1 minute.

**5)** For each sandwich, spread the roll with half of the chipotle sauce. Using tongs, add half of the chicken and cheese mixture to the roll bottom. Top with the garnishes of your choice, if desired. Cap with the roll top, cut in half, and serve hot.

> **note** To roast poblano chiles, preheat the broiler on High. Put the chiles on a broiler pan and broil, turning occasionally, until the skin is blackened and blistered (but not burned through), about 10 minutes total. Transfer to a bowl and cover. Let steam and cool for about 10 minutes. Using a paring knife, scrape off the blackened skin, discarding the seeds and ribs. Try not to rinse the chiles unless absolutely necessary.

# The Cutlet

**Makes 4 sandwiches**

This Italian-influenced example shows how important texture is in building a sandwich. The broccoli rabe is tender and plays off the crispy chicken. The rolls should not be too crusty, as you don't want them to spoil the pleasure of biting into the crunchy panko coating. The prosciutto acts not only as another flavor but as a salty seasoning to bring it all together.

---

### broccoli rabe

1 pound/455 g broccoli rabe (see Note), coarsely chopped

2 tablespoons extra virgin olive oil

2 cloves garlic, thinly sliced

¼ teaspoon crushed hot red pepper

Fine sea salt

---

### chicken

Two 10- to 12-ounce/ 280 to 340 g skinless, boneless chicken breast halves

½ cup/70 g all-purpose flour

2 large eggs

1 cup/70 g panko breadcrumbs

2 tablespoons finely chopped fresh flat-leaf parsley

2 cloves garlic, crushed through a press

½ teaspoon fine sea salt

¼ teaspoon freshly ground black pepper

Olive oil for frying

4 oblong Italian or French rolls, split lengthwise and toasted

12 rounds thinly sliced fresh mozzarella cheese

8 thin slices prosciutto

8 slices deli-style roasted red pepper, drained and patted dry, cut to fit the rolls

Balsamic glaze

**1)** **Make the broccoli rabe:** Bring a large pot of salted water to a boil over high heat. Fill a large bowl with ice water. Add the broccoli rabe to the pot of boiling water, cover, and return to a boil. Cook just until it is crisp-tender and turns a brighter green, about 2 minutes. Drain, then transfer to the ice water to cool. Drain again. Pat dry with kitchen towels or paper towels. (The broccoli rabe can be refrigerated in a resealable plastic bag for up to 1 day.) Heat the extra virgin olive oil, sliced garlic, and hot red pepper together in a large skillet over medium heat until the garlic softens, about 2 minutes. Add the broccoli rabe and cook, stirring occasionally, until heated through, about 5 minutes. Season with salt. Remove from the heat and cover to keep warm.

**2)** **Cook the chicken:** Preheat the oven to 200°F/95°C.

**3)** Pound each chicken breast between sheets of plastic wrap with the flat side of a meat pounder until it is about ½ inch/1.25 cm thick. Cut each in half crosswise to make 4 portions total. Spread the flour in a wide shallow bowl or pie plate. Beat the eggs in a second bowl (an immersion blender works best). Mix the panko, parsley, crushed garlic, salt, and pepper in a third bowl. One at a time, coat the chicken in the flour, shaking off excess flour, and coat with the eggs. Transfer to the panko and turn to coat. Transfer to a half-sheet pan.

*Recipe continues*

**note** Broccoli rabe (also called rapini) can be an underappreciated vegetable, but not by me! Before cooking, rinse it very well in bowls of water to remove any grit, as it can be sandy. Broccoli rabe is naturally bitter and is blanched first to cut some of the edge. This step is not meant to actually cook the greens, just to bring it to a still-firm tenderness.

4) Put a wire cooling rack over a second half-sheet pan and place near the stove. Pour enough olive oil to come about ½ inch/1.25 cm up the sides of a large skillet and heat over medium-high heat until shimmering. In two batches, add the chicken to the oil and cook, adjusting the heat so the chicken bubbles steadily without burning, until crisp and golden brown, 3 to 4 minutes. Transfer to the wire rack to drain. (When pierced with a small knife in the thickest part, the chicken should show no sign of pink.) Keep warm in the oven while cooking the remaining chicken.

5) For each sandwich, place a portion of chicken breast on the roll bottom. Top with 3 cheese slices, 2 prosciutto slices, 2 red pepper slices, a drizzle of balsamic glaze, and about one-quarter of the warm broccoli rabe. Cap with the roll top, cut in half crosswise, and serve hot.

# homemade breadcrumbs

Never throw away day-old, stale bread. It is easy to transform it into one of your kitchen's most useful ingredients, breadcrumbs. While virtually all kinds of breads work, Italian and French loaves or rolls are the most versatile. White sandwich bread is good, too. However, avoid enriched breads like challah and brioche because crumbs made from these sweeter loaves can burn more easily when used as coatings.

The bread should be stale, but it doesn't have to be rock-hard. (Of course, if you see any mold, toss the bread out.) In batches, rip a few bread slices into chunks and process in a food processor or heavy-duty blender to make coarse crumbs. Don't pack the bread into the machine, or it will take forever to grind into crumbs. Depending on the machine used, it can take a minute or two to reach the right consistency. Just transfer the crumbs to a resealable plastic bag and store in the freezer. Defrost the crumbs before using—it doesn't take long.

# Chicken, Fig, and Walnut Salad Sandwich

**Makes 4 sandwiches**

Fresh tarragon makes this twist on chicken salad extraordinary, but use whatever fresh herbs you have handy, if you prefer. If using other herbs, adjust the amount to taste, as some are stronger than others. If chicken salad can be classy, this is it.

### chicken

One 12-ounce/340 g skinless, boneless chicken breast half

1 small yellow onion, sliced

3 sprigs fresh flat-leaf parsley (optional) and/or the herb stalks (from the salad)

¼ teaspoon dried thyme

1 teaspoon fine sea salt

5 black peppercorns

### salad

½ cup/35 g walnuts, toasted (see Note) and coarsely chopped

⅓ cup/40 g diced (¼ inch/6 mm) celery

⅓ cup/45 g diced (½ inch/1.25 cm) moist dried figs

½ cup/120 ml mayonnaise

1 teaspoon Dijon mustard

2 teaspoons finely chopped fresh tarragon, dill, or flat-leaf parsley, or 1 teaspoon finely chopped fresh thyme or rosemary (use the stalks in the cooking broth)

Fine sea salt and freshly ground black pepper

8 slices white sandwich bread, untoasted or toasted

4 tender lettuce leaves, such as Bibb

**1) Cook the chicken:** Place the chicken, onion, parsley, if using, thyme, salt, and peppercorns in a medium saucepan and add enough cold water to cover, about 1 quart/960 ml. Bring to a simmer over medium heat. Reduce the heat to low and simmer, uncovered, until the chicken looks opaque when pierced in the thickest part with the tip of a sharp knife, about 20 minutes. Transfer the chicken to a plate and let cool. (The cooking liquid can be strained, cooled, covered, and used as chicken broth.)

**2) Make the salad:** Chop the chicken into ½ inch/1.25 cm pieces and transfer to a medium bowl. Add the walnuts, celery, figs, mayonnaise, mustard, and tarragon and mix well. Season with salt and pepper.

**3)** For each sandwich, spoon one-quarter of the chicken salad on one slice and top with the lettuce. Cap with another slice. Press together, cut in half, and serve.

**note** To toast walnuts, preheat the oven to 350°F/180°C. Spread the walnuts on a half-sheet pan and bake, stirring occasionally, until they are golden and toasted, about 10 minutes. Let cool completely before chopping.

## chicken meatballs

1 pound/455 g ground chicken or turkey (not 99% lean)

¾ cup/55 g panko breadcrumbs

½ cup/50 g freshly grated Parmigiano-Reggiano cheese

½ small yellow onion, shredded on the large holes of a box grater

1 large egg, beaten

1 teaspoon fine sea salt

¼ teaspoon ground allspice

¼ teaspoon freshly grated nutmeg

¼ teaspoon freshly ground black pepper

2 tablespoons vegetable or canola oil

## mushroom gravy

4 tablespoons/56 g (½ stick) unsalted butter

8 ounces/225 g sliced cremini mushrooms

2 tablespoons minced shallot

2 cloves garlic, minced

¼ cup/35 g all-purpose flour

2 cups/480 ml reduced-sodium beef broth

½ cup/120 ml heavy cream

⅓ cup/75 ml dry white wine, such as Pinot Grigio

2 teaspoons Worcestershire sauce

1 teaspoon Dijon mustard

2 tablespoons finely chopped fresh flat-leaf parsley, plus more for finishing

Fine sea salt and freshly ground black pepper

4 French or Italian rolls, split and lightly toasted

# Chicken Meatball and Mushroom Gravy Sub

**Makes 4 sandwiches**

Inspired by the Swedish classic, these juicy, tender meatballs with warm spices are simmered in a mushroom cream sauce. The result is a great cold-weather meal that is both hearty and comforting. If you like sweet-and-savory combinations, serve lingonberry or cranberry sauce on the side.

1) **Make the chicken meatballs:** Mix the chicken, panko, cheese, onion, egg, salt, allspice, nutmeg, and pepper (your hands work best) in a large bowl until combined but not compacted. Shape the mixture into 16 equal balls and put on a large plate.

2) Heat the oil in a large skillet over medium-high heat. Add the meatballs and cook, turning occasionally, until browned all over, 4 to 5 minutes. Using a slotted spoon, return the meatballs to the plate. Pour out the fat in the pan.

**60**

**3)** **Make the mushroom gravy:** Melt 2 tablespoons of the butter in the same skillet over medium heat. Add the mushrooms and cook, stirring occasionally, until the juices have evaporated and the mushrooms are beginning to brown, about 7 minutes. Move the mushrooms to one side of the skillet and add the remaining 2 tablespoons butter, the shallots, and garlic to the empty area. Cook, occasionally stirring the shallots and garlic, until the shallots soften, about 2 minutes. Stir into the mushrooms. Sprinkle with the flour and stir well. Stir in the broth, cream, wine, Worcestershire sauce, and mustard. Bring to a boil, stirring often. Return the meatballs and any juices to the skillet. Reduce the heat to low and simmer, uncovered, stirring occasionally, until the sauce thickens and the meatballs are cooked through, 6 to 8 minutes. Stir in the parsley and season with salt and pepper.

**4)** For each sandwich, using a large spoon, transfer 4 meatballs with their gravy onto the roll bottom. Sprinkle with more parsley. Pour any remaining gravy into a sauceboat. Close the roll, cut in half, and serve hot, with the remaining gravy.

# Nashville Hot Fried Chicken Sandwich

**Makes 4 sandwiches**

Here is another dish that has taken on the name of its place of origin. In Nashville, an enterprising restaurateur came up with a spicy dip for crunchy fried chicken, and before long, everyone in town was making their chicken this way. You'll be a convert, too. Don't forget to serve it with your favorite slaw.

## fried chicken

Two 10- to 12-ounce/ 280 to 340 g skinless, boneless chicken breast halves

2 cups/480 ml buttermilk

¼ cup/60 ml mild hot sauce, such as Frank's RedHot

1 tablespoon fine sea salt

⅔ cup/90 g all-purpose flour

1 teaspoon sweet paprika

½ teaspoon cayenne pepper

¼ teaspoon garlic powder

½ teaspoon freshly ground black pepper

Vegetable or canola oil for frying

## dip

4 tablespoons/56 g (½ stick) unsalted butter, melted

2 tablespoons honey

½ teaspoon cayenne pepper

½ teaspoon sweet or smoked paprika

¼ teaspoon garlic powder

¼ teaspoon fine sea salt

4 sandwich buns

16 dill pickle slices

**1) Prepare the chicken:** Pound each chicken breast between sheets of plastic wrap with the flat side of a meat pounder until it is about ½ inch/1.25 cm thick. Cut each in half crosswise to make 4 portions total. Whisk the buttermilk, hot sauce, and salt in a 1-gallon/3.78 L resealable plastic bag. Add the chicken, close the bag, and refrigerate, turning occasionally, for at least 2 hours or up to 18 hours.

**2) Fry the chicken:** Whisk the flour, paprika, cayenne, garlic powder, and black pepper together in a medium bowl. One at a time, remove the chicken pieces from the marinade, shaking off any excess buttermilk, and coat on both sides in the flour. Transfer to a half-sheet pan.

**3)** Preheat the oven to 200°F/95°C. Line a second half-sheet pan with a wire cooling rack and place near the stove.

**4)** Pour enough oil to come 1 inch/2.5 cm up the sides of a large saucepan and heat over high heat to 350°F/180°C on a deep-frying thermometer. Working with two pieces at a time, add the chicken to the oil and fry until the underside is golden brown, about 3 minutes. Flip the chicken and cook until the other side is golden brown, about 3 minutes more. Using a slotted spatula, transfer to the cooling rack. (If you pierce the chicken in its thickest part, there should be no sign of pink. If there is, cook longer.) Keep warm in the oven until all the chicken is fried.

**5) Make the dip:** Using a ladle, measure ½ cup/120 ml of the hot oil in a heatproof measuring cup and transfer to a heatproof bowl. Add the melted butter, honey, cayenne, paprika, garlic powder, and salt and whisk well to combine.

**6)** For each sandwich, using tongs, quickly coat one piece of chicken in the dip. Place on the bun bottom and top with 4 pickle slices. Drizzle some of the sauce on the roll top and cap the sandwich. Cut the sandwich in half and serve hot.

# Piri-Piri Chicken Sandwich

**Makes 4 sandwiches**

Piri-piri (also known as peri-peri) is a chile-based condiment in African cooking that traveled around the world via Portuguese traders. Keep this sauce in mind when you want a marinade for grilled chicken for a backyard cookout, or if you want a hot table sauce that is interesting but not too highly spiced. (But if you like a hotter sauce, swap out 3 more red chiles for the bell pepper.) I also like it because it can be made in a flash in a food processor or blender with raw peppers. The cilantro slaw, with its unexpected addition of Thai sweet chili sauce, is a keeper, too.

## piri-piri sauce

- 1 medium red bell pepper, seeded and coarsely chopped
- 1 long red cayenne or 3 Fresno or red jalapeño chiles, seeded and coarsely chopped
- ½ medium red onion, coarsely chopped
- 3 cloves garlic, crushed and peeled
- 3 tablespoons fresh lemon juice
- 2 teaspoons fine sea salt
- 2 teaspoons smoked paprika
- 1 teaspoon freshly ground black pepper
- ½ cup/120 ml extra virgin olive oil

Two 12-ounce/340 g skinless, boneless chicken breast halves (or 1½ pounds/680 g skinless, boneless thighs)

## cilantro slaw

- ½ cup/120 ml mayonnaise
- 2 tablespoons Thai sweet chili sauce (see Note, page 66)
- 2 tablespoons fresh lemon juice
- One 8-ounce/227 g bag coleslaw mix (about 2½ loosely packed cups)
- 2 tablespoons finely chopped fresh cilantro
- Fine sea salt and freshly ground black pepper

Vegetable or canola oil for the pan

4 crusty rolls, split and toasted

Pickled Red Onions (page 222)

**1) Make the piri-piri sauce:** In a food processor, pulse the bell pepper, chiles, red onion, garlic, lemon juice, salt, paprika, and black pepper until minced. With the machine running, pour in the oil through the feed tube and process until smooth. Makes about 1½ cups/360 ml sauce. Transfer ½ cup/120 ml of the sauce to a covered container and refrigerate to serve with the sandwiches.

**2)** Pound each chicken breast half between sheets of plastic wrap with a flat meat pounder or rolling pin until about ½ inch/1.25 cm thick. Cut each in half to make 4 portions total. Place in a 1-gallon/3.78 L

*Recipe continues*

resealable storage bag and pour in the remaining
1 cup/240 ml sauce. Close the bag and refrigerate,
turning occasionally, for at least 2 hours or up to
12 hours.

**3) Make the cilantro slaw:** Whisk the mayonnaise,
sweet chili sauce, and lemon juice in a medium bowl.
Add the slaw mix and cilantro and mix well. Season
with salt and pepper. (The slaw can be covered and
refrigerated for up to 2 days.)

**4)** Heat a ridged grill pan over medium heat. Remove
the chicken from the piri-piri, shaking off excess
sauce. Brush the pan with oil. Add the chicken and
cook, turning halfway through cooking, until the meat
shows no sign of pink when pierced in the thickest part
with the tip of a knife, 8 to 10 minutes. Transfer to a
plate. Discard the marinade.

**5)** Spread the split sides of the rolls with the reserved
piri-piri sauce. For each sandwich, place a chicken
portion on the roll bottom. Top with a portion of the
slaw and a few onion rings. Cap with the roll top. Cut in
half and serve with the remaining slaw on the side.

**note** Thai sweet chili sauce is the dip served
with Thai spring rolls. You will find it in Asian
markets, although it is being sold at standard
supermarkets with more regularity.

# Peking Duck Wrap

**Makes 6 servings**

Whenever I make this, it reminds me of the time my brother Octavien and I went to China and were finally able to taste classic Chinese food at the source. Peking duck is always roasted, but my skillet version is much faster and provides a fair reproduction of the dish's crisp and golden skin. The trick is to start cooking the duck in a cold skillet to render out the fat and finish cooking in the oven. Think of duck breast like flank steak—it shouldn't be cooked more than medium-rare or it will dry out, and slice it thinly on the diagonal, across the grain. While I like making individual wraps, you can also serve the duck, tortillas, hoisin sauce, slaw, and cucumbers family-style and let each guest make their own.

## napa cabbage slaw

One 2-inch/5 cm knob of fresh ginger, unpeeled

2 tablespoons rice vinegar

1 tablespoon vegetable oil

1 tablespoon toasted sesame oil

1 teaspoon soy sauce

1 teaspoon honey

3 cups/300 g shredded napa cabbage

1 scallion, white and green parts, finely chopped

Fine sea salt and freshly ground black pepper

Pinch of crushed hot red pepper

## duck

Two 1-pound/455 g boneless duck breast halves with skin (magrets; see Note)

1 teaspoon fine sea salt

½ teaspoon five-spice powder

¼ teaspoon freshly ground black pepper

———

6 burrito-sized flour tortillas, warmed

6 tablespoons hoisin sauce

One 3-inch/7.5 cm piece of seedless (English) cucumber, julienned (a mandoline works best)

1) **Make the napa cabbage slaw:** Shred the ginger on the large holes of a box grater. Squeeze the ginger in your fist over a bowl to extract the juice. You should have about 1 tablespoon ginger juice. Discard the ginger pulp. Whisk in the vinegar, vegetable and sesame oils, soy sauce, and honey. Add the cabbage and scallion and mix well. Season with salt, black pepper, and hot red pepper. Cover and refrigerate the slaw for at least 1 hour and up to 1 day. Drain before using, if needed.

*Recipe continues*

**note** Boneless duck breasts are often labeled with their French name, *magret*. Prepared from the Moulard duck variety, the flesh is very meaty and the thick skin is fatty. If your local butcher carries specialty meats, and it isn't in the refrigerator case, it might be sold frozen. Magret can also be purchased online.

**2) Prepare the duck:** Preheat the oven to 400°F/200°C. Using a sharp thin knife, cut a crosshatch pattern in the duck skin, taking care not to cut into the flesh, spacing the cuts about ½ inch/1.25 cm apart. Combine the salt, five-spice powder, and pepper and rub the mixture all over the duck breasts.

**3) Cook the duck:** Place the duck breasts, skin side down, in a large ovenproof skillet. Place over medium heat and cook until the skin is crisp and browned, 8 to 10 minutes, pouring off the copious fat as it collects. (You can refrigerate the fat for another use, keeping in mind that it will have some five-spice flavor.) Transfer the duck to a plate and discard any remaining fat. Return the duck to the skillet, skin side up. Place in the oven and roast until a meat thermometer inserted in the center of the duck reads 120°F/48°C for rare, 10 to 15 minutes. Transfer to a carving board with a well and let stand for about 5 minutes.

**4)** Using a sharp carving knife held at a slight diagonal, cut the duck across the grain into thin slices, and then vertically in half. For each sandwich, place a warm tortilla on your work surface. Spread 1 tablespoon hoisin sauce in a horizontal strip on the bottom third of a tortilla. Top with one-quarter of the slaw, a portion of the duck, and a sprinkle of cucumber. Fold up from the bottom of the tortilla to cover the filling, tucking it in tightly at the top. Fold the right and left sides 1 to 2 inches/2.5 to 5 cm inward to partially cover the filling, tucking in the corners as needed. The filling should be completely covered. Set aside, seam side down. Cut in half and serve warm.

# OG Spicy Chicken Sandwich

## with bacon and avocado

**Makes 2 sandwiches**

Along with My Favorite Tuna Melt (page 96), this is a sandwich that made me fall in love with the "stacked" genre at an early age. It is actually the first chicken sandwich I ever posted on social media, when, by chance, I decided to film one of my go-to lunches. It is inspired by a sandwich I used to order at a sandwich chain, but I now make my own version at home.

### chili chicken

One 10- to 12-ounce/ 280 to 340 g skinless, boneless chicken breast half

1 tablespoon olive oil

1 teaspoon chili powder

1 teaspoon ground cumin

1 teaspoon sweet paprika

1 teaspoon fine sea salt

6 slices thick-cut bacon

6 slices Gouda cheese

4 slices sourdough bread, toasted

Chipotle Mayonnaise (page 219)

1 ripe Hass avocado, halved, pitted, and sliced

Micro cilantro or coarsely chopped fresh cilantro

2 slices red onion, separated into thin rings

Crushed hot red pepper

**1) Make the chili chicken:** Pound the chicken breast between plastic wrap with a flat meat pounder or rolling pin until about ½ inch/1.25 cm thick. Cut in half crosswise to make 2 portions. Brush the oil on both sides. Mix the chili powder, cumin, paprika, and salt and use it to season the chicken all over.

**2)** Place the bacon in a cold empty skillet and cook over medium heat, turning occasionally, until crisp and browned, about 8 minutes. Transfer to paper towels to drain and cool. Pour out all but 1 tablespoon of the fat in the skillet and return to medium-high heat.

**3)** Add the chicken and cook, turning occasionally, until the meat shows no sign of pink when pierced in the center with the tip of a sharp knife, 8 to 10 minutes. Reduce the heat to very low. Top each chicken portion with 3 slices of cheese. Cover tightly and cook until the cheese melts, about 1 minute.

**4)** For each sandwich, spread 2 bread slices with about half of the mayonnaise. Add half of the avocado on each bottom slice. Top with a chicken portion and its cheese. Add 3 bacon strips, then a sprinkle of cilantro, a few onion rings, and a sprinkle of hot red pepper. Cap with the other bread slice, cut in half, and serve immediately.

# Grilled Chicken and Jack Quesadilla

## with creamy salsa dip

**Makes 4 quesadillas**

A tortilla quesadilla is as versatile as any bread sandwich and can be made with your favorite protein. I'm going with chicken here, but you can see the options: shrimp, ground beef, pulled pork, chorizo, sautéed vegetables. I upgrade the old favorite with a creamy dip on the side.

### mexican lime chicken

¼ cup/60 ml olive oil

3 tablespoons fresh lime juice

2 cloves garlic, minced

2 teaspoons ground cumin

2 teaspoons smoked paprika

1 teaspoon dried oregano, preferably Mexican

½ teaspoon fine sea salt

¼ teaspoon freshly ground black pepper

4 skinless, boneless chicken thighs, about 18 ounces/505 g total

### dip

½ cup/110 g Smoky Tomato Salsa (page 221) or store-bought fire-roasted salsa

½ cup/120 ml mayonnaise

½ cup/120 ml sour cream

1 teaspoon Mexican hot sauce, such as Cholula, or more to taste

2 cups/200 g shredded Monterey Jack cheese

2 cups/200 g shredded Colby Jack or mild Cheddar cheese

1 cup/50 g seeded and diced (½ inch/1.25 cm) tomatoes, patted dry with paper towels

½ cup/60 g chopped red onion

¼ cup/25 g chopped fresh cilantro

3 tablespoons seeded and minced jalapeño chile

4 burrito-sized flour tortillas

**1) Make the Mexican lime chicken:** Whisk the oil, lime juice, garlic, cumin, paprika, oregano, salt, and pepper together in a medium bowl. Pour into a 1-gallon/3.78 L resealable plastic bag, add the chicken, and close the bag. Refrigerate, turning occasionally, for at least 1 hour and up to overnight.

**2)** Heat a ridged grill pan over medium heat. Remove the chicken from the marinade, shaking off excess sauce. Add the chicken and cook, turning halfway through cooking, until the meat shows no sign of pink when pierced in the thickest part with the tip of a knife, 8 to 10 minutes. Transfer the chicken to a chopping board and let cool slightly. Chop into bite-sized pieces. Discard the marinade.

**3) Make the dip:** Whisk the salsa, mayonnaise, sour cream, and hot sauce in a medium bowl. Transfer to 4 small bowls for dipping.

**4)** Preheat the oven to 200°F/95°C.

**5)** Combine the two cheeses in a bowl. Mix the tomatoes, onions, cilantro, and jalapeño in another bowl. Heat a large grill pan, skillet, or griddle over medium heat. In batches, add a tortilla and heat just until the underside is warm, about 15 seconds. Flip the tortilla and sprinkle with 1 cup/100 g of the mixed cheese. On the lower half of the tortilla, scatter one-quarter of the tomato mixture and one-quarter of the chopped chicken. Fold the tortilla over into a half-moon shape. Grill until the underside is toasted, about 30 seconds. Flip the quesadilla and toast the other side, about 30 seconds more. Transfer to a half-sheet pan and keep warm in the oven while making quesadillas with the remaining ingredients.

**6)** Transfer the quesadillas to a chopping board. Using a large knife, cut each into 4 wedges. Transfer to plates and serve with the bowls of dip on the side.

# Turkey Crunch Sandwich

## with frico crisps

**Makes 2 sandwiches**

As the parent of these recipes, I know I'm not supposed to have a favorite turkey sandwich. But I do, and it is this Turkey Crunch. What makes the "crunch"? The Parmigiano-Reggiano crisp called *frico*, which is shredded cheese melted in a skillet to make a golden brown "chip." They are very quick to make, and you may find yourself making extra for nibbling. I usually make this with turkey from the deli, but when you have leftover turkey after a holiday dinner, make this sandwich!

### basil pesto

2 cloves garlic, crushed and peeled

1 cup packed/30 g fresh basil leaves

½ cup/50 g freshly grated Parmigiano-Reggiano cheese

¼ cup/35 g pine nuts

½ cup/120 ml extra virgin olive oil, plus more for topping

Fine sea salt and freshly ground black pepper

4 slices sourdough bread, lightly toasted

10 ounces/280 g thinly sliced turkey, preferably oven-roasted style

4 to 5 Frico Crisps (page 227)

2 red onion slices, separated into rings

Mild or hot pickled banana pepper rings

2 tablespoons Calabrian Mayonnaise (page 219)

**1)** **Make the basil pesto:** With the food processor running, drop the garlic through the feed tube to mince the garlic. Add the basil, cheese, and pine nuts and process until the basil is minced. With the machine running, gradually pour the oil through the feed tube and process until thick and smooth. Season with salt and pepper. (To store, transfer the pesto to a covered container. Pour a thin layer of additional olive oil on the surface to seal the pesto. Cover and refrigerate for up to 2 weeks or freeze for up to 3 months. If using frozen pesto, thaw before using. In either case, stir in the oil on the surface before using.)

**2)** For each sandwich, spread 1 tablespoon of the pesto on a slice of bread. Top with half of the turkey, followed by half of the crisps (broken to fit, if necessary), half of the red onion, and as many peppers as you like. Spread a second slice of bread with 1 tablespoon of the mayonnaise and use it to cap the sandwich. Cut in half and serve.

# Turkey Monte Cristo Sandwich

## with cranberry chutney

**Makes 2 sandwiches**

The Monte Cristo—basically a turkey-and-cheese sandwich on French toast—isn't as well-known as it used to be, which is too bad. I have improved on the original with a zesty cranberry chutney. You'll be glad to have this recipe when Thanksgiving rolls around, as it blows canned cranberry sauce out of the water. Choose your favorite topping—both maple syrup and confectioners' sugar have their fans.

### cranberry chutney

1 teaspoon vegetable oil

⅓ cup/45 g finely chopped yellow onion

2 tablespoons seeded and minced jalapeño chile

1 clove garlic, minced

One 14-ounce/395 g can whole berry cranberry sauce

½ cup/70 g finely diced (¼ inch/6 mm) crystallized ginger

Grated zest of 1 lime

2 tablespoons fresh lime juice

½ teaspoon ground cinnamon

½ teaspoon dry mustard

Pinch of fine sea salt

4 slices white or whole wheat sandwich bread

8 ounces/225 g sliced turkey

8 slices Swiss cheese

2 large eggs

½ cup/120 ml whole milk

¼ teaspoon fine sea salt

⅛ teaspoon freshly ground black pepper

2 tablespoons unsalted butter

Confectioners' sugar for garnish (optional)

**1)** **Make the cranberry chutney:** Heat the oil in a medium saucepan over medium heat. Add the onion, jalapeño, and garlic and cook, stirring occasionally, until the onion softens, about 3 minutes. Add the cranberry sauce, ginger, lime zest and juice, cinnamon, mustard, and salt. Bring to a simmer, stirring often. Reduce the heat to medium-low and simmer, stirring often, to blend the flavors, about 5 minutes. Let cool to room temperature. Makes about 1¼ cups/300 ml. (The chutney can be stored in a covered container in the refrigerator for up to 2 months.)

**2)** For each sandwich, spread 2 bread slices with 2 tablespoons of the chutney. On one slice, top the chutney side with one-quarter of the cheese, half of the turkey, and another quarter of the cheese. Cap with the other bread slice, chutney side down.

**3)** Whisk the eggs, milk, salt, and pepper in a wide shallow bowl. (An immersion blender does the best job.) Melt the butter in a wide nonstick skillet over medium heat. Dip each sandwich in the egg mixture, coating well on both sides. Add to the skillet and cook until the undersides are golden brown, about 2 minutes. Flip the sandwiches and cook the other sides, about 2 minutes more. Transfer to plates and cut in half. Sift confectioners' sugar on top, if desired. Serve hot, with the remaining cranberry chutney passed on the side.

# Turkey Saltimbocca Sandwich

## with sage sauce

**Makes 3 sandwiches**

*Saltimbocca* means "jump in your mouth" in Italian, and this combo of mild turkey, salty and crisp prosciutto, and sage-infused white wine sauce will do just that. My nonna makes it with veal, but I started using turkey and found it to be an excellent substitute. When cooking lean turkey breast cutlets, use medium heat, as they will toughen if the heat is too high. The cutlets are returned to the sauce for final cooking, so don't be concerned if the turkey seems undercooked at the initial browning.

---

1 pound turkey cutlets, about ¼ inch/6 mm thick, cut into 9 relatively equal pieces

Fine sea salt and freshly ground black pepper

¼ cup/35 g all-purpose flour

4 tablespoons/56 g (½ stick) cold unsalted butter, cut into tablespoons

2 tablespoons olive oil, plus more as needed

3 ounces/85 g thinly sliced prosciutto (not paper thin, if possible)

2 teaspoons finely chopped fresh sage

1 cup/240 ml dry white wine, such as Pinot Grigio

3 ciabatta rolls, split and toasted

About 1½ cups/45 g mixed baby greens

1 lemon, cut into wedges, for serving

1) Season the turkey with ¾ teaspoon salt and ½ teaspoon pepper. Spread the flour on a plate and coat the turkey on both sides, shaking off excess flour.

2) Melt 1 tablespoon of the butter with the oil in a very large skillet over medium heat. When the butter subsides, in batches, add the turkey. Cook, turning once, until very lightly browned, about 2 minutes. Do not overcook. Transfer the turkey to a platter. Add more oil to the skillet for the second batch, if needed.

3) Add the prosciutto to the skillet and cook, turning once, until crisp and lightly browned, about 1½ minutes. Add to the platter with the turkey.

4) Add 1 tablespoon of the remaining butter to the skillet and melt. Add the sage and stir until fragrant, about 30 seconds. Pour in the wine and bring to a boil, scraping up the browned bits in the skillet. Return all the turkey to the skillet. Cook, turning the cutlets in the liquid, until the sauce is very lightly thickened, about 1½ minutes. Return the turkey to the platter.

5) Remove the skillet from the heat. Add the remaining 2 tablespoons butter and whisk until it is absorbed by the sauce. Season with salt and pepper. Return the cutlets to the skillet and turn to coat in the sauce.

6) For each sandwich, place one-third of the cutlets, cut to fit as needed, with their sauce, on the roll bottom. Top with one-third of the prosciutto (folded to fit) and one-third of the greens. Cap with the roll top. Cut in half crosswise and serve hot with the lemon wedges.

**77**

# 4

# seafood

# Beer-Battered Cod Sandwich

## with jalapeño aioli

**Makes 4 sandwiches**

This sandwich is a perfect example of why it is good for home cooks to master deep-frying. Before jumping in, please read the technique tips on page 8. I use rice flour in the batter to reduce the gluten and create an especially light and crunchy tempura-like coating for the cod. For a more traditional sandwich, swap tartar sauce for the aioli. You might want to serve this with Oven French Fries (page 228) to make a fish-and-chips meal for the gods.

### red cabbage slaw

Grated zest of 1 lime

2 tablespoons fresh lime juice

Grated zest of 1 lemon

2 tablespoons fresh lemon juice

1 tablespoon cider vinegar

Fine sea salt and freshly ground black pepper

⅓ cup/75 ml extra virgin olive oil

2 cups/200 g shredded red cabbage (about ¼ small head)

½ small red onion, cut into thin half-moons

⅓ cup/35 g finely chopped fresh cilantro

### beer-battered cod

1 pound/455 g cod, scrod, or haddock fillets

Vegetable or canola oil for deep-frying

¾ cup/105 g all-purpose flour

¼ cup/40 g white rice (not sweet rice) flour or cornstarch

1 teaspoon baking powder

½ teaspoon fine sea salt

¼ teaspoon freshly ground black pepper

1 cup/240 ml lager or light beer, as needed

4 soft oblong rolls, split and lightly toasted

About ½ cup/120 ml Jalapeño Aioli (page 219)

Kosher salt for serving

Lemon wedges for serving

**1)** **Make the red cabbage slaw:** Whisk the lime zest and juice, lemon zest and juice, vinegar, ½ teaspoon salt, and ¼ teaspoon pepper in a medium bowl. Gradually whisk in the oil. Add the cabbage, onion, and cilantro and mix well. Season with more salt and pepper. Cover and refrigerate for at least 1 hour and up to 1 day. Drain before using, if needed.

**2)** Place a wire cooling rack on a half-sheet pan. Pour enough oil into a large heavy saucepan to come at least 2 inches/5 cm up the sides and heat over high heat until the oil reads 350°F/180°C on a deep-frying thermometer. Preheat the oven to 200°F/95°C.

**80**

**3)** **Make the beer-battered cod:** Cut the cod into 4 equal pieces. Whisk the all-purpose flour, rice flour, baking powder, salt, and pepper in a medium bowl. Gradually whisk in enough of the beer until the consistency is like thin pancake batter. Do not overmix; a few small lumps are fine. Dip 2 cod fillets in the batter to coat. Place on a wire spider or slotted spoon and ease into the hot oil. Let cook until the batter begins to set, about 10 seconds, and then release the cod into the oil. (This helps keep the batter from sticking to the bottom of the saucepan.) Deep-fry until golden, about 4 minutes. Using a wire spider or slotted spoon, transfer the cod to the wire rack. Blot off excess oil with paper towels and keep warm in the oven while frying the remaining cod. Be sure to let the oil return to 350°F/180°C between batches.

**4)** For each sandwich, spread a roll with about 2 tablespoons of the aioli. Sprinkle the cod with kosher salt. Place a cod fillet on the roll bottom and top with a serving of the slaw. Cap with the roll top. Cut in half and serve hot with lemon wedges and the remaining slaw on the side.

# Crab Cake Sandwich

## with old bay aioli

**Makes 4 sandwiches**

This is how they make the famous crab cakes in the Chesapeake Bay region around Baltimore. There, any crab cake worth its salt features Old Bay Seasoning and plenty of crab with just enough binder to hold it together. If you have access to fresh crabmeat, definitely choose it over the canned and pasteurized versions—it is a worthwhile indulgence.

### crab cakes

- 1 pound/455 g crabmeat, preferably fresh
- ¼ cup/60 ml mayonnaise
- 1 large egg
- 1 tablespoon Dijon mustard
- 1 tablespoon finely chopped fresh flat-leaf parsley
- 1 tablespoon finely chopped scallion (white and pale green parts)
- 1 teaspoon Old Bay Seasoning
- 1 teaspoon Worcestershire sauce
- ½ teaspoon hot red pepper sauce, such as Tabasco
- ¼ teaspoon fine sea salt
- ¼ teaspoon freshly ground black pepper
- ¼ cup/20 g panko breadcrumbs
- ¼ cup/60 ml vegetable or canola oil for frying

---

- 4 English muffins or hamburger buns, split and toasted
- About ½ cup/120 ml Old Bay Aioli (page 219)
- 4 slices ripe tomato
- 4 tender lettuce leaves, such as Bibb or butter

1) **Make the crab cakes:** Pick through the crabmeat and discard any shells or cartilage. Whisk the mayonnaise, egg, mustard, parsley, scallion, Old Bay Seasoning, Worcestershire sauce, hot sauce, salt, and pepper in a medium bowl. Add the crabmeat and panko and mix well. Divide and shape into four 4-inch/10 cm patties. Place on a waxed or parchment paper–lined baking sheet, cover with plastic wrap, and refrigerate to firm the crabcakes, at least 30 minutes and up to 4 hours.

2) Line a baking sheet with paper towels. Heat the oil in a large skillet over medium-high heat. Add the crab cakes and cook until the underside is golden brown, about 3 minutes. Flip and cook the other side, 2 to 3 minutes more. Transfer to the paper towels to drain.

3) For each sandwich, spread the cut sides of an English muffin with about 2 tablespoons of the aioli. Stack a crab cake, a tomato slice, and a lettuce leaf on one half of the muffin. Cap with the other muffin half, cut vertically, and serve.

## fennel slaw

2 tablespoons finely
chopped shallot

2 tablespoons finely
chopped fresh fennel
fronds or dill, or a
combination

2 tablespoons fresh
lemon juice

2 teaspoons cider
vinegar or white wine
vinegar

¼ teaspoon sugar

3 tablespoons extra
virgin olive oil

3 cups/240 g thinly
sliced fennel (a
mandoline or food
processor with the
thin slicing blade
work best)

Fine sea salt and freshly
ground black pepper

## salmon burgers

1½ pounds/680 g
skinless salmon
fillet, cut into
1-inch/2.5 cm pieces

1 cup/75 g panko
breadcrumbs

3 tablespoons
mayonnaise

2 tablespoons finely
chopped fresh chives
or green scallion tops

1 tablespoon finely
chopped fresh dill
(see page 86)

1 large egg yolk

1 tablespoon Dijon
mustard

1 tablespoon fresh
lemon juice

½ teaspoon fine sea salt

¼ teaspoon freshly
ground black pepper

3 tablespoons vegetable
or canola oil

6 brioche buns, toasted

About ½ cup/120 ml
Lemon-Herb
Mayonnaise (page
219)

6 tomato slices

6 tender lettuce leaves,
such as Bibb or
Boston

# Lemon-Herb Salmon Burger

## with fennel slaw

**Makes 6 burgers**

Finely chopped salmon makes great seafood burgers. I usually opt for fresh fennel as the herb, but you can substitute dill, basil, mint, tarragon, chives, chervil, or parsley, or your favorite combination. (The equal parts of the last four make up the classic French fines herbes mix, so that is a sure bet for a combo. You can skip the chervil, as it isn't all that easy to find.)

**1) Make the fennel slaw:** Whisk the shallot, fennel fronds, lemon juice, vinegar, and sugar in a medium bowl. Whisk in the oil. Add the fennel slices and mix well. Season with salt and pepper. Cover and refrigerate for at least 1 hour and up to 1 day to soften the fennel.

*Recipe continues*

2) **Make the salmon burgers:** Pulse the salmon in a food processor about 10 times, until finely chopped. Stir ⅓ cup/25 g of the panko, the mayonnaise, chives, dill, yolk, mustard, lemon juice, salt, and pepper in a medium bowl. Add the chopped salmon and mix well. Shape into six 4-inch/10 cm patties. Spread the remaining ⅔ cup/50 g panko on a plate. Coat the patties in the panko, patting to help the coating adhere. Transfer to a baking sheet, cover with plastic wrap, and refrigerate to firm the salmon cakes for at least 30 minutes or up to 4 hours.

3) Heat the oil in a very large skillet over medium heat. Add the patties and cook until the underside is golden, about 3 minutes. Flip the patties and cook until the other side is golden, about 3 minutes more. Transfer to paper towels to drain briefly.

4) For each burger, spread a bun with about 2 tablespoons of the mayonnaise. Add a patty to the bottom roll and top with a tomato slice and lettuce leaf. Add a spoonful of slaw and cap the top of the roll. Cut in half and transfer to a plate. Serve hot, with the fennel slaw on the side.

# chopping fresh herbs

When chopping fresh herbs, especially delicate ones like dill, be sure they are well dried and use a very sharp knife. A salad spinner does a good job of drying rinsed herbs, but still give them a quick pat-down with paper towels to remove every last droplet of water before chopping. The chopped herbs will keep for a few days, loosely wrapped in a dry paper towel and refrigerated in an airtight container or small resealable plastic bag.

## cilantro tequila shrimp

¼ cup/60 ml fresh lime juice

¼ cup/60 ml extra virgin olive oil, plus more for brushing

¼ cup/60 ml silver (blanco) tequila

2 tablespoons agave syrup or honey

2 tablespoons finely chopped fresh cilantro

1 tablespoon seeded and minced jalapeño chile

1 teaspoon ground cumin

½ teaspoon cayenne pepper

½ teaspoon fine sea salt

¼ teaspoon freshly ground black pepper

1¼ pounds/570 g large (31–35 count) shrimp, about 36 shrimp, peeled and deveined

## red cabbage taco slaw

Grated zest of 1 lime

2 tablespoons fresh lime juice

2 tablespoons extra virgin olive oil

½ teaspoon ground cumin

2 cups packed/200 g shredded red cabbage

Fine sea salt and freshly ground black pepper

———

24 street taco-sized corn tortillas, warmed (see Note, page 89)

Roasted Tomatillo Salsa (page 221) or store-bought green salsa, for serving

1 lime, cut into quarters, for serving

# Grilled Shrimp and Tomatillo Street Tacos

**Makes 12 small tacos, 4 servings**
**Special equipment: 8 long bamboo skewers, soaked in water to cover for at least 30 minutes, and drained**

Small "street taco" corn tortillas are now sold in supermarkets, and they do make authentic tacos. Because you get just a few bites per taco, they must be bursting with flavor, as they are here. With its zesty marinade, tart slaw, and earthy salsa, this shrimp version will go to the top of your list of favorite seafood tacos. I like the char flavor from an outdoor grill, but you can also make them in a grill pan or on a griddle.

1) **Marinate the shrimp:** Whisk the lime juice, oil, tequila, honey, cilantro, jalapeño, cumin, cayenne, salt, and pepper in a medium bowl. Pour into a 1-gallon/3.78 L resealable plastic bag, add the shrimp, and close the bag. Refrigerate for at least 30 minutes but no longer than 1 hour.

2) **Make the red cabbage taco slaw:** Whisk the lime zest and juice, oil, and cumin in a medium bowl. Add the cabbage, mix, and season with salt and pepper. Cover and refrigerate until ready to serve. The slaw is best the day it is made. *Recipe continues*

3) Prepare an outdoor grill for direct cooking over medium heat (350° to 450°F/180° to 230°C). If using a charcoal grill, let the coals burn until you can hold your hand above the grate for about 3 seconds. It should not be blazing hot. Brush the grate clean.

4) **Cook the cilantro tequila shrimp:** Remove the shrimp from the marinade. Keeping the shrimp in a C shape, thread about 9 shrimp onto 2 parallel skewers (this keeps them from spinning as they would on a single skewer). Brush the skewered shrimp with oil. Line them up on the grill, perpendicular to the grate. Slip a strip of aluminum foil under the uncovered handle ends of the skewers to protect them from the direct heat. Close the lid and grill, turning once, until the shrimp turn opaque, about 3 minutes. Slide the shrimp off the skewers onto a chopping board. Coarsely chop the shrimp and transfer to a bowl.

5) For each serving, build 3 tacos directly on a dinner plate. Make three stacks of 2 tortillas. Top each stack with a portion of the chopped shrimp, a spoonful of the slaw, and 1 tablespoon of the salsa. Fold the tacos in half and stand them next to each other for support. Add a lime wedge to each plate and serve immediately, with the remaining salsa passed on the side.

**note** Many taquerías use a double stack of tortillas as protection against wet fillings that will soak into a single tortilla and make it fall apart. If you know your tortillas are sturdy, a single layer may be enough. The easiest way to heat the tortillas in pairs is to warm 12 double stacks in a preheated 350°F/180°C oven, placing them directly on the oven rack without a baking sheet, for 4 to 5 minutes. Or warm them, one tortilla at a time, on a large griddle or heated grill, and transfer to a baking sheet in a preheated 200°F/95°C oven to keep warm until ready to use.

**Shrimp Tacos a la Plancha:** Heat a ridged grill pan or griddle over medium heat. Remove the shrimp from the marinade. Do not thread the shrimp on the skewers. Spread the shrimp in the pan and cook until the edges turn opaque, about 2 minutes. Using tongs, flip the shrimp and cook until they are opaque throughout, about 1 minute longer. Transfer the shrimp to the chopping board and chop coarsely.

# Ma's Shrimp Toast

## with spicy asian mayonnaise

**Makes 4 or 5 servings**

Here it is, the viral recipe that put me on the map. Every Asian cuisine has a version of shrimp toast, but this is the way Ma (Grandma Han) makes it. It is a fantastic way to turn a handful of shrimp into a special treat. Usually served plain, I like to bump them up with gochujang-spiced mayo. However, they are also good with small bowls of nuoc cham (page 152) for dipping, skipping the mayo on the platter.

### shrimp paste

1 medium celery rib, minced

1 scallion, white and green parts, minced

2 tablespoons minced water chestnuts

2 tablespoons finely chopped fresh cilantro

8 ounces/225 g large shrimp, peeled and deveined

1 large egg white, beaten with a fork until foamy

2 tablespoons cornstarch

2 teaspoons toasted sesame oil

1 tablespoon soy sauce

4 or 5 slices white sandwich bread, preferably day-old and slightly stale

Vegetable or canola oil for deep-frying

Spicy Asian Mayonnaise (page 219)

1 scallion, green part only, thinly sliced into rings, for serving

1 lemon for serving

**1)** **Make the shrimp paste:** Put the celery, scallions, water chestnuts, and cilantro in a medium bowl. Using a large knife, mince the shrimp well until reduced to a paste. Scrape into the bowl. Add the egg white, cornstarch, sesame oil, and soy sauce and stir well. (To make in a food processor, coarsely chop the vegetables by hand, transfer to the processor, and pulse until minced. Transfer to a bowl. Puree the shrimp in the food processor. Add the egg white, cornstarch, sesame oil, and soy sauce and pulse to combine. Return the minced vegetables to the processor and pulse to mix. Transfer to a bowl.) Cover with plastic wrap and refrigerate for about 15 minutes to firm up a bit.

**2)** Trim off the crusts from the bread (reserve for testing the oil). Divide the shrimp mixture among the bread slices. Depending on the size of the bread, you will have 4 or 5 shrimp-topped slices. Cut diagonally in half to make 2 triangles per slice.

**3)** Preheat the oven to 200°F/95°C. Place a wire cooling rack in a half-sheet pan.

**4)** Pour enough vegetable oil in a large deep skillet to come ½ inch/1.25 cm up the sides and heat over high heat until the oil shimmers. (A cube of bread crust will start to sizzle and brown immediately when added to the oil.) In batches, add the triangles, shrimp side down, to the oil. Cook until the shrimp paste is browned and set, about 2 minutes, adjusting the heat as needed to keep the oil bubbling around the toasts. Carefully flip the toasts and fry until the bread is golden brown, about 1 minute more. Using a slotted spatula, transfer to the wire rack and keep warm in the oven until all the toasts are fried.

**5)** Fill a plastic squeeze bottle with the spicy Asian mayonnaise. Arrange the shrimp on a platter. Squeeze zigzags of the mayonnaise on the toast. Sprinkle with the scallions. Using a zester, finely grate the lemon zest on top, then cut the lemon into wedges. Serve immediately with the lemon wedges and remaining mayonnaise on the side.

## remoulade

1 cup/240 ml
mayonnaise

2 tablespoons dill pickle
relish or minced dill
pickle

2 tablespoons fresh
lemon juice

1 tablespoon prepared
horseradish

1 tablespoon finely
chopped fresh flat-
leaf parsley

2 teaspoons Creole or
whole-grain mustard

1 teaspoon
Worcestershire sauce

1 clove garlic, crushed
through a press

½ teaspoon Cajun or
Creole seasoning

½ teaspoon smoked
paprika

## snapper

1 cup/140 g all-purpose
flour

½ teaspoon sweet
paprika

½ teaspoon garlic
powder

½ teaspoon fine sea salt

½ teaspoon freshly
ground black pepper

⅛ teaspoon cayenne
pepper

1 cup/240 ml buttermilk

2 tablespoons hot
red pepper sauce,
preferably Louisiana,
such as Crystal

1 cup/150 g yellow
cornmeal

Vegetable oil for deep-
frying

Four 6-ounce/170 g
red snapper fillets,
skinned

4 soft oblong rolls, split

16 ripe tomato slices

2 cups/150 g shredded
iceberg lettuce

Dill pickle slices
(optional)

# Snapper Po'boy

## with remoulade

**Makes 4 sandwiches**

Po'boy gets its name from the story of how the sandwiches were made for the "poor boys" who ate them as cheap meals in nineteenth-century New Orleans. Snapper makes a great po'boy, but so do shucked oysters, shrimp, or catfish nuggets, so I've included variations on that theme following the master recipe. Feel free to try them all!

**1)** **Make the remoulade:** Whisk the mayonnaise, relish, lemon juice, horseradish, parsley, mustard, Worcestershire sauce, garlic, Cajun seasoning, and paprika together. (The remoulade can be covered and refrigerated for up to 1 week.)

**2)** **Prepare the snapper:** Whisk the flour, paprika, garlic powder, salt, and black and cayenne peppers together in a shallow bowl or pie plate. Whisk the buttermilk and hot sauce in another bowl or pie plate.

*Recipe continues*

Spread the cornmeal in a third bowl or pie plate. Place an empty plate nearby. Place a wire cooling rack on a half-sheet pan near the stove.

3) Pour enough oil into a large heavy saucepan to come about 1 inch/2.5 cm up the sides and heat over medium-high heat until the oil reads 350°F/180°C on a deep-frying thermometer. Preheat the oven to 200°F/95°C.

4) **Cook the snapper:** Working with 2 fillets at a time, dredge each fillet into the seasoned flour, then shake off excess flour. Dip into the buttermilk mixture, and then into the cornmeal to coat. Place on the plate. Carefully add the fillets to the oil and fry until golden brown, 2½ to 3 minutes. Using a slotted spatula, transfer the snapper to the wire rack. Blot excess oil with paper towels and keep warm in the oven while frying the remaining snapper.

5) For each sandwich, spread each roll generously with 2 to 3 tablespoons of the remoulade. Place a snapper fillet on the roll bottom. Top with 4 tomato slices and ½ cup of the lettuce. Add pickles, if using. Cap with the roll top, cut in half, and serve immediately, with the remaining remoulade on the side.

**Oyster Po'boy:** Substitute 24 to 32 shucked oysters for the snapper.

**Shrimp Po'boy:** Substitute 1½ pounds/680 g medium (31–36 count) peeled and deveined shrimp for the snapper.

**Catfish Po'boy:** Substitute 1½ pounds/680 g catfish fillets for the snapper.

# Shrimp Puttanesca Roll

**Makes 4 rolls**

Puttanesca sauce is supposed to be made quickly, the opposite of my nonna's slow-simmered tomato sauce on page 115. While it is usually made with canned tuna to put on pasta, I like it paired with shrimp as a hot sandwich. According to Italian cooking "rules," which were passed down to me by Chef Daniella, you are not supposed to serve cheese with seafood, but if you were to grate some Parmigiano on top, I won't tell anyone.

## puttanesca sauce

2 tablespoons olive oil

6 anchovy fillets in oil, drained and minced, or 2 teaspoons anchovy paste

2 cloves garlic, minced

¼ teaspoon crushed hot red pepper

One 14-ounce/390 g can diced tomatoes

¼ cup/40 g pitted and chopped kalamata olives

2 tablespoons drained nonpareil capers

1 tablespoon chopped fresh basil

1 tablespoon olive oil, plus more for brushing

1 pound/455 g large (31–35 count) shrimp, peeled and deveined

4 crusty oblong rolls, split

1 large clove garlic for rubbing

Chopped fresh basil for serving

Lemon wedges for serving

**1)** **Make the puttanesca sauce:** Heat the oil, anchovies, and garlic in a medium saucepan over medium heat, stirring often, until the garlic softens and the anchovies melt, about 2 minutes. Stir in the hot red pepper, followed by the tomatoes and their juice. Bring to a boil over high heat. Reduce the heat to medium and cook at a brisk simmer until the juices thicken, about 7 minutes. Stir in the olives, capers, and basil, reduce the heat to low, and simmer to blend the flavors, about 3 minutes.

**2)** Heat 1 tablespoon of the oil in a large skillet over medium-high heat. Spread the shrimp in a single layer in the skillet. Cook, without stirring, until lightly browned on the underside, about 2 minutes. Flip the shrimp and brown just to sear, about 30 seconds. Do not overcook. Add the warm sauce, bring to a simmer, and cook until the shrimp are opaque throughout, about 1 minute. Remove from the heat.

**3)** Brush the cut sides of the rolls with oil and toast in a broiler or toaster oven (or on a griddle or grill pan). For each sandwich, rub the crisp, browned sides of the roll with the garlic clove. Fill the roll with one-quarter of the shrimp and sauce. Sprinkle with basil. Close the roll, cut in half, and serve hot with lemon wedges.

# My Favorite Tuna Melt

**Makes 2 sandwiches**

When I was about twelve, our family took a vacation in Bali. Although I considered myself a grown-up, I still got a charge by ordering from the kids' menu. That's when I first had this incredible open-faced tuna melt sandwich, loaded with vegetables and herbs, and I was instantly obsessed. So much so that I have been perfecting it ever since. If you've never had tuna packed in olive oil, you are in for a treat, as it has much better flavor and texture than the water-packed variety.

## tuna salad

Two 5-ounce/142 g cans tuna in olive oil

¼ cup/35 g finely chopped celery

¼ cup/30 g finely chopped red onion

4 to 6 pepperoncini (pickled peppers), stemmed and finely chopped

¼ cup/60 ml mayonnaise, homemade (page 218) or store-bought

1 tablespoon finely chopped fresh flat-leaf parsley

1 tablespoon finely chopped fresh dill

1 teaspoon Dijon mustard

Grated zest of ½ lemon

1 tablespoon fresh lemon juice

Fine sea salt and freshly ground black pepper

2 sesame bagels

12 slices wide tomato, such as beefsteak or an heirloom variety

4 ounces thinly sliced Fontina cheese, preferably Italian

1 cup/35 g radish or alfalfa sprouts

**1)** **Make the tuna salad:** Empty the tuna into a medium bowl (no need to drain) and flake with a fork. Add the celery, onion, pepperoncini, mayonnaise, parsley, dill, mustard, and lemon zest and juice and mix. Season with salt and pepper.

**2)** Position a broiler rack about 4 inches/10 cm from the source of heat and preheat on High. For each sandwich, place an open bagel on a broiler pan and top both halves of the bagel with half of the tuna salad, half of the tomatoes, and half of the cheese. Broil until the cheese is melted, 1 to 2 minutes. Transfer, open-faced, to a plate, top with half of the sprouts, and serve.

## tuna: lunch in a can

Before the early twentieth century, the most popular canned fish was salmon, which could be easily mixed with mayonnaise for a salad topping or sandwich filling. Sardines also had a large piece of the canned fish market. Around 1900, fishing equipment improved and larger fish could be caught. About the same time, the sardine catch in Southern California failed. To replace the loss, a local canning factory tried the process on albacore tuna, which was considered an overabundant trash fish at the time. Surprisingly (although not perhaps to Italian immigrants from southern Italy, where tuna was a part of the culinary landscape), the "new" fish took off. When someone used it instead of salmon to make their lunchtime sandwich, a star was born. Within twenty years, the California fish population was overfished, and canners had to move to Mexico and other points south for their catch. Tuna has lost some of its popularity, but I still love it as a nostalgic treat.

# Lobster Tempura Bao

## with cilantro mayonnaise

**Makes 16 bao, 4 servings**

I asked my good friend and fellow food-content creator, H Woo Lee, for a lobster roll recipe, and he provided this one, which is more Korean than New England, as I should have expected. It's served in the traditional Asian manner of a communal platter so diners can help themselves. Prepare the various components ahead of time (add the liquids to the dry ingredients in the batter at the last minute), and all you'll have to do is fry the lobster tempura. One of H Woo's secrets to his light tempura batter is vodka—its alcohol has a crisping effect on the crust. This is a luxurious meal to share with your besties.

### lobster tempura

Two 10- to 12-ounce/ 280 to 340 g lobster tails

1 cup/140 g all-purpose flour

2 tablespoons potato starch or cornstarch

1 teaspoon baking soda

¾ cup/180 ml chilled club soda, plus more as needed

1 large egg, cold from the fridge

2 tablespoons chilled vodka

3 ice cubes

Vegetable oil for deep-frying

———

Shichimi togarashi (see Note) for serving

Fine sea salt for serving

16 Steamed Buns (page 147), warm

Cilantro Mayonnaise (page 219; H Woo recommends the shiso variation)

Spicy Cucumber Pickles (page 225)

1) **Prepare the lobster tails:** Turn the lobster tail so the hard top is facing down. Using kitchen shears, cut down one side of the "belly," where it meets the hard shell, and repeat on the other side. Pull off and discard the thin belly shell and feelers. Slip a dessertspoon, bowl facing up, under the shell and work around the shell to loosen the tail meat. Pull both sides of the hard shell apart and away from the tail meat at the same time to reveal the tail meat. Discard the shell. Repeat with the second lobster tail. Cut the lobster meat crosswise into 16 relatively equal medallions about 1 inch/2.5 cm thick.

2) **Make the tempura batter:** Whisk the flour, potato starch, and baking soda together in a medium bowl. Using a dinner fork, mix the club soda, egg, and vodka in another bowl. Add to the flour mixture and stir with the fork just until combined—the batter should be a little lumpy. Adjust the thickness with more club soda, if needed, to reach the consistency of a pancake batter, just thick enough to cling to the lobster meat. Add the ice cubes to keep the batter cold.

3) **Make the lobster tempura:** Preheat the oven to 200°F/95°C. Line a half-sheet pan with a wire cooling rack and place near the stove.

4) Pour enough oil to come 2 inches/5 cm up the sides of a large, deep saucepan and heat over high heat until the oil reads 350ºF/180ºC on a deep-frying thermometer. In two batches, dip the lobster medallions into the batter, let the excess batter drip back into the bowl, and add to the oil. Deep-fry until golden brown, about 2½ minutes. Using a wire spider or a slotted spoon, transfer the lobster to the cooling rack and keep warm in the oven until all the lobster is cooked.

5) Arrange the lobster on a platter. Sprinkle with the shichimi togarashi and salt. Serve immediately with the steamed buns, cilantro or shiso mayonnaise, pickles, and the bottle of shichimi togarashi. Let each guest fill their own bao.

**note** Shichimi togarashi is a blend of dried chiles, spices, sesame seeds, and dried orange peel that is a popular Japanese condiment. It is sold in small, pocket-sized bottles because many diners like to carry a personal supply. You'll find it at Japanese grocers.

# 5

# beef, veal, and lamb

# Not-So-Classic Cheesesteak

**Makes 2 sandwiches**

Philadelphia is the birthplace of the cheesesteak. At its bare bones, the filling is sliced steak cooked with lots of onions piled onto a roll and finished with a blanket of melty cheese. The first time I had it, it was a quick meal between planes at the Philly airport. I savored it so slowly that I almost missed my flight! For extra kick, top it with sliced pickled peppers, such as cherry peppers, which is the way many fans like it. My version also has a tangy sauce that you won't find in the plainer versions.

---

1 pound/455 g boneless rib eye steak

⅓ cup/80 ml ketchup

2 tablespoons reduced-sodium soy sauce

1 tablespoon Worcestershire sauce

2 teaspoons sriracha

2 tablespoons vegetable or canola oil

1 medium sweet onion, cut into thin half-moons

1 tablespoon finely grated fresh ginger

2 cloves garlic, finely chopped

¾ teaspoon fine sea salt

½ teaspoon freshly ground black pepper

¾ cup/75 g shredded low-moisture mozzarella cheese

¾ cup/75 g shredded unsmoked provolone cheese

2 crusty French or Italian rolls, partially split lengthwise and opened like a book

Sliced hot or sweet pickled cherry peppers

**1)** Freeze the steak until firm and partially frozen, about 30 minutes. On a carving board, cut across the grain into ¼-inch/6 mm slices. Stir the ketchup, soy sauce, Worcestershire sauce, and sriracha together.

**2)** Position the broiler rack about 4 inches/10 cm from the source of heat and preheat the broiler on High.

**3)** Heat a large heavy skillet, preferably cast iron, over high heat. Add the oil, then the onions, ginger, and garlic. Cook, stirring occasionally, until the onions begin to brown, about 3 minutes. Move the onions to the edges of the pan and add the steak strips to the center. Spread out the steak as much as you can to have contact with the skillet. Cook the steak until seared on the underside, about 2 minutes. Flip the steak and cook until seared but still rare, about 2 minutes more. Stir the steak and onions together and season with the salt and pepper. Stir in the ketchup mixture and bring to a simmer. Remove from the heat.

**4)** Combine the mozzarella and provolone cheeses. For each sandwich, open a roll and heap half of the steak mixture on the bottom half. Top with half of the cheese. Place the open-faced sandwiches on a broiler pan. Broil until the cheese is melted, about 1 minute. Add the pickled peppers as desired. Close the roll, cut in half, and serve hot.

# Chicago Italian Beef Sandwich

**Makes 8 sandwiches**

I love Chicago Italian beef sandwiches so much that I have been known to mail order a "make-your-own" kit from my favorite place, Portillo's. Every great Italian beef shop in the Windy City has its own secret recipe, and this is my personal mash-up of many versions, so if you think it's not the same as the one on *The Bear*, you are probably right and let's not disagree. The big question about Chicago beef is whether to serve it dry, wet, or dipped. You'll find your sweet spot. Note that the cooked beef needs to refrigerate overnight to firm it up before carving it into the thinnest slices you can manage. One more tip: Be sure your bread is sturdy enough to hold up to a dip in the juices. If it is too fluffy, it will fall apart—a big problem. A very sharp carving knife is essential, and if you are lucky enough to have a home-model meat slicer, use it. Rome was not built in a day.

2 tablespoons olive oil, plus more as needed

One 4½-pound/1.8 kg top round beef roast

1½ teaspoons fine sea salt

½ teaspoon freshly ground black pepper

2 medium green bell peppers, seeded and cut lengthwise into strips about 1 inch/2.5 cm wide

1 large Spanish onion, cut into half-moons about ½ inch/1.25 cm thick

4 cloves garlic, coarsely chopped

1 cup/240 ml hearty red wine, such as Shiraz

1 quart/960 ml reduced-sodium beef broth

Soft Italian rolls, partially split and opened like a book

Windy City Giardiniera (recipe follows), at room temperature, for serving

**1)** Preheat the oven to 300°F/150°C.

**2)** Heat the oil in a Dutch oven over medium-high heat. Rub the beef all over with the salt and black pepper. Add to the pot and cook, turning occasionally, until browned on all sides, about 10 minutes. Transfer to a plate.

**3)** Add more oil to the pot, if needed. Add the bell peppers, onion, and garlic and cook, stirring occasionally, until the onions soften, about 5 minutes. Pour in the wine and bring to a boil, scraping up the browned bits in the pot. Return the beef to the pot and pour in the broth. Add water, if needed, to cover the beef by three-quarters up the sides and bring to a boil over high heat.

**4)** Cover tightly and bake, turning the beef every hour or so, until it is very tender when pierced with a meat fork, about 3 hours. Remove from the heat. Transfer the beef to a carving board with a well, reserving the cooking liquid in the pot. Using a slotted spoon, transfer the peppers and onions to a bowl. Cool the roast, vegetables, and cooking liquid to

*Recipe continues*

**104**

room temperature. Wrap the roast in foil. Transfer the vegetables and liquid to separate containers and cover. Refrigerate the roast, vegetables, and liquid for at least 1 day and up to 2 days.

5) Using a sharp carving knife, cut the cold beef crosswise into very thin slices, and then into pieces that will fit the rolls. Don't worry about any meat that crumbles, and just save it. (The sliced beef can be refrigerated in a plastic storage bag for 1 day.)

6) To serve, bring the broth to a simmer in a large, wide saucepan over high heat. Reduce the heat to very low to keep the broth very hot but not simmering. Reheat the peppers/onions separately in a small skillet or microwave oven. Transfer the sliced beef (and any bits) to the hot broth. Let stand just until heated through, about 1 minute.

7) For each sandwich, determine if it will be served dry, wet, or dipped (see below).

**For a dry sandwich:** Add a serving of the sliced beef and its clinging broth to a roll. Follow with some of the peppers and as much giardiniera as you like. Close the roll, cut in half, and serve.

**For a wet sandwich:** Use the tongs to first dip the cut side of the rolls in the hot broth, and then add the beef with any clinging broth, the peppers, and the giardiniera. Close the roll, cut in half, and serve.

**For a dipped sandwich:** Make the dry version, with peppers and giardiniera as desired. Close the roll, cut it in half, stab each half onto a meat fork, and use the tongs to hold it together as you submerge it into the broth until the roll is wet but not soaked, 2 to 3 seconds. You don't want the roll to fall apart. The wet sandwich is very sloppy but outrageously good, and a Chicagoan would never eat it with a fork and knife. But then again, it would be wrapped in deli paper. You can do the same. Place the wet sandwich on a sheet of deli paper, wrap it up like a burrito, cut it in half, and serve.

**106**

# Windy City Giardiniera

**Makes 1 quart/960 ml**
**Special equipment:** 1-quart/960 ml glass
canning jar

The colorful chopped vegetable condiment is
essential on Chicago beef, but it is an excellent side
dish for any sandwich. A couple of tips: Rather than
buy out the produce section, you might want to
purchase smaller amounts of veggies at the salad
bar or get a crudité platter. Also, plan your time
accordingly, as the vegetables are brined overnight
to help keep them crisp, and then marinated for a
day or two. This method of preserving vegetables is
called *sott'olio* ("under oil") in Italian. You will find
many other sandwiches that will benefit from this
crunchy giardiniera. To make a mild version, leave
out the jalapeño. Sometimes I divide the giardiniera
between two 1-pint/480 ml jars, adding half of the
jalapeño to just one jar to end up with one jar of hot
pickles and one of mild.

1 cup/120 g seeded and
diced (¼ inch/6 mm)
green bell pepper

1 cup/130 g diced
(¼ inch/6 mm) yellow
onion

⅔ cup/55 g coarsely
chopped cauliflower
florets

½ cup/55 g diced
(¼ inch/6 mm) carrot

½ cup/65 g diced
(¼ inch/6 mm) celery

2 cloves garlic, finely
chopped

½ jalapeño chile, seeded,
cut into ¼-inch/6 mm
rounds, then
quartered

2 tablespoons fine sea
salt

½ cup/75 g sliced
pimiento-stuffed
olives or salad olives

1 teaspoon dried oregano

¼ teaspoon freshly
ground black pepper

1 cup/240 ml olive oil, as
needed

1) Combine the bell pepper, onion, cauliflower, carrot,
celery, garlic, and jalapeño in a medium bowl. You want
about 4 cups of chopped vegetables. Add the salt and
toss to coat. Pour in 1 quart/960 ml water and stir to
dissolve the salt. Let stand for 12 hours.

2) Drain the vegetables and rinse under cold running
water. Return to the bowl and stir in the olives, oregano,
and pepper. Transfer to a clean 1-quart/960 ml glass
canning jar. Pour in enough oil to cover the vegetables.
Cover and refrigerate for 1 to 2 days before serving.
(Store the giardiniera in the refrigerator for up to
2 months. Bring to room temperature before using.)
Use a slotted spoon to serve.

# Tuscan Pot Roast Sandwich

**Makes 4 sandwiches**

Since the dawn of time, grandmothers have taken a humble cut of meat and turned it into a wonderful meal. My nonna is no different. This is how she makes her Tuscan pot roast (stracotto), and it just happens to make an incredible sandwich. The braising liquid is so delicious that I have been known to pour it into cups to use as a dip for the sandwich.

### stracotto

½ cup packed/15 g dried porcini mushrooms

1 cup/240 ml boiling water

3 tablespoons olive oil

One 2½-pound/1.2 kg beef chuck roast

Fine sea salt and freshly ground black pepper

1 medium yellow onion, chopped

2 cloves garlic, coarsely chopped

1 cup/240 ml hearty red wine, such as Chianti or Shiraz

1¾ cups/420 ml reduced-sodium beef broth

2 tablespoons tomato paste

1 large sprig fresh rosemary or ½ teaspoon dried

4 sprigs fresh thyme or ½ teaspoon dried

4 ciabatta or other Italian rolls, split and toasted

1 cup/30 g baby arugula

**1) Make the stracotto:** Soak the dried mushrooms in the boiling water in a small heatproof bowl until the mushrooms soften, about 20 minutes. Lift out the soaked mushrooms and squeeze them over the bowl to remove excess liquid. Line a fine wire sieve with a moistened paper towel and put it over a second bowl. Strain the soaking liquid through the sieve, leaving the gritty liquid in the bottom of the soaking bowl. Coarsely chop the soaked mushrooms. Reserve the strained soaking liquid.

**2)** Heat 2 tablespoons of the oil in a Dutch oven over medium-high heat. Season the beef with 2 teaspoons salt and 1 teaspoon pepper. Add to the pot and cook, turning occasionally, until browned on all sides, 8 to 10 minutes. Transfer the beef to a plate.

**3)** Heat the remaining 1 tablespoon oil in the Dutch oven over medium heat. Add the onion and garlic to the pot and cook, stirring occasionally, until the onion softens, about 3 minutes. Add the wine and bring to a boil, stirring up the browned bits in the pot. Add the broth, ¼ cup/60 ml water, the tomato paste, rosemary, and thyme and bring to a boil, stirring to dissolve the tomato paste. Return the beef to the pot and return to a simmer. Reduce the heat to medium-low, cover tightly, and simmer until the beef is fork tender, about 2 hours. Transfer the beef to a plate, season with salt and pepper, and cover with foil to keep warm. Keep the braising liquid warm. Discard the herb stems.

**4)** Cut the beef across the grain into thick slices— the meat will fall apart. For each sandwich, transfer a serving of the beef to a roll. Top with a handful of arugula and a few spoonfuls of the braising liquid. Close the roll, cut in half, and serve hot.

# Chopped (Beef and) Cheese

**Makes 4 sandwiches**

Some New York City bodegas make "chopped cheese" sandwiches on their griddles. The name might be confusing because it is actually a kind of free-form cheeseburger, and not cheese alone. It is always served with the meat well-done, which is why it is important to use fatty chuck to keep the filling nice and moist. Save the lean ground sirloin for another recipe. I add onions and bell peppers to my version and season the meat with the Latino spice blend known as adobo. (Don't have any adobo? No problem because I am including a recipe for making it from scratch.) If you want it spicier, top it with some pickled jalapeños.

1¼ pounds/570 g ground beef chuck (80% lean)

1½ teaspoons adobo seasoning (see Note, page 110)

½ teaspoon fine sea salt

½ teaspoon freshly ground black pepper

¼ cup/60 ml mayonnaise

¼ cup/60 ml ketchup

4 oblong sandwich rolls, split

3 tablespoons unsalted butter, at room temperature

½ cup/70 g diced (¼-inch/6 mm) sweet onion, such as Vidalia

½ cup/65 g diced (¼-inch/6 mm) green bell pepper

8 slices American cheese

8 slices beefsteak tomato

2 cups/150 g shredded iceberg lettuce

**1)** Heat a large griddle or heavy skillet over medium heat. Preheat the oven to 200°F/95°C.

**2)** Mix the ground beef, adobo seasoning, salt, and black pepper in a medium bowl. Shape into 2 oblong patties about ½ inch/1.25 cm thick.

**3)** Mix the mayonnaise and ketchup together in a small bowl to make a pink mayonnaise. Spread the rolls with 2 tablespoons of the butter and set the rolls aside.

**4)** Add the remaining 1 tablespoon butter to the center of the griddle and melt. Add the onion and green pepper to the butter and cook, stirring occasionally, until softened, about 3 minutes. Move the vegetables to the two sides of the griddle. Add the patties to the empty area of the griddle and cook until the underside is browned, about 2 minutes. Flip and lightly brown the other side, about 1 minute more. Scoop the vegetables onto the patties. Using the long side of a pancake turner, chop the meat and vegetables together, breaking up the patties well and cooking until the beef loses its raw look, 1 to 2 minutes longer. Divide into 4 servings that are approximately the size of the roll bottoms. At the same time, add the

*Recipe continues*

**109**

buttered rolls, cut side down, to the griddle and cook until toasted. Transfer the rolls to the oven to keep warm. Reduce the heat to low. Top each serving of the beef with 2 slices of cheese and let the cheese melt, about 1 minute longer.

**5)** Spread the pink mayonnaise on the rolls. For each sandwich, use the pancake turner to lift and transfer a serving of the chopped beef and cheese to the bottom of a roll. (A second pancake turner or spatula will help with the transfer.) Cover with 2 tomato slices and a quarter of the lettuce. Cap with the top of the roll, cut in half, and serve immediately.

**note** In Latino cooking, adobo is an essential spice blend. (However, in the Philippines, it is a method of stewing meat or poultry in soy sauce.) You'll find Latino adobo in the international foods or spice sections of the supermarket. To make it yourself, combine 1 teaspoon ground turmeric, 1 teaspoon garlic powder, 1 teaspoon well-crumbled dried oregano, 1 teaspoon chili powder, 1 teaspoon ground cumin, 1 teaspoon fine sea salt, 1 teaspoon freshly ground black pepper, and $\frac{1}{2}$ teaspoon sugar. Store in a small jar in a cool dry place.

# French Onion Burger

**Makes 4 burgers**

While a lot of burgers are designed for quick meals, this one will take some time, although much of it is unattended as the sauce simmers and the onions cook down. Caramelized onions always need patience to cook correctly. And for the demi-glace, a classic French beef-based sauce that normally takes hours (if not days) to make, I offer a cheater's version with gelatin to provide the proper body. Serve plenty of napkins with this one.

## quicker demi-glace

1 tablespoon vegetable or canola oil

1 small yellow onion, coarsely chopped

1 small carrot, coarsely chopped

4 ounces/115 g ground chuck (80% lean)

½ cup/120 ml hearty red wine, such as Shiraz

2 cups/480 ml reduced-sodium beef broth

Pinch of dried thyme or one 2-inch sprig fresh thyme

1 envelope (about 2¼ teaspoons) unflavored gelatin powder

Fine sea salt and freshly ground black pepper

## burgers

1¼ pounds/570 g ground chuck (80% lean)

1½ teaspoons fine sea salt

½ teaspoon freshly ground black pepper

4 ounces/115 g thinly sliced Gruyère cheese

4 brioche burger buns, split and toasted

Caramelized Onions (see page 120)

**1) Make the demi-glace:** Heat the oil in a medium saucepan over medium-high heat. Add the onion and carrot and cook, stirring occasionally, until very well browned, about 6 minutes. Stir in the ground chuck and cook until the meat is browned, about 5 minutes. Pour in the wine and scrape up the browned bits in the saucepan. Boil until reduced by half, about 4 minutes. Pour in the broth, add the thyme, and bring to a boil. Reduce the heat to medium-low and simmer until reduced by half, about 20 minutes. Strain through a wire sieve into a bowl and let stand 5 minutes. Discard the solids in the sieve. Skim the fat from the surface of the enriched broth. Clean the saucepan.

**2)** Return the enriched broth to the saucepan and bring to a boil over high heat. Boil until reduced to about 1 cup/240 ml, 5 to 10 minutes. Meanwhile, pour ¼ cup/60 ml water into a small ramekin or custard cup. Sprinkle the gelatin on top and let stand 5 minutes to soften and stir to combine. Stir the softened gelatin into the boiling broth and cook, stirring often, until reduced to about ¾ cup/180 ml, 5 to 10 minutes. Season with salt and pepper. Remove from the heat and let cool until warm and slightly thickened, about 10 minutes. (The demi-glace can be cooled, covered, and refrigerated for up to 3 days. Reheat over low heat, whisking often, until just warm and fluid before using.)

**3) Cook the burgers:** Mix the ground chuck, salt, and pepper in a medium bowl. Shape into four 4-inch/10 cm patties. Heat a large, heavy skillet or griddle, preferably cast-iron, over medium-high heat. Add the burgers and cook until browned on the underside, about 4 minutes. Flip the burgers and cook until the other side is browned, 2 to 3 minutes for medium-rare. During the last minute, top each burger with one-quarter of the cheese and cover to melt the cheese.

**4)** For each serving, open a bun onto a dinner plate. Spoon about 3 tablespoons of the demi-glace on the top and bottom of the bun. Top the bun bottom with a burger, then a serving of the onions. Cap with the roll top and serve hot.

# The Ultimate French Dip

**Makes 8 servings**

The French dip is another sandwich of the "dunk" school, where the bread is submerged in a flavorful liquid. It has been around for over a hundred years and was supposedly invented when a sandwich maker accidentally dropped a roll in roast beef pan drippings. Too many people just warm up some beef broth for the "dip." There's more to it than that. The roast beef's drippings are the base to a terrific French dip, so, in this recipe, beef bones are added to be sure that you get lots of those essential browned bits in the roasting pan.

Olive oil

One 3½-pound/1.6 kg rump roast

Fine sea salt

½ teaspoon garlic powder

Freshly ground black pepper

2 pounds/910 g flanken-style short ribs, cross-cut beef shank, or beef marrow bones

2 medium carrots, cut in half crosswise

1 large yellow onion, quartered

1 sprig fresh rosemary or ½ teaspoon dried

3 sprigs fresh thyme or ½ teaspoon dried

6 cups/1.4 L reduced-sodium beef broth

8 crusty French or Italian rolls, split

16 slices Swiss or unsmoked provolone cheese (optional)

Hot and spicy mustard for serving

Pepperoncini for serving

**1)** Drizzle oil over the rump roast and rub to coat. Combine 2 teaspoons salt, the garlic powder, and ½ teaspoon pepper in a small bowl and sprinkle all over the roast. Put the flanken, carrots, onion, rosemary, and thyme in a metal roasting pan, drizzle with oil, and toss to coat. Place the roast, fat side down, on the vegetables and flanken. Let stand at room temperature for about 1 hour.

**2)** Preheat the oven to 450°F/230°C. Roast until the beef is beginning to brown, about 20 minutes. Flip the roast over, fat side up.

**3)** Reduce the oven temperature to 350°F/180°C. Roast until an instant-read thermometer inserted in the center of the beef reads 125°F/51°C, about 30 minutes more. Transfer the beef to a carving board with a well and let cool for 20 to 30 minutes.

**4)** Meanwhile, make the jus: Transfer the flanken and vegetables from the roasting pan to a bowl. Pour the rendered fat out of the pan. Place the pan over medium-high heat and heat until it sizzles. Add the broth and bring to a broil, scraping up the browned bits in the pan with a wooden spatula. Return the flanken

*Recipe continues*

**112**

and vegetables to the pan, reduce the heat to low, and cook at a bare simmer to blend the flavors with minimal reduction for about 20 minutes. Strain the mixture through a wire sieve into a large saucepan, pressing hard on the vegetables. You should have about 5 cups/1.2 L jus. Boil the jus down in the saucepan or add water as needed. Discard the solids in the sieve. Season the jus with salt and pepper. Return the jus to the roasting pan and keep it warm, but not simmering, over low heat.

5) Using a thin sharp knife (or, better yet, an electric meat slicer, if you have one), carve the meat crosswise into thin slices, then cut the slices in half to fit the rolls. Add any carving juices to the jus. Divide the meat into 8 servings.

6) If using cheese, position a broiler rack about 4 inches/10 cm from the heat source and preheat the broiler on High.

7) Divide the cheese over the rolls, tearing the cheese to fit. Broil until the cheese melts, about 1 minute.

8) For each sandwich, using tongs, add a serving of beef in the jus for a few seconds to warm the meat and place it on the roll bottom. Cap with the roll top and cut in half. Pour the remaining jus into ramekins or custard cups. Cut the sandwiches in half and serve with the jus for dipping and the mustard and pepperoncini on the side.

## meatballs

1½ cups/55 g plain soft breadcrumbs, from crusty stale bread (see page 58)

¾ cup/180 ml whole milk

1 pound/455 g ground chuck (80% lean)

8 ounces/225 g sweet Italian pork sausage, casings removed

½ large yellow onion, grated on the large holes of a box grater

2 cloves garlic, minced

½ cup/50 g freshly grated Parmigiano-Reggiano cheese

3 tablespoons finely chopped fresh flat-leaf parsley

1 large egg, lightly beaten

1½ teaspoons fine sea salt

½ teaspoon freshly ground black pepper

## tomato sauce

3 tablespoons extra virgin olive oil

½ large yellow onion, finely chopped

2 cloves garlic, minced

One 28-ounce/795 g can crushed tomatoes, preferably San Marzano

2 tablespoons coarsely chopped fresh basil

½ teaspoon sugar

Salt and freshly ground black pepper

———

4 crusty Italian rolls, partially split lengthwise and opened like a book

12 slices low-moisture mozzarella cheese

½ cup/50 g freshly grated Parmigiano-Reggiano cheese

# Nonna's Meatball Sandwich

**Makes 4 sandwiches**

My nonna's recipe for meatballs is as classic as they come. Note that she does not brown the meatballs but instead poaches them in the copious tomato sauce (she called it *sugo di pomodoro*, but you might know it as marinara) so they are extra-tender. Another tip: Use moderate heat when cooking the onions and garlic—burned garlic is the enemy of a good tomato sauce. Finally, fresh basil makes all the difference. You will probably have leftover sauce, ready to store for another meal, which is a great bonus for an already outrageous recipe.

**1) Prepare the meatballs:** Combine the breadcrumbs and milk in a small bowl and set aside for 5 minutes. Drain in a wire sieve and press out the milk. Crumble the bread into a large bowl. Add the ground chuck, sausage, onion, garlic, Parmigiano-Reggiano cheese, parsley, egg, salt, and pepper and mix with clean hands until combined. Using hands rinsed under cold water, shape into 16 meatballs and transfer to a baking sheet. Refrigerate while making the sauce to firm them up.

**2) Make the tomato sauce:** Pour the oil into a large Dutch oven and add the onion and garlic. Place over medium heat and cook, stirring often, until the onion is

*Recipe continues*

**115**

golden, 5 to 7 minutes. Take your time with this, as you do not want to brown the garlic—starting the cooking in a cold pot will help. Stir in the tomatoes. Fill the can with water and stir the water into the sauce. This will dilute the sauce but also allow you to simmer for longer as it reduces and gains flavor. Add the basil and sugar and cover. Increase the heat to high and bring to a boil, stirring often.

**3) Cook the meatballs:** Reduce the heat to medium so the sauce is gently boiling. Season with salt and pepper. One at a time, reshape the meatballs and drop them into the sauce. Adjust the heat so the sauce is simmering. Cook, uncovered, without stirring, until the meatballs have set, 10 to 15 minutes. Give them a gentle stir. Reduce the heat to medium-low so the sauce is cooking at a low simmer. Cook, uncovered, stirring occasionally, until the sauce reduces by about one-third and turns deep red with some oily patches, 2 to 2½ hours. Using a slotted spoon, transfer the meatballs to a bowl.

**4)** Arrange a broiler rack about 4 inches/10 cm from the source of heat and preheat on High.

**5)** Arrange the rolls, cut sides up, on a baking sheet. Top each roll with 3 slices of mozzarella cheese. Broil the rolls until the cheese is melted, 1 to 2 minutes. Add 4 meatballs and cut each meatball in half with the side of the spoon (this helps make the sandwich more compact). Spoon about ¼ cup/60 ml of the sauce on top. Sprinkle with 2 tablespoons of Parmigiano cheese. Close the roll, cut in half, and serve with the warm remaining sauce on the side. (The leftover sauce can be cooled, covered, and refrigerated for up to 3 days or frozen for up to 6 months.)

# New Orleans Debris Po'boy

**Makes 6 sandwiches**

Po'boys are a classic of New Orleans cuisine, but they aren't always made with seafood (page 92), as good as that version may be. The debris here refers to the shredded look of the braised beef, which is served up with a beautiful gravy. The classic has both mayo and gravy—this isn't your standard-issue hot roast beef sandwich.

1 tablespoon salt-free Cajun seasoning

Fine sea salt

Freshly ground black pepper

One 3½-pound/1.6 kg beef chuck roast

2 tablespoons vegetable or canola oil

1 medium yellow onion, coarsely chopped

1 medium carrot, coarsely chopped

1 medium celery rib, coarsely chopped

6 cloves garlic, unpeeled, crushed under a knife

1 quart/960 ml reduced-sodium beef broth

2 tablespoons tomato paste

¼ teaspoon dried thyme

2 dried bay leaves

2 tablespoons unsalted butter

2 tablespoons all-purpose flour

6 soft oblong rolls, partially split lengthwise and opened like a book

Cajun Aioli (page 219)

12 slices unsmoked provolone cheese

12 slices ripe beefsteak tomato

2 cups/150 g thinly sliced iceberg lettuce

Hot sauce, such as Tabasco or My Hot Sauce (page 226), for serving

**1)** Preheat the oven to 300°F/150°C.

**2)** Mix the Cajun seasoning, 2 teaspoons salt, and ½ teaspoon pepper in a small bowl and rub all over the beef. Heat the oil in a large Dutch oven over medium-high heat. Add the beef and cook, turning occasionally, until browned on all sides, about 10 minutes. Transfer to a plate.

**3)** Add the onion, carrot, celery, and garlic and stir to loosen the browned bits in the pot. Cook, stirring occasionally, until softened, about 3 minutes. Stir in the broth, tomato paste, thyme, and bay leaves. Bring to a boil, scraping up the browned bits in the pot with a wooden spatula. Return the beef to the pot.

**4)** Cover tightly and bake until the beef is very tender when pierced with a meat fork, 3 to 3½ hours. Transfer the beef to a carving board with a well and let stand while making the gravy.

**5)** To make the gravy, strain the broth through a wire sieve into a 1-quart/960 ml glass measuring cup or bowl. Press hard on the solids, then discard them. Let the broth stand 3 minutes, then skim off the fat on the surface. You should have about 2½ cups/600 ml cooking liquid. Boil the broth down in the pot over high heat or add water as needed. Melt the butter in the Dutch oven over medium heat. Whisk in the flour. Let bubble until lightly browned, about 2 minutes. Whisk in the cooking liquid and bring to a simmer, whisking often. Reduce the heat to medium-low and simmer, whisking often and scraping down any browned bits on the sides of the pot, until smooth, thickened, and slightly reduced, about 10 minutes. Season with salt and pepper.

**6)** Position a broiler rack about 4 inches/10 cm from the heat and preheat on High.

**7)** Carve the beef crosswise into thick slices, discarding any clumps of fat, and transfer to a medium bowl. Using two forks, shred the beef. Add the beef and any juices to the simmering gravy and mix. (The beef can be cooled, covered, and refrigerated for up to 2 days. Reheat in a large saucepan over low heat until simmering.)

**8)** For each sandwich, spread a roll with about 2 tablespoons of the Cajun aioli. Heap a serving of the shredded beef with gravy onto an opened roll and top with 2 slices of cheese. Place the opened sandwiches on a broiler pan. Broil until the cheese melts, about 1 minute. Top with 2 tomato slices and a handful of lettuce. Close the roll, cut in half, and serve hot, with the hot sauce on the side.

# OG Steak Sandwich

## with caramelized onions and aioli

**Makes 2 sandwiches**

Sliced steak makes one of the most perfect of sandwiches, especially with lots of sweet, caramelized onions and punchy aioli. Skirt is perfect for this sandwich because it is fattier than other steaks and it cooks up with lots of browning, both conditions that give extra flavor. The grain in the steak will look like an accordion, so when slicing, cut across and almost perpendicular to the grain to get the most tender slices. And everyone should know how to make caramelized onions. One important rule: Don't rush them!

### caramelized onions

2 tablespoons olive oil

2 large yellow onions (about 1½ pounds/680 g), cut into thin half-moons

½ teaspoon fine sea salt

¼ teaspoon freshly ground black pepper

### steak

Extra virgin olive oil

1 pound/455 g skirt steak, cut in half vertically

½ teaspoon fine sea salt

¼ teaspoon freshly ground black pepper

___

2 crusty French or Italian rolls, split and lightly toasted

4 ounces/115 g thinly sliced Gruyère cheese

¼ cup/60 ml Aioli (page 219)

1 cup packed/30 g arugula leaves

½ lemon

**1) Caramelize the onions:** Heat the oil in a large skillet over medium-high heat. Add the onions, salt, and pepper and cover. Cook, stirring once or twice, until the onions are beginning to brown, about 7 minutes. Reduce the heat to very low and cook, uncovered, stirring occasionally, until the onions are very tender and deep beige with some well-browned bits, 30 to 40 minutes. Makes about 1 cup/200 g. (The onions can be cooled, covered, and refrigerated for up to 3 days. Reheat before using.)

**2) Cook the steak:** Drizzle oil all over the steak and sprinkle with the salt and pepper. Thoroughly heat a large heavy skillet, preferably cast iron, over medium-high heat. Add the steak and cook until the underside is well browned, about 3 minutes. Flip the steak and brown the other side, 3 minutes more. The steak should remain rare. Transfer to a carving board with a well and let stand for about 5 minutes.

**3)** Position a broiler rack about 4 inches/10 cm from the heat and preheat the broiler on High.

**4)** Place the open rolls on a broiler pan and divide the cheese over the bottom halves. Broil until the cheese is melted, about 1 minute. Remove from the broiler.

**5)** Holding a sharp knife at a slight angle, cut the steak across the grain into thin slices. For each sandwich, spread half of the aioli on the top half of the roll. Place half of the steak and half of the onions over the cheese on the bottom half. Top with half of the arugula and a squeeze of lemon juice. Drizzle with any carving juices. Close the roll, cut in half crosswise, and serve.

**120**

**OG Steak Hoagie:** This sandwich is great for serving a few hungry folks who have gathered to watch a television sports event, or make it as a grilled sandwich for a backyard cookout. This recipe is the big sandwich on the cover of this book. Cook 1½ pounds/680 skirt steak. Cut an entire loaf of French bread in half lengthwise and lightly toast it. Increase the aioli to about ½ cup/120 ml, the Gruyère to 6 ounces/170 g, and the arugula to about 1½ cups/45 grams. Use the entire batch of caramelized onions. When the sandwich is built, cut the bread into 4 to 6 portions and serve.

# Steak au Poivre and Frites Sandwich

**Makes 2 sandwiches**

Steak au poivre shows French food at its best, especially when it comes to the pan sauce, where the flavorful browned bits in the skillet after cooking the meat are deftly turned into a great accompaniment. I go further by topping the steak and sauce with some oven fries.

Two 8-ounce/225 g filets mignons, each cut 1 inch/2.5 cm thick

Fine sea salt and freshly ground black pepper

3 tablespoons unsalted butter

2 tablespoons minced shallots

¼ cup/60 ml brandy or Cognac

1 cup/240 ml reduced-sodium beef broth

1 cup/240 ml heavy cream

2 teaspoons whole black peppercorns, coarsely crushed in a mortar with a pestle, or under a small heavy saucepan

2 crusty oblong rolls, split and toasted

Oven French Fries (page 228)

Chopped fresh flat-leaf parsley for serving

**1)** Sprinkle the steaks all over with 1 teaspoon salt and ½ teaspoon pepper. Let stand at room temperature for 30 minutes to 1 hour.

**2)** Heat an empty heavy skillet, preferably cast-iron, over medium-high heat until it is very hot. Add the filets and cook until the underside is browned, about 3 minutes. Turn and brown the other side, about 3 minutes more. During the last 2 minutes, add 2 tablespoons of the butter, let it melt, and baste the steaks with the melted butter. The filets should be rare—an instant-read thermometer inserted through the side of a filet into the center should read 125°F/51°C. If you want them more well done, reduce the heat to medium-low and cook for 1 to 2 minutes longer. Transfer to a carving board with a well and let rest while making the sauce.

**3)** Add the shallots and the remaining 1 tablespoon butter together to the skillet and cook over medium-low heat, stirring occasionally, until the shallots soften, about 2 minutes. (The skillet will be very hot from residual heat, so watch out for burning.) Have a lid for the skillet handy. Carefully pour the brandy into the skillet. Using a long match or butane grill lighter, ignite the brandy. Let it burn until it extinguishes by itself and has reduced to about 1 tablespoon, about 1 minute. If the brandy is still flaming, cover the skillet tightly with the lid to extinguish the flame. Add the broth, cream, and crushed peppercorns. Bring to a boil, scraping up the browned bits in the skillet with a wooden spoon, and cook, stirring often, until the sauce is reduced by about half, about 3 minutes. (A finger run through the sauce on the spoon will cut a swath.) Remove from the heat. Season with salt.

**4)** On the carving board, cut the filets across the grain into slices about ¼ inch/6 mm thick. For each sandwich, cover the bottom half of the roll with half of the beef and drizzle with some of the carving juices. Add a handful of fries. Pour half of the sauce on top and sprinkle with the parsley. Cap with the roll top and cut in half. Serve hot with the remaining fries on the side.

# Roast Beef Sandwich

## with caper-dill mayonnaise

**Makes 4 sandwiches**

No one really loves airline food, but on one flight I was served roast beef and caper mayonnaise. It has been one of my favorite combinations ever since, and here I present it as a sandwich. I probably don't have to tell you how great this is with a side of potato chips. Eye of round is a flavorful cut, but it must be roasted no more than medium-rare to remain moist. My local butcher taught me the trick of topping it with pork fat before roasting.

### roast beef

1 teaspoon finely chopped fresh rosemary

1 teaspoon finely chopped fresh thyme

1 teaspoon garlic powder

1 teaspoon sweet paprika

¾ teaspoon fine sea salt

½ teaspoon freshly ground black pepper

2 tablespoons olive oil

One 2½-pound/1.2 kg beef eye of round roast

5 ounces/140 g pork fat, thinly sliced (see Note), or thick-cut bacon

4 crusty oblong French or Italian rolls, toasted

About ¾ cup/180 ml Caper-Dill Mayonnaise (page 219)

½ small red onion, cut into thin rings

About 2 cups/115 g watercress, tough stems trimmed

1) **Make the roast beef:** Mix the rosemary, thyme, garlic powder, paprika, salt, and pepper in a small bowl. Rub the oil all over the beef, followed by the herb mixture. Drape the fat over the top and sides of the beef and tie it in place with a few loops of kitchen twine or unwaxed and unflavored dental floss. Let stand at room temperature for about 30 minutes.

2) Preheat the oven to 500°F/260°C.

3) Place the beef in a roasting pan. Roast for 15 minutes. Reduce the oven temperature to 300°F/150°C and continue roasting until an instant-read thermometer inserted in the center reads 130°F/54°C for medium-rare, 25 to 35 minutes. Transfer to a wire rack on a carving board with a well and let cool for 30 to 45 minutes.

4) Discard the twine and remaining pork fat. On the carving board, using a sharp knife, slice the beef crosswise as thinly as possible.

5) For each sandwich, spread a roll with about 3 tablespoons of the caper mayonnaise. Shingle one-quarter of the roast beef on the bottom half and drizzle with some carving juices. Top with a few red onion rings and a handful of watercress. Cap with the roll top. Cut in half crosswise and serve.

**note** Pork fatback is fresh, solid, white fat trimmed from pork loin. It is commonplace at Asian butchers and often sold in supermarkets. Sliced bacon (preferably unsmoked) or fresh pork belly are passable substitutes. To slice whole fatback, freeze until it is firmer, about 30 minutes. Using a sharp knife, cut it horizontally into slices about ⅛ inch/3 mm thick. It doesn't matter if it isn't perfectly sliced, as it is going to melt anyway.

123

# Beef Shawarma with Fries

**Makes 4 servings**

Another one of my "greatest hits" according to the number of TikTok views it racked up, beef shawarma is a riot of tastes and textures, starting with a bold yogurt and spice marinade. I think shawarma is even better when homemade fries are rolled into the wrap, and I know you will agree. Time the cooking of the French fries so they are done about the same time as the beef.

### marinated beef

1¼ pounds/570 g beef rib eye or flank steak

¼ cup/60 ml plain low-fat yogurt (not Greek yogurt)

3 tablespoons olive oil

2 tablespoons red wine vinegar

1 teaspoon ground cumin

1 teaspoon ground allspice

½ teaspoon ground cinnamon

½ teaspoon garlic powder

½ teaspoon onion powder

1 teaspoon fine sea salt

½ teaspoon freshly ground black pepper

Pinch of crushed hot red pepper

½ medium white onion, cut into thin half-moons

### tomato salad

2 plum tomatoes, halved lengthwise and cut into ½-inch/1.25 cm slices

½ medium white onion, cut into thin half-moons

3 tablespoons finely chopped fresh flat-leaf parsley

2 teaspoons ground sumac

Fine sea salt

3 tablespoons vegetable or canola oil, plus more as needed

1 cup/240 g store-bought hummus

4 extra-large laffa or flat pita breads, about 12 inches/30.5 cm in diameter (see Note, page 126)

Yogurt-Tahini Sauce (page 137)

Oven French Fries (page 228)

2 cups packed/150 g shredded iceberg lettuce

**1) Marinate the beef:** Freeze the steak until partially frozen, about 30 minutes. On a carving board, using a sharp knife held at a slight diagonal, cut the meat across the grain into slices about ¼ inch/6 mm thick. Whisk the yogurt, olive oil, vinegar, cumin, allspice, cinnamon, garlic powder, onion powder, salt, black pepper, and hot red pepper in a medium bowl. Add the sliced beef and onion and mix well. Cover and refrigerate for at least 30 minutes and up to 2 hours.

*Recipe continues*

**2) Make the tomato salad:** Mix the tomatoes, onion, parsley, and sumac together in a medium bowl. Season with salt. (The salad can be stored at room temperature for up to 2 hours.)

**3) Cook the marinated beef:** Heat 2 tablespoons of the vegetable oil in a very large nonstick skillet or on a griddle over high heat. Add the meat and onions and cook without disturbing for 2 to 3 minutes. Flip the mixture and continue cooking until the meat loses its raw look, about 3 minutes more. Remove from the heat.

**4)** Place a baking sheet near your work surface. For each shawarma, spread about ¼ cup/65 g hummus in the center of the laffa and top with one-quarter of the meat. Using a slotted spoon, add one-quarter of the tomato salad, then drizzle with about 2 tablespoons of the tahini sauce and a handful of fries. Top with a handful of the lettuce. Fold up from the bottom to cover the filling, then fold the right and left sides inward 1 to 2 inches/2.5 to 5 cm to partially cover the filling. Roll up from the bottom to close the shawarma, tucking in the corners as needed. The filling should be completely covered. Set aside on a baking sheet, seam side down.

**5)** Heat the remaining 1 tablespoon vegetable oil in a large skillet or griddle over high heat. In batches, if necessary, add the shawarmas, seam side down, and cook until the undersides are browned, about 1 minute. Flip and brown the other side, about 1 minute more. Return to the baking sheet. Repeat with the remaining servings, adding more oil as needed. Cut in half crosswise and serve.

**note** Laffa looks similar to pita, but it is bigger, thicker, softer, and sturdier for holding saucy fillings like shawarma. Extra-large pita, 12 to 13 inches/30.5 to 33 cm, is a good substitute. Both can be purchased at Middle Eastern grocers. If neither is available, change your folding strategy and use 6 to 8 standard pocket pitas instead. Cut the top 2 inches/5 cm from the top of each pita and open to make pockets. Smear 2 tablespoons of hummus inside of each. Fill with the beef mixture, tomato salad, lettuce, fries, and a drizzle of sauce. You can also simply top a round, un-pocketed pita with the fillings and fold it in half like a taco.

# Grilled Tri-Tip and Chimichurri Sandwich

**Makes 6 sandwiches**

When I moved to California, it didn't take me long to discover tri-tip, a uniquely West Coast sirloin cut that is treated like a big flank steak (meaning it is cooked rare and sliced across the grain for serving). It isn't very common outside of the Golden State, but you will find it for sale by mail order online. While it is not an enormous cut, it is rich and chewy, and an average roast will yield six to eight servings. Chimichurri, the sauce you will find at every Argentine steak house, is the perfect match. Note that this herbaceous condiment should be somewhat thin—it isn't pesto. The secret to my version is orange zest and juice.

### california tri-tip

½ cup/120 ml extra virgin olive oil

½ cup/120 ml fresh lime juice

3 cloves garlic, minced

2 teaspoons chili powder

2 teaspoons ground cumin

2 teaspoons sweet paprika

1 teaspoon dried oregano

1½ teaspoons fine sea salt

1 teaspoon freshly ground black pepper

1 tri-tip beef roast, about 2½ pounds/ 1.2 kg (see Notes, page 129)

### chimichurri

¾ cup/45 g finely chopped fresh flat-leaf parsley

½ cup/50 g finely chopped fresh cilantro or additional parsley

4 cloves garlic, finely chopped

1 tablespoon seeded and finely chopped fresh hot red chile, such as Fresno or jalapeño

1 teaspoon dried oregano

Fine sea salt

Grated zest of ½ orange

¾ cup/180 ml extra virgin olive oil

3 tablespoons red wine vinegar

2 tablespoons fresh orange juice

6 sourdough rolls, split lengthwise

Pickled Red Onions (page 222)

1) **Marinate the tri-tip:** Whisk the oil, lime juice, garlic, chili powder, cumin, paprika, oregano, salt, and pepper in a medium bowl and pour into a 1-quart/960 ml resealable plastic bag. Add the tri-tip, seal the bag, and let stand at room temperature, turning occasionally, for 30 minutes to 1 hour. (Or refrigerate for at least 4 hours and up to 1 day. Let the tri-tip stand at room temperature for 1 hour before cooking.)

*Recipe continues*

**127**

**2)** **Make the chimichurri:** Stir the parsley, cilantro, garlic, chile, oregano, ½ teaspoon salt, and orange zest in a medium bowl. Stir in the oil, vinegar, and orange juice. The thickness should remind you more of vinaigrette than pesto. Season with additional salt. Let the chimichurri stand at room temperature for 15 minutes to blend the flavors. Makes about 1½ cups/360 ml. (The chimichurri can be covered and refrigerated for up to 2 days. Bring to room temperature before using.)

**3)** Preheat a gas grill on High (600°F/315°C). Leave one side of the grill on High and turn the other side off for indirect heat. For a charcoal grill, build a charcoal fire and let it burn until the coals are coated in white ash. Move the coals to one side of the grill, leaving the other side empty. Brush the grill grate clean.

**4)** **Grill the California tri-tip:** Remove the tri-tip from the marinade, shaking off excess marinade. Place on the hot side of the grill. Cover and grill until the underside is browned, about 5 minutes. Flip the tri-tip and brown the other side, about 5 minutes more. Move to the cooler side of the grill. Cover and grill with indirect heat until an instant-read thermometer inserted in the thickest part of the beef reads 125°F/51°C for medium-rare, 20 to 25 minutes. Transfer to a carving board with a well and let stand for 5 to 10 minutes.

**5)** Place the rolls on the hotter side of the grill, cut sides down, and grill until toasted, about 1 minute. Remove from the grill. Using a sharp thin knife, cut the tri-tip across the grain into slices about ¼ inch/6 mm thick.

**6)** For each sandwich, spoon about 2 tablespoons of the chimichurri over the cut sides of a toasted roll. Add a portion of the sliced beef over the bottom half, drizzle with some of the carving juices, and top with some pickled onions. Cap with the top of the roll, cut in half, and serve with the remaining chimichurri on the side.

## notes

- One mail-order source for tri-tip is wildforkfoods.com. They also have retail stores.

- To roast the tri-tip: Preheat the oven to 350°F/180°C. Remove the tri-tip from the marinade and shake off excess marinade. Heat 1 tablespoon olive oil in a large ovenproof skillet (preferably cast iron) over high heat. Add the tri-tip and cook until the underside is browned, about 4 minutes. Flip and brown the other side, about 4 minutes more. Transfer the skillet and tri-tip to the oven and roast until an instant-read thermometer inserted in the thickest part of the roast reads 125°F/51°C for medium-rare, 25 to 30 minutes.

**129**

# Sirloin Tidbits Sandwich

## with crispy onion rings

**Makes 2 sandwiches**

This is a steak sandwich on steroids, with big flavors of fresh and roasted garlic, as well as crispy onions. Save it for when you are really hungry and have invited a friend with a huge appetite. It is a steak house in a roll.

### marinated steak tidbits

⅓ cup/80 ml reduced-sodium soy sauce

1 tablespoon Worcestershire sauce

2 cloves garlic, minced

½ teaspoon fine sea salt

½ teaspoon freshly ground black pepper

1 pound/455 g top sirloin steak, cut into 1-inch/2.5 cm cubes

### roasted garlic butter

4 tablespoons/56 g (½ stick) unsalted butter, softened

1 tablespoon mashed Roasted Garlic (page 230)

1 tablespoon extra virgin olive oil

¼ teaspoon crushed hot red pepper

Fine sea salt

2 tablespoons vegetable or canola oil

6 slices low-moisture mozzarella cheese

2 oblong rolls, partially split lengthwise, and opened like a book

Crispy Onion Rings (page 227)

**1)** **Marinate the steak tidbits:** Combine the soy sauce, Worcestershire sauce, garlic, salt, and pepper in a 1-quart/960 ml resealable plastic bag. Add the steak, close, and let stand at room temperature, turning occasionally, for 30 minutes to 1 hour, or refrigerate for up to 8 hours.

**2)** **Make the roasted garlic butter:** Mash the butter, roasted garlic, olive oil, and hot red pepper in a small bowl. Season with the salt.

**3)** Position a broiler rack about 4 inches/10 cm from the heat source and preheat on High.

**4)** **Cook the marinated steak tidbits:** Drain the steak and pat dry with paper towels. Heat a large ovenproof skillet over high heat and add the vegetable oil. When the oil is very hot, add the steak cubes and sear on the underside, about 1 minute. Flip the cubes and cook until the other side is browned, about 1 minute more. Do not overcook. Remove from the heat. Move the steak cubes together and top them with the mozzarella. Broil until the cheese is melted, about 1 minute. Remove the skillet from the broiler.

**5)** Spread the roasted garlic butter on the cut sides of the rolls. Broil, cut sides up, until toasted, about 1 minute. For each sandwich, use a wide spatula to add half of the steak to the bottom half of the roll and top with a few onion rings. Drizzle with the pan juices. Close the sandwiches and cut in half crosswise. Serve with the remaining onion rings on the side.

## vodka sauce

2 tablespoons unsalted
  butter

1 medium yellow onion,
  chopped

2 cloves garlic, minced

2 teaspoons crushed
  Calabrian chiles in oil,
  or more to taste (see
  Note)

½ cup/120 ml vodka

One 28-ounce/794 g
  can crushed
  tomatoes, preferably
  San Marzano

1 teaspoon sugar

½ cup/120 ml heavy
  cream

Fine sea salt and freshly
  ground black pepper

## veal

12 ounces/340 g thinly
  sliced veal cutlets,
  cut crosswise into
  12 equal pieces

½ cup/70 g all-purpose
  flour

½ teaspoon fine sea salt

¼ teaspoon freshly
  ground black pepper

3 large eggs

1 cup/130 g plain dried
  breadcrumbs

¾ cup/75 g freshly
  grated Parmigiano-
  Reggiano cheese

¼ cup/60 ml olive or
  vegetable oil for
  frying, plus more as
  needed

8 ounces/225 g fresh
  mozzarella cheese,
  cut into thin rounds

4 crusty oblong Italian
  rolls, split lengthwise
  and lightly toasted

2 tablespoons chopped
  fresh basil

# Veal Vodka Parmesan Hero

**Makes 4 sandwiches**

Veal "Parm" sandwiches are probably sold at your corner pizza place, but I doubt they are this delicious. The difference is in the creamy and spicy sauce, which completes this masterpiece. You will have leftover sauce. I suppose you could make half a batch of sauce, but it won't save you any time and it is great to have leftover sauce, which is perfect on pasta, too, of course.

1) **Make the vodka sauce:** Heat the butter in a medium saucepan over medium heat. Add the onion and garlic and cook, stirring occasionally, until the onion is golden, about 5 minutes. Stir in the chiles. Add the vodka, bring to a boil, and let it cook until reduced by half, about 3 minutes. Stir in the tomatoes and sugar and bring to a boil. Reduce the heat to low and simmer, stirring often, until the sauce is slightly reduced, about 20 minutes. Stir in the cream and cook until reduced to its former consistency, about 20 minutes more. Season with salt and pepper. Keep the sauce warm. (The sauce can be cooled, covered,

and refrigerated up to 2 days ahead or frozen for up to 2 months. Thaw, if necessary, and reheat over low heat before using.)

2) **Prepare the veal:** Pound each piece of veal between sheets of plastic wrap with the flat side of a meat pounder until it is about ¼ inch/6 mm thick. Put the flour in a wide, shallow bowl or baking dish and season with the salt and pepper. Beat the eggs in a second bowl. (An immersion blender works best.) Mix the breadcrumbs with ½ cup/50 g of the Parmigiano cheese in a third bowl. Place a wire rack over a half-sheet pan near the stove. One at a time, dip a veal cutlet in the flour to coat, then into the eggs, and then into the breadcrumbs, and place the coated cutlets on another half-sheet pan.

3) **Cook the veal cutlets:** Heat the oil in a large skillet over medium heat until shimmering. In batches, add the cutlets and cook until the underside is light golden brown, about 45 seconds. Flip the cutlets and cook until the other side is light golden brown, about 45 seconds more. Do not overcook. Using a slotted pancake turner, transfer the cutlets to the wire rack.

4) Position a broiler rack about 4 inches/10 cm from the source of heat and preheat the broiler.

5) Arrange the veal cutlets, overlapping as needed, on a broiler rack or half-sheet pan, to make 4 portions, 3 cutlets to a portion. Move the portions closely together and top each portion with an equal amount of the mozzarella cheese. Top with a sprinkling of the remaining ¼ cup/25 g Parmigiano cheese. Broil until the cheese is melted, 1 to 2 minutes.

6) For each sandwich, spoon about 2 tablespoons of the sauce on the roll bottom. Add a veal portion with its cheese and spoon another 2 tablespoons of sauce on top. Add a sprinkle of basil. Add the roll top, cut in half, and serve hot with the remaining sauce in a bowl on the side for those who want a saucier sandwich.

**note** Calabrian chiles are preserved in oil and sold in jars either whole or chopped (crushed). They are hot and spicy with a fruity undertone. The heat level changes from brand to brand, so use caution when adding them to dishes until you have a handle on the spiciness of your jar.

STACKED

# Bistro Grilled Lamb Sandwich on Sourdough

**Makes 8 sandwiches**

Grilled lamb is the start of an amazingly good sandwich. This has Provençale flavors straight out of a restaurant in the south of France. Wine, lemon, fresh herbs, olive oil, and garlic all come into play. The lamb can also be broiled in your kitchen if you don't have an outdoor grill. This recipe uses all the lamb to make eight sandwiches. But, of course, if you serve less, you can use the leftover lamb to top a salad for another meal.

### marinated lamb

¾ cup/180 ml extra virgin olive oil

½ cup/120 ml hearty red wine, such as Shiraz

3 tablespoons red wine vinegar

Grated zest of 1 lemon

3 tablespoons fresh lemon juice

1 tablespoon finely chopped fresh rosemary

1 tablespoon finely chopped fresh thyme

4 cloves garlic, minced

1 teaspoon fine sea salt

½ teaspoon freshly ground black pepper

One 4¼-pound/1.9 kg boneless leg of lamb, trimmed of fat and fell (membrane), cut in half vertically to make two "roasts," and each roast butterflied

16 slices sourdough bread

¾ cup/180 ml Aioli (page 219)

2 to 3 large tomatoes, cut into 16 slices

1 cup/100 g crumbled feta cheese

2 cups/60 g baby arugula

**1)** **Marinate the lamb:** Whisk the oil, red wine, vinegar, lemon zest and juice, rosemary, thyme, garlic, salt, and pepper in a medium bowl. Pour into a 1-quart/960 ml resealable plastic bag. Add the lamb, close the bag, and refrigerate, turning occasionally, for at least 2 hours and up to 1 day. Let the lamb stand at room temperature for 1 hour before cooking.

**2)** Heat a gas grill to High (about 600°F/315°C). Leave one side of the grill on High and turn the other side off for indirect heat. For a charcoal grill, build a charcoal fire and let it burn until the coals are coated in white ash. Move the coals to one side of the grill, leaving the other side empty. Brush the grill grate clean.

**3)** **Grill the marinated lamb:** Remove the lamb from the marinade, shaking off excess marinade. Place on the hot side of the grill. Cover and grill until the underside is browned, about 5 minutes. Flip the lamb and brown the other side, about 5 minutes more.

**134**

Move to the cooler side of the grill. Cover and cook with indirect heat until an instant-read thermometer inserted in the thickest part of the lamb reads 125°F/51°C for medium-rare, 10 to 15 minutes. Transfer to a carving board with a well and let stand for 5 minutes.

**4)** Put the bread on the hotter side of the grill and toast, turning once, 1 to 2 minutes. Using a sharp carving knife, cut the lamb across the grain into very thin slices. For each sandwich, spread 2 bread slices with about 2 tablespoons of aioli. Top one slice with a portion of the lamb and drizzle with any carving juices. Add 2 tomato slices, about 2 tablespoons feta, and a handful of arugula. Cap with the other slice of bread, cut in half, and serve.

**note**  To oven-roast the lamb, preheat the oven to 350°F/180°C. Remove the lamb from the marinade and shake off excess marinade. Heat 1 tablespoon olive oil in a large ovenproof skillet over high heat. Add the lamb "roasts" and cook until the underside is browned, about 4 minutes. Flip and brown the other side, about 4 minutes more. Transfer to the oven in the skillet and roast until an instant-read thermometer inserted in the thickest part of the roast reads 125°F/51°C for medium-rare, about 25 minutes. Toast the bread in a toaster, toaster oven, or the broiler.

# Lamb-Stuffed Pitas (Arayes)

## with yogurt-tahini sauce

**Makes 8 arayes**

Arayes are Lebanese and out of the ordinary in every way. While they could be thought of as lamb burgers, their unique shape makes them much more than that. They can be cooked on an outdoor grill, or indoors in a sandwich pan or skillet. In either case, the heat should be moderate to allow the filling to heat through without burning the bread. Serve tabbouleh or a chopped tomato and cucumber salad on the side.

### yogurt-tahini sauce

¾ cup/180 ml plain low-fat yogurt (not Greek yogurt)

¼ cup/60 ml tahini

3 tablespoons fresh lemon juice

2 cloves garlic, minced and mashed with a pinch of salt into a paste

½ teaspoon hot sauce, such as Tabasco

### lamb filling

1 firm ripe plum tomato

½ medium yellow onion

1¼ pounds/570 g ground lamb, ground chuck, or a combination

½ cup/30 g finely chopped fresh flat-leaf parsley

3 cloves garlic, minced

1¼ teaspoons fine sea salt

1 teaspoon baharat (seven-spice blend; see Note)

½ teaspoon ground cumin

¼ teaspoon ground cinnamon

½ teaspoon Urfa biber flakes (see Note)

¼ teaspoon cayenne pepper

½ cup/100 g crumbled feta cheese

4 pocket pitas

Olive oil for brushing

**1)** **Make the yogurt-tahini sauce:** Mix the yogurt, tahini, lemon juice, garlic paste, and hot sauce together in a small bowl. Cover and refrigerate until ready to serve.

**2)** **Make the lamb filling:** Using the large holes of a box grater, shred the tomato into a large bowl, discarding the remaining skin. Grate the onion into the bowl. Add the lamb, parsley, garlic, salt, baharat, cumin, cinnamon, Urfa biber flakes, and cayenne and mix with clean hands. Add the cheese and mix again.

**3)** Cut each pita in half and open each fully into a pocket. Spread one-eighth of the filling into each pita half, pressing it into a thin layer.

**4)** Preheat a gas grill to medium (about 350°F/180°C). For a charcoal grill, build a fire and let it burn until the coals are covered with white ash and you can hold your hand above the grid for about 4 seconds. The key to this recipe is moderate heat—you're not searing a steak. Brush the pitas with oil and place them on the grill. Cover and cook until the underside is toasted and seared with grill marks, about 3 minutes. Flip the pitas and toast on the other side, about 3 minutes more. (The pitas can also be toasted in a ridged sandwich grill with a sandwich press on top for about the same time. Keep the filled and toasted pitas warm in a 200°F/95°C oven until they are all cooked.) The pitas should be crisp and the filling should be well done. Transfer to a chopping board. Cut each in half and serve hot, with the sauce in small bowls as a dip.

**note** **Baharat** is a combination of seven spices (garam masala is a good substitute). **Urfa biber** is a purple-red dried chile with smoky, fruity, and spicy flavors, sold flaked. Both spices are sold in Middle Eastern specialty grocers and online.

**137**

# 6

# pork and cold cuts

# BLT&R

## with green tomatoes

**Makes 4 sandwiches**

A BLT with ranch dressing and cornmeal-coated green tomatoes is an over-the-top way to enjoy one of the best claasic sandwiches. Treat yourself to some really good bacon for this version. It's best to make it when green, unripe local tomatoes are at your farmers' market. And nothing beats the tangy creaminess of from-scratch ranch dressing.

### ranch dressing

- 1 cup/240 ml plain low-fat Greek yogurt or mayonnaise
- ⅓ cup/80 ml buttermilk
- 2 tablespoons fresh lemon juice
- 1 tablespoon finely chopped fresh dill or 1 teaspoon dried
- 1 tablespoon finely chopped fresh flat-leaf parsley
- 1 teaspoon garlic powder
- 1 teaspoon onion powder
- Fine sea salt and freshly ground black pepper

### green tomatoes

- ¼ cup/35g all-purpose flour
- 1 large egg
- ¼ cup/35 g standard yellow cornmeal
- ⅛ teaspoon fine sea salt
- ⅛ teaspoon freshly ground black pepper
- Vegetable or canola oil for frying
- 1 large firm unripe green tomato, cored and sliced crosswise into 4 rounds about ½ inch/1.25 cm thick

- 8 slices enriched bread, such as challah or brioche loaf, toasted
- 1 large clove garlic, whole but peeled
- 16 slices thick-cut bacon, cooked (see page 7)
- 4 leaves Bibb lettuce

**1)** **Make the ranch dressing:** Whisk the yogurt, buttermilk, lemon juice, dill, parsley, garlic powder, and onion powder until combined. Season with salt and pepper. Cover and refrigerate for at least 30 minutes and up to 1 week before using. Makes about 1½ cups/360 ml dressing.

**2)** **Cook the green tomatoes:** Preheat the oven to 200°F/95°C.

**3)** Line a half-sheet pan with a wire cooling rack. Spread the flour in a wide shallow bowl or pie plate. Beat the egg in a second bowl or pie plate. (An immersion blender works best.) Mix the cornmeal, salt, and pepper in a third bowl or pie plate. Pour enough oil into a large skillet to come 1 inch/2.5 cm up the sides and heat over medium-high heat until the oil is shimmering. Dip each tomato slice in the flour, then the egg, and then the cornmeal to coat. Place the coated tomatoes on another half-sheet pan. Add to the oil and fry, turning once, until golden, about 3 minutes, adjusting the heat so the tomatoes bubble steadily without burning. Transfer to the cooling rack and keep warm in the oven while frying the remaining tomatoes.

**4)** For each sandwich, rub one side of each toast slice with the garlic clove. Spread with 2 tablespoons of the ranch dressing. Top one slice of bread with 4 bacon slices, 1 tomato slice, and a lettuce leaf. Top with the second slice, cut in half, and serve, with the remaining dressing on the side.

**141**

# Brotherly Love Roast Pork, Broccoli Rabe, and Provolone Sandwich

**Makes 6 sandwiches**

Philadelphia is one helluva sandwich town. Of course there is the cheesesteak, but here is another Sandwich Hall of Famer, served at Tommy DiNic's deli stand at the city's Reading Terminal Market. Tender pork, sharp cheese, rustic broccoli rabe, all layered in a crusty roll moistened with lots of cooking juices. Think of it as the porky relative of Chicago's Italian beef sandwich.

## pork

One 3- to 3½-pound/
   1.4 to 1.6 kg boneless
   pork shoulder (butt or
   Boston butt), netting
   removed and skin
   discarded

2 teaspoons fine sea salt

2 teaspoons Italian herb
   seasoning

1 teaspoon fennel seeds,
   crushed with a mortar
   in a pestle or under a
   heavy pan

1 teaspoon garlic
   powder

1 teaspoon freshly
   ground black pepper

½ teaspoon crushed hot
   red pepper

2 tablespoons olive oil

½ cup/120 ml dry white
   wine

½ cup/120 ml reduced-
   sodium chicken broth

## broccoli rabe

1 pound/455 g broccoli
   rabe (see Note,
   page 57)

2 tablespoons olive oil

2 cloves garlic, thinly
   sliced

¼ teaspoon crushed hot
   red pepper

Fine sea salt

6 oblong French or
   Italian rolls, partially
   split lengthwise and
   opened like a book

18 slices unsmoked
   provolone cheese

**1) Cook the pork:** Open up the pork so the smoother side is facing down (boned side up). Butterfly the pork: Using a large knife, cut diagonally into the thicker areas of the pork and open them up as flaps to increase the surface area of the pork. Mix the salt, Italian seasoning, fennel seeds, garlic powder, black pepper, and hot red pepper. Rub half of the herb mixture over the boned side of the pork. Roll up the pork back into its original shape. Using loops of kitchen twine, tie the pork crosswise and lengthwise into a compact roast. Brush the pork with the oil and rub the remaining herb mixture all over the pork. Let stand at room temperature for about 1 hour. (Or, if you have the time, wrap in aluminum foil or plastic wrap and refrigerate for 12 to 24 hours. Let stand at room temperature for 2 hours before cooking.)

**2)** Preheat the oven to 450ºF/230ºC.

**3)** Place the pork, fat side up, in a roasting pan. Roast, uncovered, until the pork is browned, about 20 minutes. Remove from the oven and reduce the oven temperature to 325ºF/165ºC. Pour the wine and broth into the pan and cover it tightly with aluminum foil. Return to the oven and cook, basting occasionally with the pan juices, until an instant-read thermometer inserted in the center reads at least 180ºF/82ºC, about 1½ hours. Transfer the meat to a carving board with a well, tent with aluminum foil, and let rest for about 15 minutes. Pour the cooking juices into a small saucepan and keep warm over low heat.

**4) Meanwhile, prepare the broccoli rabe:** Bring a large pot of salted water to a boil over high heat. Fill a large bowl with ice water. Add the broccoli rabe, cover, and return to a boil. Cook, uncovered, just until it is crisp-tender and bright green, 1 to 2 minutes. Drain, then transfer to the ice water to cool. Drain again. Pat dry with a kitchen towel or paper towels. Coarsely chop the broccoli rabe. (The broccoli rabe can be refrigerated in a resealable plastic bag for up to 1 day.)

**5)** While the pork is resting, finish the broccoli rabe: Heat the oil, sliced garlic, and hot red pepper together in a large skillet over medium heat until the garlic begins to brown, 2 to 3 minutes. Add the broccoli rabe and cook, stirring occasionally, until hot, about 5 minutes. Season with salt. Remove from the heat and cover to keep warm.

**6)** Position a broiler rack about 4 inches/10 cm from the source of heat and preheat the broiler on High. Using a carving knife, thinly slice the pork. Add any carving juices to the cooking juices. For each sandwich, place an opened roll on a broiler pan. Add a serving of the pork and top with 3 cheese slices. Broil until the cheese melts and the roll is toasted, 1 to 2 minutes. Add a portion of the broccoli rabe and a few tablespoons of the cooking juices. Close the roll, cut in half, and serve.

# Pork Belly Burnt Ends Banh Mi

**Makes 6 sandwiches**

This concept came to me one day, and I could hardly wait to get into the kitchen to try it out. The pork belly cooks low and slow to yield caramelized nuggets of melt-in-your mouth pork in a terrific Asian-inspired sauce. This cut shrinks a lot during cooking, so don't be surprised. Served as a Vietnamese sandwich with pickles and cilantro and cucumber to add freshness, it is even better than I had imagined.

## pork belly burnt ends

2½ pounds/1.2 kg pork belly, skin removed

2 tablespoons light brown sugar

2 tablespoons five-spice powder

1 tablespoon onion powder

1 tablespoon fine sea salt

1 teaspoon freshly ground black pepper

½ cup/120 ml reduced-sodium soy sauce

¼ cup/60 ml hoisin sauce

¼ cup/60 ml honey

2 tablespoons unseasoned rice vinegar

1 tablespoon toasted sesame oil

1 tablespoon grated fresh ginger

3 cloves garlic, minced

---

4 oblong, thin-crusted French or Italian rolls, split lengthwise

½ cup/120 ml mayonnaise, preferably Kewpie

1 jalapeño chile, sliced into thin rounds, loose seeds shaken out

Asian Pickles for Banh Mi (page 225), drained

Fresh cilantro sprigs

½ seedless (English) cucumber, cut into thin rounds

2 scallions, white and green parts, thinly sliced

2 limes, cut into wedges

**1)** **Make the pork belly burnt ends:** Preheat the oven to 300°F/150°C.

**2)** Cut the pork belly into 1- to 2-inch/2.5 to 5 cm cubes so that each piece includes a strata of meaty and fat layers. Transfer to a large bowl. Mix the brown sugar, five-spice powder, onion powder, salt, and pepper in a small bowl. Sprinkle over the pork and toss well to coat. Spread the pork in a 9 × 13-inch/23 × 33 cm metal baking pan, preferably nonstick. Cover tightly with aluminum foil.

**3)** Bake for 1¼ hours. Remove the foil, stir the pork, and increase the oven temperature to 350°F/180°C. Bake until the pork is dark brown and tender when pierced with the tip of a sharp knife, about 30 minutes. If the pork seems to be getting too dark, tent the pan with aluminum foil.

*Recipe continues*

**144**

**4)** Whisk the soy sauce, hoisin sauce, honey, vinegar, sesame oil, ginger, and garlic in a large bowl. Drain the pork in a colander, discarding the fat. Add the pork to the sauce and mix well to coat. Return the sauced pork to the pan.

**5)** Return the pan to the oven and bake, stirring occasionally, until the sauce is reduced into a dark glaze and the pork has crisp edges, about 15 minutes. (If you want the pork even more crisp, broil it in the pan for a few minutes.) Remove from the oven. Divide the pork and sauce into 4 servings.

**6)** For each sandwich, spread the roll with 2 tablespoons of mayonnaise. Spoon a portion of the pork and its sauce on the bottom. Add a few slices of jalapeño, a scattering of the drained pickles, a few cilantro sprigs, a few cucumber slices, and a sprinkle of scallions. Cap with the roll top and cut in half. Serve immediately with the lime wedges.

## banh mi

Vietnam may seem an unlikely place to be famous for its sandwiches, but then again, that only proves the universality of food between bread. *Banh mi* literally means "wheat bread" in Vietnamese, but what originally referred to only a loaf of bread over the years came to refer to the entire sandwich. More than a century of French colonization brought the baguette to Vietnam, with the Asian version evolving to be more tender than its European counterpart. Besides the rolls, my recipe includes other touchstones of a great banh mi, such as tangy pickles, crunchy cucumber, and fresh hot chiles, for an interplay of textures and flavors. One thing I left out, but many purists may want on their sandwich, is a schmear of liver pâté. Purchase the canned version at a specialty market or happily settle for some liverwurst from the deli, seasoned with a pinch of five-spice powder.

# Bao with Hoisin Pork Burnt Ends

**Makes 16 buns, 4 to 6 servings**
**Special equipment:** One two-tier (10-inch/25 cm diameter) bamboo steamer; parchment paper for lining trays (cut to fit the steamer tiers or buy precut paper rounds for steamers)

When I created the Pork Belly Burnt Ends Banh Mi (see the previous recipe), I realized I had to share the classic Asian presentation for pork belly as the centerpiece of a family-style meal where everyone helps themselves and stuffs the meat into steamed buns. I'm including a recipe for homemade buns, but you can also buy refrigerated or frozen Chinese steamed buns (chimei gua bao) at Asian markets. Or just substitute leafy green lettuce and make lettuce wraps, also an Asian tradition. They're both great ways to feed a group.

### steamed buns (bao)

2⅔ cups/345 g cake flour (not self-rising; see Note, page 148), plus more for kneading and shaping

2 tablespoons sugar

1½ teaspoons instant (also called quick-rising or bread-machine) yeast

1 teaspoon baking powder

½ teaspoon fine sea salt

½ cup/120 ml hot tap water

¼ cup/60 ml whole milk

2 tablespoons vegetable or canola oil, plus more for the bowl and brushing

---

Pork Belly Burnt Ends (page 144)

Asian Pickles for Banh Mi (page 225)

Cilantro Slaw (page 65)

**1)** **Make the steamed buns:** Combine the flour, sugar, yeast, baking powder, and salt in the bowl of a heavy-duty stand mixer. Mix the hot water, milk, and oil together in a small bowl and add to the dry ingredients. Stir with a wooden spoon until the mixture comes together. Attach the kneading hook and knead on medium speed to make a smooth and tacky dough that lightly sticks to the bottom of the bowl and passes the windowpane test (see page 239), about 6 minutes. This is a soft and sticky dough. If the dough is very sticky, you may mix in flour, 1 tablespoon at a time. Conversely, if the dough seems too dry, you may mix in 1 tablespoon water for each addition.

To make the dough by hand: Combine the flour, sugar, yeast, baking powder, and salt in a large bowl. Mix the hot water, milk, and oil together and stir into the dry ingredients to make a soft dough. Turn out the dough onto a well-floured work surface. Using a dough scraper (or even a pancake turner), lift up the dough and slap it down onto your work surface until the dough is smooth and tacky and passes the windowpane test (see page 239), 6 to 8 minutes. This is a sticky dough, and easiest to make in a mixer. However, this special "slapping" technique will help deal with the sticky dough.

**2)** Transfer the dough to a floured surface and shape into a ball. Transfer to a lightly oiled bowl, smooth side down, and turn to coat with oil, leaving the smooth side up. Cover tightly with plastic wrap and let stand in a warm place (such as an oven with the door ajar so the light is on) until the dough looks very well risen and has at least doubled in bulk, about 1½ hours.

**3)** Line the bottoms of the steamer tiers with rounds of parchment paper, cutting them a bit smaller than the diameter to allow the steam to circulate. Turn out the dough onto a floured work surface. Divide the dough into 16 equal pieces, shape into balls, place on a floured area, and sprinkle the tops with more flour. One ball at a time, working on the floured surface, press the dough under the heel of your hand

*Recipe continues*

**147**

(or use a rolling pin) to flatten into an oval about 4 inches/10 cm long, 2½ inches/6 cm wide, and ¼ inch/6 mm thick, pulling the oval as needed to lengthen it. Lightly brush the top with the vegetable oil. Fold in half from top to bottom, leaving the bottom half peeking out, but do not seal closed, making a folded bun about 2 inches/5 cm long. Transfer the bun to a lined basket. As shaped, space the buns close together but not touching. Loosely cover each tier with plastic wrap. Let stand in a warm place until the buns look puffed but not quite doubled, about 1 hour.

4) Choose a large saucepan that will singly hold the stacked steamer on top without any leakage of steam. Add enough water to come 1 inch/2.5 cm up the sides and bring to a full boil over high heat. Discard the plastic wrap. Stack the steamer tiers, cover with the steamer lid, and place on the saucepan over the boiling water. Reduce the heat to medium and cook with a full head of steam until the buns have risen and spring back when pressed, about 8 minutes. Don't worry if the steamed buns are touching—they pull apart easily. If the buns on the bottom tier are done first, remove the bottom tier and continue steaming the buns in the top a few minutes more, until the buns are cooked. To keep the buns warm, turn off the heat

and let the buns stand in the tiers over the hot water with the top lid ajar for up to 15 minutes. (The buns are best the day they are made. They can also be cooled, covered with plastic wrap, and stored at room temperature for up to 8 hours. Or freeze on a baking tray, transfer to a freezer bag, and freeze the buns for up to 3 months. When ready to serve, thaw the buns at room temperature. To reheat, place the buns in the steamer baskets and place over boiling water for about 5 minutes. The buns can also be reheated in freezer bags in the microwave in batches of 8 buns at High/100% power for about 20 seconds.)

5) To serve, put out a platter of the warm buns with bowls of the pork, pickles, and slaw. Let each guest fill their own bao.

note Cake flour (such as Softasilk or Swans Down) will make the most tender bao. Be sure to use a brand that is not self-rising, To store, freeze the remaining flour in a plastic freezer bag, where it will keep for up to 2 years. Let the cold flour come to room temperature before using.

# Carolina Pulled Pork

## with bbq slaw

**Makes about 12 servings**

When people talk about barbecue, the words "low and slow" always comes up. That's what we're doing here, allowing time and low temperatures to gently melt the fat and tough parts of the pork into juicy submission. While true barbecue requires outdoor cooking, I developed this slow-baked version for people without an outdoor grill. Pulled pork is perhaps the very best meal for serving a crowd in the Southern style. Even if you aren't giving a party, leftover pork is great to find in the freezer for other meals. Important note: This thin, sweet-tart sauce is meant to be a condiment on the sandwich and is not applied during cooking. It is not a thick and gooey sauce.

### carolina bbq sauce

- 2½ cups/600 ml distilled white vinegar
- ¼ cup/50 g granulated sugar
- ½ teaspoon garlic powder
- ½ teaspoon fine sea salt
- 1 tablespoon ketchup
- 1 tablespoon crushed hot red pepper

### pulled pork

- One 5- to 6-pound/2.3 to 2.7 kg pork shoulder or butt, with the bone
- 2 teaspoons hickory-flavored liquid smoke (optional)
- 1 tablespoon fine sea salt
- 2 teaspoons light brown sugar
- 1 teaspoon smoked paprika
- 1 teaspoon chili powder
- 1 teaspoon freshly ground black pepper
- ½ teaspoon garlic powder
- ½ teaspoon onion powder
- ¼ teaspoon cayenne pepper
- One 12-ounce/360 ml bottle lager beer

### bbq slaw

- ¾ cup/180 ml vegetable oil
- Two 14-ounce/397 g packages coleslaw mix
- 1 small yellow onion, grated on the large holes of a box grater (about 3 tablespoons grated onion)
- ½ teaspoon celery seeds
- Fine sea salt and freshly ground black pepper

12 soft sandwich buns

**1) Make the Carolina BBQ sauce:** Bring 1 cup/240 ml of the vinegar, the granulated sugar, garlic powder, and salt to a boil over high heat in a small saucepan, stirring to dissolve the sugar and salt. Remove from the heat and whisk in the remaining 1½ cups/360 ml vinegar with the ketchup and hot red pepper. Let cool. (The sauce can be refrigerated in a covered container at room temperature for up to 3 days.)

*Recipe continues*

**2) Prepare the pork:** If the pork has skin, use a thin knife to score it in a crisscross pattern just down to where the fat meets the flesh. Slice the fat cap with its skin from the flesh as a flap, keeping it hinged to the meat on one side. Brush the hickory flavoring, if using, all over the pork flesh. Mix the salt, brown sugar, paprika, chili powder, black pepper, garlic powder, onion powder, and cayenne in a small bowl. On a large sheet of aluminum foil to catch the rub, massage the rub all over the exposed flesh, including under the fat cap. Put the fat cap back in place. Wrap in the foil, using more foil as needed. Let stand at room temperature for 1 hour. (Or, if you have the time, refrigerate for 12 to 24 hours. Let stand at room temperature for 2 hours before cooking.)

**3)** Preheat the oven to 300°F/150°C.

**4) Cook the pork:** Unwrap the pork and place it, fat side up, on a wire rack or collapsible steamer (or make a ring out of aluminum foil to hold the pork) in a Dutch oven, pour in the beer, and cover. Roast until the meat is fork-tender (an instant-read thermometer inserted in the thickest part will read at least 195°F/90°C), about 3½ hours. Remove the lid, increase the oven temperature to 350°F/180°C, and bake so the outside of the pork develops a brown crust (bark), about 30 minutes. The meat should be pulling away from the bone.

**5)** Wrap the pork in a large sheet of heavy-duty aluminum foil. Let stand for 1 to 2 hours before shredding the meat. This rest period allows the residual heat in the pork to melt any remaining tough bits and retains the juices. Pour the cooking liquid into a small bowl and reserve.

**6) Meanwhile, make the BBQ slaw:** Whisk ¾ cup/180 ml Carolina BBQ sauce and the oil in a large bowl. Add the coleslaw mix, onion, and celery seeds and mix well. Season with salt and pepper. Cover and refrigerate for 1 to 2 hours until serving. (The slaw can be made up to 2 days ahead.)

**7)** Pour the remaining sauce into a squeeze bottle or syrup dispenser for serving. Transfer the pork to a work surface and unwrap the pork, leaving it in the foil. Using two large forks, pull the pork apart into shreds, discarding any bones and large pieces of fat. Even better: Wear protective gloves and shred the meat with your fingers. Transfer the meat to a serving bowl. Mix in any juices from the foil and a few tablespoons of the cooking juices to moisten. (The meat should still be warm. If necessary, reheat the meat and reserved juices in the Dutch oven over medium heat, stirring often, until hot, about 5 minutes.) Transfer the meat to a bowl and serve with the slaw, sauce, and buns, allowing the guests make their own sandwiches.

**Pulled Pork Doughnut:** This is very rich, but a lot of BBQ fans swear by it. Just substitute glazed yeast doughnuts for the buns.

# Vietnamese Pork Summer Rolls

**Makes 8 rolls, 2 rolls per serving**
**Special equipment: Mandoline or plastic slicer**

Summer rolls are fun to make because you can personalize them. Many recipes use cooked shrimp instead of pork, but the pork makes the rolls a bit more substantial. If you've never worked with rice paper rounds before, you may sacrifice a couple until you get the hang of dealing with the moistened papers, as they are quite sticky. (But there are plenty in a package, so don't worry.) The rolls can be covered and refrigerated for a few hours before serving.

## marinated pork

- ¼ cup/60 ml fish sauce
- 2 tablespoon fresh lime juice
- 2 tablespoons vegetable oil
- 2 teaspoons light brown sugar
- 2 cloves garlic, minced
- ½ fresh Thai chile, seeded and minced
- Two 3- to 4-ounce/85 to 115 g boneless center-cut pork loin cutlets, pounded to ½ inch/1.25 cm thickness

## nuoc cham dip

- 3 tablespoons hot tap water
- 2 tablespoons granulated sugar, preferably superfine
- 2 tablespoons fish sauce
- 2 tablespoons fresh lime juice
- 2 cloves garlic, minced
- ½ fresh Thai chile, seeded and minced, or to taste

## summer rolls assembly

- 2 small skeins (3.5 ounces/100 g) rice vermicelli (also called rice sticks or bun)
- Vegetable oil for the rice vermicelli
- Eight 9-inch/23 cm rice paper rounds (spring/summer roll wrappers)
- 8 green lettuce leaves, torn to fit the rolls
- ½ seedless (English) cucumber, julienned (a mandoline works best)
- 1 small carrot, julienned (a mandoline works best)
- ¼ cup loosely packed/ 7 g fresh cilantro or mint leaves
- ¼ cup/30 g coarsely chopped roasted peanuts, plus more for garnish

**1) Marinate the pork:** Whisk the fish sauce, lime juice, oil, brown sugar, garlic, and chile in a small bowl to dissolve the sugar. Pour into a 1-quart/960 ml resealable plastic bag. Add the pork and close the bag. Refrigerate for 1 to 2 hours, turning occasionally.

**2) Make the nuoc cham dip:** Mix the hot water and sugar in a small bowl to dissolve the sugar. Stir in the fish sauce, lime juice, garlic, and chile. Let stand at room temperature until ready to serve.

**3) Cook the marinated pork:** Heat a ridged grill pan over medium heat. Remove the pork from the marinade. Place on the grill and cook, turning once, until well seared on both sides and cooked through, about 5 minutes. Transfer the meat to a carving board with a well and let cool for 5 minutes. Using a sharp carving knife, cut the pork into strips about ¼ inch/6 mm wide. Transfer to a small bowl.

**4) Prepare the summer rolls:** Bring a medium saucepan of water to a boil over high heat. Add the vermicelli, stirring often to separate the strands, and cook until just tender, about 4 minutes. Drain and rinse well under cold running water; drain well. Transfer to a small bowl and toss with a teaspoon or so of vegetable oil to reduce sticking and use kitchen scissors to randomly snip the noodles into pieces about 6 inches/15 cm long.

**5)** Line a half-sheet pan with parchment or waxed paper. Add enough hot tap water to a pie plate to fill it halfway. Arrange the pie plate, rice paper rounds, and bowls of the lettuce, vermicelli, pork, cucumber, carrot, cilantro, and peanuts on a work surface. For each summer roll, dip a rice paper round in the hot water just until it softens, about 5 seconds, depending on the brand. Shake off excess water and place the round flat on the work surface. Top with a lettuce leaf and one-eighth portions of the vermicelli, pork, cucumber, and carrot, arranging them vertically about 1 inch/2.5 cm from the left side of the round. Sprinkle with a few cilantro leaves and some peanuts. Fold in the top and bottom to partially cover the filling by about ¼ inch/6 mm, then fold the left side over. Roll from left to right, tucking in the ingredients in the round as you go. The rice round will stick to itself. Transfer to the prepared pan. Do not let the summer rolls touch each other. (The rolls can be loosely covered with plastic wrap and refrigerated for up 4 to 6 hours.) Serve at room temperature or chilled, with the nuoc cham in small bowls or ramekins for dipping.

# Cubano Sandwich

**Makes 4 sandwiches**

I ate plenty of Cuban sandwiches during my time in Florida. Crusty on the outside, filled with two kinds of pork and melty Swiss cheese, with sharp notes from the mustard and pickles, it is always satisfying. To help the cheese melt, warm up the ham in a microwave or in a skillet, just about 30 seconds or so to heat it. While Cuban sandwiches are often made with pulled pork (lechon asado or pernil), lately I've been using marinated pork tenderloin because it is quicker to cook and equally tasty.

## marinated pork

Grated zest of 1 orange

½ cup/120 ml fresh orange juice

¼ cup/60 ml fresh lime juice

3 tablespoons olive oil

2 tablespoons finely chopped fresh cilantro

2 cloves garlic, minced

1 teaspoon ground cumin

1 teaspoon dried oregano

½ teaspoon crushed hot red pepper

½ teaspoon fine sea salt

¼ teaspoon freshly ground black pepper

1 pork tenderloin (about 1 pound/455 g), trimmed of silverskin

———

1 tablespoon olive oil

4 soft oblong rolls, such as Cuban, split

½ cup/120 ml Dijon mustard

8 slices Swiss cheese, cut to fit the rolls

8 slices Black Forest or boiled ham, cut to fit the rolls, briefly warmed in a microwave or skillet

Dill pickle slices

3 tablespoons unsalted butter, melted

**1) Marinate the pork:** Whisk the orange zest and juice, lime juice, oil, cilantro, garlic, cumin, oregano, hot red pepper, salt, and black pepper together in a medium bowl. Pour into a 1-gallon/3.78 L resealable plastic bag. Add the pork and close the bag. Refrigerate for at least 1 hour or overnight, turning the bag occasionally.

**2)** Preheat the oven to 350°F/180°C.

**3) Cook the marinated pork:** Remove the pork from the marinade and blot it with paper towels. Heat the oil in a large ovenproof skillet over medium-high heat. Add the pork and cook, turning occasionally, until browned on all sides, about 6 minutes. Transfer the pork in the skillet to the oven and bake until an instant-read thermometer inserted in the center of the pork reads 145°F/63°C, 20 to 25 minutes. Transfer to a carving board with a well and let cool for about 5 minutes. Using a sharp carving knife held at a slight angle, cut the tenderloin into 12 thin medallions.

**4)** Heat a griddle or large skillet over medium heat. For each sandwich, spread a roll with 2 tablespoons of the mustard. Stack the ingredients on the bottom half of the roll in this order: 1 cheese slice, 1 ham slice, 3 pork medallions with their carving juices, a few pickles, a second ham slice, and a second cheese slice. Cap with the roll top. Press firmly to condense the sandwich. Brush the sandwich on both sides with melted butter.

**5)** Place the sandwiches on the griddle, cover with a half-sheet pan, and weight with a few heavy cans. (If you were cooking a single sandwich, you would use a sandwich press, but this method allows you to press a few Cubanos at once.) Adjusting the heat so the sandwich is cooking steadily without burning, cook until the underside is toasted, about 2 minutes. Flip the sandwiches, replace the pan and cans, and cook until the other side is toasted, about 2 minutes more. Transfer to a chopping board. Cut crosswise in half on a sharp diagonal. Transfer to plates and serve hot.

# The Godmother

**Makes 4 sandwiches**

I call this Italian deli extravaganza the Godmother because I picture a woman at her local panini store who can't make up her mind, so she orders a panino with a little bit of everything. Load up the cart at your favorite Italian deli, go home, and make this sandwich. It is even better if made ahead so the flavors can meld, so keep it in mind for a picnic, trip to the beach, tailgate party, or other times when you want a sandwich that needs to travel. This sandwich has it all!

### italian dressing

½ cup/120 ml extra virgin olive oil

3 tablespoons red wine vinegar

1 small clove garlic, minced

½ teaspoon dried oregano

¼ teaspoon dry mustard

¼ teaspoon fine sea salt

¼ teaspoon freshly ground black pepper

Pinch of crushed hot red pepper

4 crusty Italian rolls, split

½ cup/120 ml mayonnaise or Aioli (page 219)

12 slices soppressata

12 thin slices prosciutto

12 slices Black Forest ham (see Note, page 159)

12 slices mortadella

12 slices unsmoked provolone cheese

8 slices tomato

4 slices red onion, separated into rings

2 pepperoncini, cut into rings

1 cup/30 g baby arugula

**1) Make the Italian dressing:** Process the oil, vinegar, garlic, oregano, mustard, salt, black pepper, and hot red pepper in a blender until smooth. (Or shake the ingredients well in a jar.) Makes about ¾ cup/180 ml. (The dressing can be covered and refrigerated for up to 1 week.)

**2)** For each sandwich, drizzle about 2 tablespoons of the dressing over the cut sides of the roll. Spread with 2 tablespoons mayonnaise. Layer 3 slices each of the soppressata, prosciutto, ham, mortadella, and provolone on the bottom of the roll, cutting or folding the meats to fit. Top with 2 tomato slices, a few onion rings, a few pepperoncini slices, and a handful of arugula. Cap with the top of the roll. (If you have the time, wrap each sandwich in plastic wrap and let stand for a couple of hours before serving.) Cut in half and serve.

## you say baloney, i say bologna

While I don't have any bologna sandwiches in this book, I do have mortadella, which is very similar. Bologna (usually pronounced "baloney" in the US, although named for the central Italian city where it originated, pronounced "bol-owhn-yah") is actually an Americanized version of mortadella. When I would open my school lunchbox, I had mortadella and mozzarella while the other kids had to make do with ham and cheese. Both versions are made from a very smooth paste of pork, but mortadella is studded with white chunks of pork fat and green pistachios whereas bologna is plain. (There are local variations of bologna, such as spiced and Lebanon, but most of us know the good old beige version.) Mortadella is not sold at all delicatessens, but it is required at Italian ones.

156

# Bresaola, Goat Cheese, and Arugula Panino

**Makes 2 sandwiches**

A true panino is made on sliced bread and toasted to a golden turn, and here is one of my favorite versions. Most Americans are acquainted with prosciutto, but this sandwich is a chance to get to know its beefy cousin, bresaola. This is inspired by my sister, Olimpia, who always ordered an off-the-menu salad with these ingredients (but she liked shaved Parmigiano as the cheese) when our family would go out for dinner at our favorite Italian restaurant, Mediterraneo, in Sarasota, Florida. While I use Italian goat cheese (caprino) whenever I can find it for this panino, any country's version will do.

4 slices sourdough bread

Extra virgin olive oil

5 ounces/140 g spreadable goat cheese, preferably Italian, at room temperature

4 ounces/115 g thinly sliced bresaola (see Note)

About ½ cup/15 g baby arugula

Lemon wedges for serving

**1)** Heat a ridged grill pan over medium heat.

**2)** For each sandwich, brush one side of 2 bread slices with oil and place, oiled side down, on a work surface. Spread with half of the goat cheese. Top a slice with half of the bresaola, folded to fit. Add a handful of arugula. Cap with the second bread slice, cheese side down. Brush the top of the sandwich with oil.

**3)** Place the sandwiches on the heated pan and weight down with a sandwich press. Cook until the underside is golden brown and toasty, about 2 minutes. Flip the sandwiches, weight with the press, and cook until the second side is toasted, about 2 minutes more. Transfer to a chopping board and cut in half. Transfer to plates and serve, with the lemon wedges.

**note** Bresaola is simply beef cured like prosciutto. Instead of pork leg, lean beef round is rubbed with salt, herbs, and spices and then air-dried. The resulting meat is dry and dark purple. In addition to this sandwich, try it in a salad with arugula, lemon juice, top-quality extra virgin olive oil, and a few grinds of pepper. You will find it at Italian delicatessens and well-stocked supermarkets.

# Honeyed Ham and Brie Baguette

**Makes 2 sandwiches**

If you have ever traveled to France, you probably have come across a baguette jambon beurre, a ubiquitous sandwich of cold ham and butter on a split baguette sold at every French snack shop and roadside restaurant. Baking the sandwich to warm the ham and melt the Brie improves something that is pretty satisfying to start with, and I have replaced the butter with more flavorful ingredients.

1 baguette, cut in half crosswise into 2 pieces about 10 inches/25 cm long, and split lengthwise

6 tablespoons/90 ml Dijon Mayonnaise (page 219)

5 ounces/140 g thinly sliced Black Forest ham (see Note)

8 ounces/225 g Brie cheese, rind included, cut into ½-inch-/1.25 cm thick slices

2 to 3 tablespoons honey, or as needed

1 cup/30 g baby arugula

1 lemon, cut into wedges

**1)** Preheat the oven to 400°F/200°C.

**2)** For each sandwich, spread the baguette halves with 3 tablespoons of the Dijon mayonnaise. Top one side of the baguette with half of the ham, folded to fit. Place half of the sliced Brie on the other baguette half to cover it without the cheese hanging over the edges (overhanging cheese will melt onto the baking sheet and make a mess). Place the baguette halves, open faced, on a half-sheet pan and bake until the cheese is melted, about 10 minutes.

**3)** Depending on the size of the bread, drizzle about 1 tablespoon of the honey over each of the cheese-covered baguette halves. Top each with a handful of arugula. Close the baguettes. Cut in half crosswise and serve with the lemon wedges.

**note** Black Forest ham originated in Germany and is heavily smoked and unglazed. The domestic version is easy to find at delis and supermarkets. Any ham without a sweet and sticky coating can be substituted.

# Mortadella with Pistachio Pesto

## on schiacciata

**Makes 2 sandwiches**

There is pesto and then there is *this* pesto. Fava beans and pistachios lend their pastel colors to deep green basil leaves for this beautiful sandwich spread (and it is good tossed with pasta, too). You can find the fava beans at Latino and Italian grocers, but lima beans or even peas are a good substitute. Mortadella takes me right back to my Italian cold cut roots, as it remains my favorite salume, but you can certainly substitute sliced ham if you aren't close to an Italian deli. Try to make this in the authentic Italian fashion, on schiacciata (page 234), or use thick focaccia from a bakery.

### pistachio pesto

½ cup/65 g shelled pistachios

½ cup/70 g thawed frozen fava or lima beans, or peas

⅓ cup/35 g freshly grated pecorino Romano cheese

1 cup packed/30 g fresh basil leaves

2 tablespoons fresh lemon juice

⅔ cup/160 ml extra virgin olive oil, plus more for storage

Fine sea salt and freshly ground black pepper

2 rectangles Overnight Schiacciata (page 234) or store-bought focaccia, split

6 ounces/170 g thinly sliced mortadella (see page 156)

½ cup/130 g stracciatella (see Note)

Freshly ground black pepper

1 lemon, cut in half

**1)** **Make the pistachio pesto:** Bring a medium pot of water to a boil over high heat. Add the pistachios and boil for 2 minutes to loosen their skins and set the green color. Drain and rinse under cold running water. Pinch off as many of the brown skins as you have patience for; you do not have to do them all.

**2)** Pulse the pistachios, beans, and cheese a few times in a food processor until chopped. Add the basil and lemon juice and pulse again to chop the basil. With the machine running, gradually pour the oil through the feed tube. Season with salt and pepper. Transfer to a covered container. Top the pesto with a thin layer of oil to cover and seal the surface. Makes about 1¼ cups/345 g. (The pesto can be refrigerated for up to 1 week. Stir well before using.)

**3)** For each sandwich, spread the cut sides of the schiacciata with about 3 tablespoons of the pesto. Fold and layer the mortadella on the bottom half. Top with half of the stracciatella, add a few grinds of pepper, and squeeze the juice of a lemon half on top. Close the sandwich, cut in half, and serve.

**note** Stracciatella (which means "little rag" or "little shreds" in Italian) is a soft, spreadable fresh cheese made from stretched and shredded mozzarella curds and heavy cream. When this mixture is wrapped inside a mozzarella ball, it becomes burrata. If your cheese vendor sells burrata, they might also have stracciatella, but if you can't find the latter, just chop up a burrata ball, filling and all.

# Prosciutto Piadina

**Makes 4 sandwiches**

If you don't have bread in the house, with a few pantry items, you can have fresh, homemade piadina, a stuffed Italian flatbread. It might remind you of calzone but is cooked in a skillet. Do as Italian cooks do and consider piadine as a way to use leftovers (see some ideas on page 164). Whenever I make one, I can't help but think of my brothers, Oliver and Octavien, who could eat a stack in one sitting. But that is true of me, too.

## piadine dough

2 cups/280 g unbleached all-purpose flour, plus more for kneading and rolling

1 teaspoon fine sea salt

½ teaspoon baking powder

½ cup/120 ml warm water, or as needed

¼ cup/60 ml extra virgin olive oil

8 fresh round mozzarella cheese slices, about 6 ounces/170 g

8 ripe beefsteak tomato slices, drained on paper towels

Fine sea salt and freshly ground black pepper

4 tablespoons coarsely torn fresh basil leaves

Balsamic glaze for drizzling

4 ounces/115 g thinly sliced prosciutto

**1) Make the piadine dough:** Whisk the flour, salt, and baking powder in a medium bowl. Mix the warm water and oil together. Make a well in the flour, pour in the liquid, and stir until combined. (You may need more or less of the liquid. If too dry, add more water, a tablespoon at a time. If too wet, sprinkle in flour, a teaspoon at a time.) Turn out onto a lightly floured work surface. Knead until the dough is smooth and elastic, about 5 minutes. (To make in a food processor, pulse the flour, salt, and baking powder until combined. Combine the water and oil. With the machine running, add the liquid through the feed tube and let run until the dough forms a ball that rides on the blade with some dough bits in the bottom of the bowl, about 20 seconds. Let run for 45 seconds to knead. Remove from the processor.)

**2)** Divide the dough into 4 equal pieces. Shape each into a smooth ball. Place on a lightly floured work surface, cover loosely with a kitchen towel or plastic wrap, and let stand for 20 to 30 minutes.

**3)** On a lightly floured work surface, roll out each ball into an 8-inch/20 cm disk. Place the disks on a plate, dusting each with flour, and cover loosely with the towel or plastic wrap until ready to cook, up to 30 minutes.

**4)** Preheat the oven to 200°F/95°C.

**5)** Heat a large skillet or griddle over medium-high heat. Bring the dough rounds and filling ingredients next to the stove. One at a time, add a disk to the skillet and cook until the top is puffing and the bottom is blistered and lightly browned, about 1½ minutes. The flatbread must remain flexible enough to fold in half, so do not overcook. Flip the round over. On one half, add 2 cheese rounds and 2 tomato rounds. Sprinkle with salt and pepper and 1 tablespoon of the basil. Drizzle with the balsamic glaze. Top with one-quarter of the prosciutto slices, folded to fit.

*Recipe continues*

**162**

Fold the empty side of the round over the filling and press down slightly so the dough stays in place. Cook until both sides of the folded piadina are spotted brown, flipping as needed, 2 to 3 minutes. Transfer to a baking sheet and keep warm in the oven while making the remaining piadine.

**6)** Transfer to plates, cut each in half, and serve warm.

## personalized piadina

Create your own ideas for easy piadine, served right out of the skillet. If it sounds like it will make a great pizza, it will also make a great piadina. Here are some combinations to get your creative juices going.

Cooked broccoli rabe, cooked and crumbled Italian sausage, and Italian Fontina cheese

Salami, roasted red pepper, fresh oregano, and low-moisture mozzarella

Smoked sausage, cooked potato slices, sautéed green cabbage, and Italian Fontina cheese

Sautéed mushrooms, garlic, and Italian Fontina cheese

Sliced meatballs, tomato sauce, and fresh mozzarella

# Backyard Hot Dog

## with homemade relish

**Makes 8 servings**

Hot dogs are very popular at backyard cookouts, but how do you make them into something special? My suggestion is homemade relish and some added crunch from potato chips. My relish recipe makes enough for a big party but can easily be halved. (I give an indoor cooking method, but throw the hot dogs and buns on the grill, if you prefer.) Mustard is really the only other required condiment, but if you are a ketchup person, go for it.

### homemade sweet relish

1 seedless (English) cucumber, cut into chunks

1 medium green bell pepper, seeded and cut into chunks

1 medium sweet onion, cut into chunks

2 pepperoncini, finely chopped

2 tablespoons fine sea salt

1 cup/240 ml distilled white vinegar

½ cup/100 g sugar

½ teaspoon celery seeds

½ teaspoon yellow mustard seeds

¼ teaspoon ground turmeric

———

8 hot dogs

Your favorite mustard

8 hot dog buns, toasted

2 plum tomatoes, halved lengthwise and sliced into thin half-moons

About 1½ cups/70 g crushed potato chips

**1)** **At least one day before serving, start the sweet relish:** In two batches, pulse the cucumber, bell pepper, onion, and pepperoncini in a food processor until finely chopped into pieces about ¼ inch/6 mm square. Transfer to a colander and toss with the salt. Let drain in a sink or on a plate for at least 3 hours or overnight. Transfer the vegetables to a clean 1-quart/960 ml canning jar or covered container.

**2)** Bring the vinegar, sugar, 1 cup/240 ml water, the celery seeds, mustard seeds, and turmeric to a boil in a medium saucepan, stirring to dissolve the sugar. Pour into the jar to cover the relish (you may not need all the liquid). Stir with a long spoon to submerge the relish. Cover immediately. Let cool to room temperature. Refrigerate overnight. Makes about 1 quart/960 ml. (The relish can be stored in the refrigerator for 2 to 3 months.)

**3)** Heat a large heavy skillet (preferably cast iron) over medium-high heat. Add the hot dogs and ½ cup/120 ml water. Bring to a boil and cover. Cook for 3 minutes. Uncover and cook until the water has evaporated and the hot dogs are beginning to brown, about 5 minutes.

**4)** Spread the mustard in the buns. Tuck a hot dog and a few tomato slices into each bun, add some relish, and sprinkle with some crushed chips. Serve hot.

# Golden Korean Reuben

**Makes 4 sandwiches**

The Reuben has a contentious history because two restaurants, one in Omaha and one in New York, lay claim to inventing the stack of corned beef, sauerkraut, and Swiss cheese on rye. I bring this classic into the twenty-first century by swapping kimchi, also a kind of fermented cabbage, for the sauerkraut. I also share a special method for griddling the sandwich that you can apply to other recipes. You may be surprised to know that mayonnaise can be used to give a golden sheen to the bread (try it on your next grilled cheese).

---

12 ounces/340 g thinly
　sliced corned beef

8 slices rye bread,
　preferably marble rye

About ⅔ cup/165 ml
　mayonnaise

8 slices Swiss cheese

1 cup/240 g well-
　drained and coarsely
　chopped kimchi

Sriracha for serving
　(optional)

**1)** Heat a griddle or very large skillet over medium heat. Add the corned beef and cook, turning occasionally, until heated through. (You can also heat the corned beef, covered, in a microwave-safe plate for about 1 minute in a microwave on High/100% power.) Transfer to a plate. Wipe off the griddle with paper towels.

**2)** For each sandwich, spread 2 bread slices with about 2 tablespoons of the mayonnaise. Layer with a cheese slice, ¼ cup/60 g of the kimchi, a serving of the warm corned beef, and another cheese slice. Cap with another slice of bread, mayonnaise side down. Spread about ½ tablespoon of mayonnaise in a thin layer on the top of the sandwich. Place the sandwiches, mayonnaise side down, on the griddle. Grill, adjusting the heat as needed so the sandwiches brown at a steady pace to melt the cheese without burning the bread, until the underside is golden and lightly toasted, about 3 minutes. As the sandwich cooks, occasionally press it firmly with a pancake turner to help build the crust and to distribute the heat.

**3)** Spread another thin layer of mayonnaise on top of the sandwiches in the skillet. Flip the sandwiches over. Cook, occasionally pressing the sandwiches with the turner, until the underside is golden and toasted, about 3 minutes more. Transfer to a carving board, cut in half, and serve hot, with sriracha, if you wish.

# Double Salami and Roasted Onion Spread Sandwich

**Makes 2 sandwiches**

For the person who loves picnics (which means just about all of us), I offer this sandwich. It has all the good stuff I would want in my picnic basket, such as crusty bread, spicy cold cuts, creamy cheese, and tender greens—you provide your favorite wine. And it only gets better if it melds for a few hours before serving. The roasted onion spread adds punch to any sandwich and is worth making on a weekend afternoon to have on hand for whenever you need it. You will find cipollini, squat miniature onions, at well-stocked produce markets and Italian grocers. And the dressing just might become your "house" dressing for everyday salads.

## roasted onion spread

8 ounces/225 g cipollini onions

3 tablespoons extra virgin olive oil

1 tablespoon coarsely chopped fresh thyme

Fine sea salt and freshly ground black pepper

1 cup/100 g drained sun-dried tomatoes in oil, coarsely chopped

## balsamic basil dressing

½ cup packed/15 g fresh basil leaves

2 teaspoons dried oregano

2 tablespoons balsamic vinegar

2 tablespoons fresh lemon juice

¼ cup plus 2 tablespoons/90 ml extra virgin olive oil

Fine sea salt

———

1 baguette, cut crosswise into 2 equal pieces, split lengthwise

4 ounces/115 g thinly sliced Genoa salami

4 ounces/115 g thinly sliced hot soppressata

4 slices unsmoked provolone or Fontina cheese, preferably Fontina d'Aosta

1 cup/30 g tender mixed greens

**1)** **Make the roasted onion spread:** Bring a medium saucepan of water to a boil over high heat. Add the onions, return to a boil, and cook for 30 seconds to loosen the skins. Drain and rinse the onions under cold water. Using a sharp paring knife, peel the onions, trimming off the tops and bottoms in the process.

**2)** Position a rack in the center of the oven and preheat the oven to 400°F/200°C.

**3)** Transfer the onions to a small baking dish to hold them in a single layer. Drizzle with 1 tablespoon of the oil. Sprinkle with the thyme, ½ teaspoon salt, and ¼ teaspoon pepper and toss to combine. Roast, stirring every 15 minutes for even browning, until tender and golden brown, about 45 minutes. Let cool.

*Recipe continues*

**169**

4) Transfer the roasted onions to a food processor and pulse a few times to coarsely chop them. Add the sun-dried tomatoes and remaining 2 tablespoons oil and pulse to chop into a chunky spread. Season with salt and pepper. Transfer to a bowl. Makes about 1 cup/350 g spread. (The spread can be stored in an airtight container in the refrigerator for up to 5 days.)

5) **Make the balsamic basil dressing:** Gradually add the basil leaves to a mortar and crush with a pestle to make a coarse paste. Mash in the oregano. Mashing with the pestle, gradually add the vinegar and lemon juice, then the olive oil. (Or blend all the ingredients together in a bowl with an immersion blender.) Season with salt. Transfer to a bowl. (The dressing is best used soon after making, as the basil discolors.)

6) Position a broiler rack about 4 inches/10 cm from the source of heat and preheat the broiler on High. For each sandwich, spread the roll with about 2 tablespoons of the spread. Add half of the salami and soppressata. Top with half of the cheese. Broil until the cheese is melted, about 1 minute. Add half of the greens on each, then drizzle with about 2 tablespoons of the dressing. Cap with the baguette top. Press down on top to compress the sandwich. Cut in half and serve.

## salami, salume

In Italy, all cured pork products that are encased, cured, and sliced are called *salume*. (Just as French charcuterie is also a big category, running from pâtés to sausages.) In America, only the ground and spiced pork with peppercorns cured in a tube is called *salami*. There are a number of varieties, and the choice of salami is up to you. Genoa salami is highly flavored with garlic, pepper, and wine. Hard salami is similar, but aged so more moisture evaporates and the meat is chewier. (It is best paired with firm, crusty bread.) Soppressata is a kind of hard, narrower salami that utilizes virtually all parts of the pig, and it comes in hot and "sweet" (mild) versions. Beef salami is often made by cultures that don't eat pork and is found at Jewish and Middle Eastern delicatessens.

# Crispy Speck and Tomato Butter Sandwich

**Makes 2 sandwiches**

Speck is another member of the prosciutto family. Both are cured pork leg, but speck is also lightly smoked and a specialty of the mountainous Tyrol region of Italy. (The really good Italian version is labeled "Alto Adige" to note its source.) You can buy it, freshly sliced, at well-stocked Italian grocers, or you may find it pre-sliced and packaged. Regular prosciutto is a good substitute. With its firm texture and amped-up flavor, speck is perfect for sandwiches, and a quick trip to the skillet to crisp it up brings even more to the party.

## tomato butter

4 tablespoons/56 g (½ stick) unsalted butter, softened

2 teaspoons minced shallot

½ clove garlic, crushed through a press

2 tablespoons tomato paste

1 tablespoon finely chopped fresh flat-leaf parsley

1 tablespoon finely chopped fresh basil

Pinch of crushed hot red pepper

Fine sea salt and freshly ground black pepper

3 ounces/85 g thinly sliced speck or prosciutto (about 8 slices)

2 oblong sourdough rolls, split

½ cup/65 g stracciatella (see page 161) or finely chopped burrata cheese

1 cup packed/30 g arugula leaves

1 lemon

Extra virgin olive oil

**1)** **Make the tomato butter:** Mash the butter, shallot, garlic, tomato paste, parsley, basil, and hot red pepper in a small bowl with a rubber spatula until combined. Season with salt and black pepper.

**2)** Position a broiler rack about 4 inches/10 cm from the source of heat and preheat the broiler on High.

**3)** Heat a large skillet over medium heat. In batches, add a single layer of the speck and cook, turning once, until crisp and lightly browned, about 4 minutes. Transfer to paper towels to drain.

**4)** Spread the tomato butter on the rolls. Broil the rolls, cut sides up, until the butter is bubbling, about 2 minutes. Remove from the broiler.

**5)** For each sandwich, spread the bottom half of the roll with half of the stracciatella. Top with half of the speck, followed by half of the arugula. Using a zester, grate half of the lemon on top and drizzle with some olive oil. Cap with the top of the roll. Cut in half crosswise. Serve immediately.

171

# 7

# vegetarian

# Veggie Burger

## with roasted vegetables and quinoa

**Makes 5 burgers**

With the popularity of plant-based cuisine, veggie burgers are no longer niche fare. I have lots of tips for this first-class recipe. The roasting step evaporates excess liquid from the veggies and concentrates the flavors. Freeze any extra patties to have handy for another meal. Don't skip rinsing the quinoa, as it removes its bitter natural coating. You will have leftover cooked quinoa to save for another use (add it to salads). And the avocado crema is also a fantastic salad dressing for crisp greens. The burger itself is vegan, so just swap out the cheese for some mashed avocado or guacamole if you want a dairy-free meal. (And check the bun's ingredients.)

### avocado crema

- ½ Hass avocado, pitted and coarsely chopped
- ½ cup packed/15 g fresh cilantro leaves
- ¼ cup/60 g minced yellow onion
- ¼ cup/60 ml plain Greek yogurt
- 2 tablespoons fresh lime juice
- 1 tablespoon olive oil
- Fine sea salt and freshly ground black pepper

---

### veggie burgers

- 1 cup/175 g quinoa
- 2 cups/480 ml vegetable broth
- Fine sea salt
- 1 cup/100 g coarsely chopped white mushrooms
- 1 medium carrot, cut into ½-inch/1.25 cm dice (¾ cup/100 g)
- 1 medium yellow onion, cut into ½-inch/1.25 cm dice
- 1 cup/175 g corn kernels, fresh (from 2 ears) or thawed frozen
- ½ jalapeño chile, seeded and cut into 4 chunks
- 2 cloves garlic, peeled
- 4 tablespoons extra virgin olive oil
- ¼ cup/25 g ground (milled) flax seeds
- 2 tablespoons reduced-sodium soy sauce
- 1 tablespoon chili powder
- 1 teaspoon sweet paprika
- 1 teaspoon fine sea salt
- ½ teaspoon freshly ground black pepper
- ¼ teaspoon cayenne pepper
- One 15-ounce/439 g can black beans, drained and rinsed
- ¾ cup/55 g panko breadcrumbs
- 5 slices pepper Jack cheese

---

- 5 leaves butter lettuce
- 5 brioche buns, split
- 5 slices tomato
- ½ medium red onion, thinly sliced into rings
- Alfalfa sprouts for serving

**1) Make the avocado crema:** In a mini food processor or blender, puree the avocado, cilantro, onion, yogurt, lime juice, and oil with ¾ cup/180 ml water. Season with salt and pepper. Makes about 1½ cups/360 ml. (The crema can be refrigerated in an airtight container for up to 3 days.)

*Recipe continues*

**174**

2) **Make the veggie burgers:** Rinse the quinoa well in a wire sieve under cold running water and drain. Bring the quinoa, broth, and ½ teaspoon salt to a boil in a medium saucepan. Cover tightly and reduce the heat to low. Simmer until the liquid is absorbed and the quinoa is tender, 15 to 20 minutes. Uncover and let cool. You will have 3 cups cooked quinoa. Fluff with a fork and reserve 1 cup/175 g cooked quinoa. (Leftover quinoa can be cooled, covered, and refrigerated for up to 3 days.)

3) While the quinoa is cooking, preheat the oven to 400°F/200°C.

4) Spread the mushrooms, carrot, onion, corn, jalapeño, and garlic on a half-sheet pan. Toss with 2 tablespoons of the oil. Roast, stirring occasionally, until the onion is tender, about 15 minutes. Let cool.

5) Mix the flax seeds and ¼ cup/60 ml water in a small bowl and let it stand and thicken for about 3 minutes. Stir in the soy sauce, chili powder, paprika, salt, black pepper, and cayenne. Add the beans to the food processor (no need to clean it) and pulse into a puree. Add the flax mixture, the reserved 1 cup/175 g quinoa, and the panko and pulse just to combine. Scrape into a large bowl. Add the roasted vegetables to the processor (no need to clean the machine) and pulse until the vegetables are finely chopped. Add to the bean mixture and mix well. (Your hands do the best job.)

To make by hand: Finely chop the roasted vegetables with a large knife. Soak the seeds and mix in the soy sauce, chili powder, paprika, salt, black pepper, and cayenne. Mash the beans well in a large bowl with a large fork or potato masher. Stir in the flax seed mixture, panko, roasted vegetables, and the reserved 1 cup/175 g quinoa and mix well with your hands.

6) Line a baking sheet with waxed or parchment paper. Shape the vegetable mixture into five 4-inch/10 cm patties. Transfer to the prepared baking sheet. Refrigerate for 15 to 45 minutes to firm the patties.

7) Heat the remaining 2 tablespoons oil in a very large nonstick skillet or griddle over medium-high heat. Add the patties and cook until the underside is browned, about 2 minutes. Flip and cook until the other side is lightly browned, about 2 minutes more. Reduce the heat to medium-low and cover. Cook for 1 minute. Top each with a slice of cheese, cover, and cook until the cheese is melted, about 1 minute more.

8) For each burger, place a lettuce leaf on the brioche bun bottom. Top with a patty, a generous spoonful of the crema, a tomato slice, a few onion rings, and a sprinkle of sprouts. Cap with the bun top, cut in half, and serve.

# Zucchini, Corn, and Pinto Burrito

**Makes 6 burritos**

Of course, you don't need meat to make a burrito, as this vegetable version proves. The three main ingredients used here, zucchini, corn, and pinto beans, are a perfect combination with roots in Mexican cuisine and culture. Here's my favorite burrito hack: Use single-serving containers of precooked yellow rice instead of cooking up a batch.

2 tablespoons olive oil

1 zucchini, cut into ½-inch/1.25 cm dice (about 2 cups)

1 cup/175 g corn kernels, fresh (from 2 ears) or thawed frozen

2 tablespoons finely chopped fresh cilantro or oregano

½ medium yellow onion, chopped

1 jalapeño chile, seeds and ribs removed, minced

2 cloves garlic, minced

One 15.5-ounce/439 g can pinto beans, rinsed and drained

One 4.2-ounce/125 g container precooked yellow rice (about ½ cup; see Note)

Fine sea salt and freshly ground black pepper

1 cup/100 g shredded Mexican cheese blend

6 burrito-sized flour tortillas, warmed

Extra filling(s): Smoky Tomato Salsa (page 221), Roasted Tomatillo Salsa (page 221), sour cream, chopped avocado, thinly sliced iceberg lettuce

Mexican hot sauce, such as Cholula

**1)** Heat 1 tablespoon of the oil in a large skillet over high heat. Add the zucchini and cook, stirring occasionally, until lightly browned, about 3 minutes. Move the zucchini to one side of the skillet. Add the corn to the empty side and let cook without stirring until the corn begins to brown, then continue to cook, stirring once or twice, for about 2 minutes. Add the cilantro and mix well. Transfer to a bowl.

**2)** Add the remaining 1 tablespoon oil to the skillet. Add the onion, jalapeño, and garlic and reduce the heat to medium. Cook, scraping up the browned bits in the skillet with a wooden spoon, until the onion softens, about 3 minutes. Stir in the pinto beans and rice and cook until heated through, about 3 minutes. Stir in the reserved zucchini and corn. Season with salt and pepper. Reduce the heat to low. Sprinkle the cheese on top and cook until the cheese melts, about 2 minutes. Remove from the heat. Divide the vegetable mixture into 4 servings in the skillet.

**3)** For each burrito, place a warm tortilla on a work surface. Spread a serving of the vegetable mixture on the bottom third of the tortilla, about 1 inch/2.5 cm from the bottom. Add the extra filling(s) as desired. Fold the tortilla up from the bottom to cover the filling, tucking tightly at the top. Fold the right and left sides inward 1 to 2 inches/2.5 to 5 cm to partially cover the filling. Roll up from the bottom to close the burrito, tucking in the corners as needed. The filling should be entirely enclosed. Set aside, seam side down.

**4)** Cut each burrito in half, transfer to a dinner plate, and serve, with hot sauce on the side.

**note** If cartons of precooked yellow rice are unavailable, stir ¼ teaspoon each ground turmeric, dried oregano, ground cumin, garlic powder, and onion powder into an individual-serving container of precooked white or brown rice. Heat according to package directions. Stir well before using.

**177**

# Vegetable Egg Rolls

**Makes 12 to 14 egg rolls**

Egg rolls fit into my definition of a sandwich because the filling is encased in a grain-based wrapper. And, besides, I have memories of Ma, my Chinese grandmother, making a pork version for our family reunions. These are fun to make, and while some people may think of them as an appetizer, they can certainly be a fun meal. This makes a reasonable batch of about a dozen egg rolls, but if you are having a big party, just multiply the amounts to get the yield you need. You could also make the filling ahead and have your guests roll their own servings for a hands-on event.

One 1.6-ounce/50 g skein mung bean threads (see Notes)

5 dried shiitake mushroom caps (see Notes)

Boiling water

3 tablespoons reduced-sodium soy sauce

1 tablespoon vegetarian or standard oyster sauce, or more soy sauce

1 tablespoon rice wine or dry sherry

1 tablespoon cornstarch, plus more for the baking sheet

1 teaspoon sugar

1 teaspoon toasted sesame oil

¼ teaspoon freshly ground white or black pepper

3 tablespoons vegetable oil, plus more for deep-frying

3 scallions, white and green parts, finely chopped

1 tablespoon peeled or unpeeled finely grated fresh ginger

2 cloves garlic, minced

4 cups/400 g thinly sliced Chinese cabbage, core discarded (about ¼ small head)

2 carrots, julienned (a mandoline works best), about 1 cup/100 g

3 celery ribs, cut crosswise into very thin slices (a mandoline works best), about 1 cup/100 g

12 to 14 egg roll wrappers (see Notes)

1 large egg, beaten with 1 teaspoon water, for an egg wash

Hot Chinese mustard and duck sauce (see Notes) for serving

**1)** Place the noodles and mushrooms in separate bowls and cover with boiling water. Let the noodles stand until softened, 10 to 15 minutes. Drain, rinse under cold water, drain well, and pat dry to remove excess water. Return to the bowl and use kitchen scissors to snip into pieces about 2 inches/5 cm long. Let the mushrooms stand until softened, about 20 minutes more. Drain and chop into ¼-inch/6 mm dice. You should have about ½ cup/70 g diced mushrooms.

**2)** Heat a wok or large skillet over high heat. (If making in a frying pan, you may have to cook the filling in batches, as the cabbage takes up a lot of space in the pan until it wilts.) Stir the soy sauce, oyster sauce, rice wine, cornstarch, sugar, sesame oil, and white pepper together in a small bowl. When the wok is hot, add the vegetable oil and swirl to coat the inside. Add the diced mushrooms and cook, stirring occasionally, until they are heated through, about 1 minute (cook fresh mushrooms until browned, about 3 minutes). Add the scallions, ginger, and garlic and stir-fry until fragrant, about 30 seconds. Add the cabbage (in batches, if necessary), carrots, and celery and cook, stirring often, until the cabbage is tender and wilted, about 3 minutes. Stir the soy sauce mixture to recombine, mix into the vegetables, and cook until the liquid boils and thickens, about 15 seconds. Spread the mixture on a half-sheet pan (it will cool faster than in a bowl) and let cool completely, stirring occasionally. Stir in the bean threads. The filling must be cooled completely before using. (The filling can be cooled, covered, and refrigerated for up to 1 day. Drain off excess liquid before using.)

**3)** Dust a half-sheet pan with cornstarch. Place a wrapper on a work surface with the top point facing at 12 o'clock. Spoon about 2 tablespoons of the cooled filling on the bottom third of the wrapper, about 1 inch/2.5 cm above the bottom point, and shape the filling into a log. Fold the bottom point up and over to cover the filling, being sure the wrapper is taut against the filling. Fold the right and left points to the center, pleating the wrapper in at the ends of the filling as needed for a tight fit and to be sure the filling is completely covered. Working from the bottom, roll up the wrapper into a tight cylinder. When only the tip of the top point is exposed, dab it with some of the egg wash and complete the rolling, pressing the point to seal the roll. There should be no exposed filling at the ends. Transfer, sealed side down, to the baking sheet. Cover with plastic wrap and refrigerate until ready to fry, up to 8 hours.

**4)** Preheat the oven to 200°F/95°C and place a wire cooling rack over a half-sheet pan.

**5)** Pour enough vegetable oil to come 2 inches/5 cm up the sides of a large saucepan and heat over high heat until the oil registers 350°F/180°C on a deep-frying thermometer. In batches, without crowding, carefully add the egg rolls and fry, turning as needed, until golden, about 3 minutes. Using a slotted spoon, transfer the egg rolls to the wire rack and keep warm in the oven until serving. Serve hot, with the hot mustard and duck sauce in small bowls for dipping.

## notes

- Bean threads (also called glass or cellophane noodles) are made from mung bean starch and are almost transparent after soaking. Dried shiitake mushroom caps have a denser texture and deeper flavor than fresh, although fresh shiitakes can be substituted, if you wish. Both bean threads and dried shiitakes are soaked to soften before using.

- Egg roll (also called spring roll) wrappers are sold refrigerated or frozen in 1-pound/455 g packages, 20 to 24 wrappers per package. Of course, all of these are sold at Asian markets, but increasingly at standard supermarkets as well.

- For homemade hot mustard, stir ¼ cup/15 g dry mustard (preferably Chinese hot mustard powder) with 2 tablespoons hot water in a small bowl to make a paste. Add more water, as needed, to adjust the consistency. Let stand, uncovered, for 1 hour before serving.

- For a tasty duck sauce substitute, whisk ½ cup/170 g apricot preserves, 2 tablespoons hot water, 2 teaspoons soy sauce, 1 teaspoon rice vinegar, 1 teaspoon finely grated fresh ginger, 1 small clove garlic crushed through a press, and ½ teaspoon sriracha.

# Crispy and Spicy Eggplant Sandwich

**Makes 4 sandwiches**

Except for its breaded eggplant cutlet, this bears little resemblance to a pizzeria eggplant "Parm" sandwich. This sandwich was created when my mom, who is vegan, came for a visit, and I wanted to make something I knew she would love. (For Mom, I use egg substitute and vegan mayonnaise and skip the cheese.)

1 large eggplant, about 1 pound/455 g

Fine sea salt

1 cup/140 g all-purpose flour

¼ teaspoon freshly ground black pepper

3 large eggs

1 cup/130 g plain dried breadcrumbs

1 teaspoon Italian herb seasoning

½ teaspoon garlic powder

Canola oil for frying

4 crusty Italian rolls, split

8 slices unsmoked provolone cheese

Calabrian Mayonnaise (page 219)

2 cups/60 g baby arugula

Pickled banana pepper rings

**1)** Using a large knife held at a slight diagonal, cut the eggplant into ovals about ½ inch/1.25 cm thick. Sprinkle generously on both sides with salt. Transfer to a colander and let stand and drain in the sink for about 20 minutes. Using paper towels, wipe off the moisture from the eggplant rounds. Do not rinse.

**2)** Put the flour into a wide, shallow bowl or baking dish and season with ½ teaspoon salt and the pepper. Beat the eggs in a second bowl. (An immersion blender works best.) Combine the breadcrumbs, Italian seasoning, and garlic powder in a third bowl. Place a wire rack over a half-sheet pan near the stove. One at a time, dip an eggplant round in the flour tocoat, then into the eggs, and then into the breadcrumbs, and place the coated rounds on another half-sheet pan.

**3)** Preheat the oven to 200°F/95°C.

**4)** Pour enough oil to come about ½ inch/1.25 cm up the sides of a large skillet. Heat over medium-high heat until the oil is shimmering. (To check the oil temperature, dip the edge of an eggplant round in the oil—it should bubble immediately.) In batches without crowding, fry the eggplant, turning once, until crispy and deep golden brown, 3 to 4 minutes. Transfer to the rack to drain and keep warm in the oven. Be sure to let the oil reheat between batches.

**5)** If your broiler is in your oven, remove the eggplant on the rack from the oven. Heat the broiler with the top rung about 4 inches/10 cm from the heat source. Place the rolls on a baking sheet, cut sides up, and add 2 cheese slices to each bottom roll half. Broil to melt the cheese, 1 to 2 minutes.

**6)** For each sandwich, spread a roll with the Calabrian mayonnaise. Add one-quarter of the eggplant rounds, a handful of arugula, and a few banana pepper rings. Cap with the top of the roll, cut in half, and serve immediately.

**181**

# Grilled Cheese Panino and Roasted Tomato Soup

**Makes 4 sandwiches**

I've created an Italian-inspired version of an all-American lunch, grilled cheese and tomato soup. It deserves to be a classic in both countries. The soup is best with really ripe farmstand tomatoes. If you are using supermarket tomatoes, let them ripen at room temperature for a few days before using.

### tomato and basil soup

- 4 large tomatoes (about 1½ pounds/680 ml), cored, cut in half crosswise, and seeded
- 2 heads garlic, unpeeled, cut in half crosswise
- One 12-ounce/340 g container cherry tomatoes
- 1 medium yellow onion, halved and peeled
- 4 sprigs fresh thyme
- ¼ cup/60 ml extra virgin olive oil, plus more for the pan
- Fine sea salt and freshly ground black pepper
- Crushed hot red pepper
- 3 cups/720 ml vegetable broth (see Note, page 184)
- ½ cup/120 ml heavy cream
- ¼ cup packed/7 g fresh basil leaves

### italian cheese sandwiches

- 6 ounces/170 g sliced Fontina cheese, preferably Fontina d'Aosta
- 6 ounces/170 g thinly sliced fresh mozzarella cheese
- 8 slices crusty Italian bread
- ¼ cup/60 ml Pistachio Pesto (page 161) or store-bought pesto
- 8 slices ripe tomato, drained on paper towels
- Fine sea salt and freshly ground black pepper
- About 4 tablespoons/56 g (½ stick) unsalted butter, at room temperature

**1) Make the tomato and basil soup:** Preheat the oven to 400°F/200°C. Lightly oil a half-sheet pan.

**2)** Place the halved tomatoes cut sides up on the prepared pan. Add the garlic, cut sides down, followed by the cherry tomatoes, onion, and thyme. Drizzle with the oil. Season with ½ teaspoon salt, ¼ teaspoon black pepper, and a pinch of hot red pepper. Bake until the onion is lightly browned, about 45 minutes. Let cool until easy to handle. Squeeze the flesh from the garlic hulls and discard the hulls. Discard the tomato skins (no need to skin the cherry tomatoes) and thyme stems. Transfer the contents of the pan with their juices to a medium saucepan.

*Recipe continues*

3) Add the broth to the saucepan, bring to a simmer over medium heat, and simmer for about 5 minutes to blend the flavors. Stir in the cream and basil and heat just until the cream comes to a simmer. Using an immersion blender, puree the soup (or puree in batches in a blender, draping a kitchen towel over the blender jar instead of covering with the lid). Season with salt, black pepper, and hot red pepper. (The soup can be cooled, covered, and refrigerated for up to 2 days. Reheat before serving.) Keep the soup warm over low heat.

4) **Make the Italian cheese sandwiches:**
Combine the Fontina and mozzarella cheeses and divide into 4 portions. For each sandwich, spread 2 bread slices with the pesto. Top 1 bread slice with a portion of the cheeses and 2 tomato slices. Season the tomatoes with salt and pepper. Cap with the second bread slice, pesto side down. Spread about ½ tablespoon of the butter on the top of the sandwich and place on a half-sheet pan, buttered side up.

5) Heat a large grill pan or griddle over medium heat. Add the sandwiches, buttered side down, and top with a flat pot lid that will fit inside the grill. Cook until the undersides are golden brown and seared with marks from the ridges, about 2 minutes. Spread the tops of the sandwiches in the skillet with the remaining butter. Flip the sandwiches, top with the lid, and cook to brown the other side and melt the cheese, about 2 minutes more. Transfer to a chopping board, cut in half, and serve hot alongside individual bowls of soup.

**note** Although I usually buy canned vegetable broth, making it at home is easy, and you might even have all the ingredients on hand. Heat 2 tablespoons olive oil in a large saucepan over medium-high heat. Add 1 yellow onion, 1 carrot, 2 celery ribs, and 1 small, unpeeled baking potato (all coarsely chopped) and cook until the onion softens, about 4 minutes. Add 1 quart water, ½ teaspoon fine sea salt, a pinch of dried thyme, 5 black peppercorns, and 1 bay leaf and bring to a boil. If you have them on hand, add ¼ cup/7 g dried porcini mushrooms. Reduce the heat to medium-low and simmer until slightly reduced, 30 to 40 minutes. Drain through a colander into a bowl. (The cooked vegetables can be blended with chicken broth or more vegetable broth or milk to make a soup.)

# Roasted Portobello Mushroom Dip Sandwich

**Makes 4 sandwiches**

The original "dip" sandwiches use roast beef, but I'm applying the concept to roasted portobellos. (They can be grilled, too.) Portobellos are oversized cremini mushrooms, and the best choice for a mushroom sandwich. I've been tempted to try other big mushrooms, such as king (sold at Asian markets), but portobellos are flavorful enough to stand up to the bread. Be sure the mushrooms are good and clean before roasting.

8 large portobello mushrooms

2 large leeks, pale green and white parts only, cut into strips about ¼ inch/6 mm wide and 3 inches/7.5 cm long (about 2 cups/100 g leek strips)

### mushroom broth dip

½ cup packed/15 g dried porcini mushrooms

2 cups/480 ml boiling water

2 tablespoons olive oil

¼ cup/30 g finely chopped shallots

¼ cup/35 g finely chopped carrot

¼ cup/30 g finely chopped celery

½ cup/120 ml dry white wine, such as Pinot Grigio

1 teaspoon Maggi sauce or reduced-sodium soy sauce

3 sprigs fresh thyme or ¼ teaspoon dried thyme

Fine sea salt

6 black peppercorns

### garlic oil

3 tablespoons olive oil

1 large clove garlic, crushed and peeled

### frizzled leeks

1 cup/240 ml vegetable oil

Fine sea salt and freshly ground black pepper

4 crusty French or Italian rolls, split

12 slices unsmoked provolone or Swiss cheese

**1)** Snap the portobello stems from the caps and trim and coarsely chop the stems. Reserve the stems for the broth. Wipe the caps clean with a wet paper towel. Put the leek strips in a medium bowl of cold water and massage them in the water, letting any grit fall to the bottom of the bowl. Lift out the leeks, spread on a kitchen towel, and roll up the towel to dry them well. (Moisture on the leeks will make the oil splatter, so be sure they are as dry as possible.)

**2) Make the mushroom broth dip:** In a small heatproof bowl, soak the dried mushrooms in the boiling water until the mushrooms are tender, about 20 minutes. Squeeze the liquid from the mushrooms back into the bowl. Line a fine wire sieve with a moistened paper towel and place over a second bowl.

*Recipe continues*

Strain the soaking liquid through the sieve, leaving the gritty liquid in the bottom of the soaking bowl. Coarsely chop the soaked mushrooms. Reserve the soaking liquid.

3) Heat the oil in a medium saucepan over medium-high heat. Add the shallots, carrot, and celery and cook, stirring occasionally, until the shallots often, about 2 minutes. Stir in the chopped portobello stems and cook, stirring often, until softened, about 2 minutes more. Pour in the chopped porcini and their soaking liquid, the wine, ½ cup/120 ml water, the Maggi, thyme, a pinch of salt, and the peppercorns. Bring to a boil and reduce the heat to low. Simmer until richly flavored, 30 to 40 minutes. Season with additional salt. Strain through a fine wire sieve over a heatproof bowl, pressing hard on the solids. Discard the solids in the sieve. You should have about 2 cups/480 ml broth. Add water as needed. Rinse the saucepan, return the broth to the saucepan, and keep warm over low heat. (The broth can be made up to 2 days ahead. Reheat before using.)

4) **Make the garlic oil:** Heat the oil and garlic together in a small saucepan over medium heat until the garlic is sizzling and golden, about 3 minutes. Using a slotted spoon, remove and discard the garlic. Let the oil cool until tepid.

5) While the broth is simmering, roast the portobello caps. Preheat the oven to 400°F/200°C.

6) Place the portobello caps on a half-sheet pan. Brush on both sides with the garlic oil and season with salt and pepper. Set the remaining garlic oil aside. Roast until the mushrooms are tender, about 20 minutes. Transfer the mushrooms to a carving board. Cut the caps in half vertically. Return to the pan and keep warm in the turned-off oven with the door ajar.

7) **Meanwhile, cook the leeks:** Line a half-sheet pan with paper towels. Heat the oil in a medium skillet over medium-high heat until the oil is shimmering. A handful at a time, add the leeks to the oil and fry just until crisp and golden brown, about 1 minute. Do not overcook or the leeks will be bitter. Using a wire spider or slotted spoon, quickly transfer the leeks to the paper towels to drain. Season the leeks with salt and pepper.

8) Position a broiler rack about 4 inches/10 cm from the source of heat and preheat the broiler on High. For each sandwich, place an opened roll on a broiler pan and top with 4 mushroom halves followed by 3 cheese slices. Brush the exposed roll half with garlic oil. Broil until the bread is toasted and the cheese is melted, 1 to 1½ minutes. Add a handful of leeks to each sandwich. Pour the hot mushroom broth into 4 ramekins or custard cups. Cut each sandwich in half and serve immediately, with the broth and any remaining leeks on the side. While eating, dip the sandwich in the broth before taking a bite.

**Grilled Portobello Mushroom Dip Sandwich:** Grill the oil-brushed portobello caps on a heated grill over medium heat (400°F/200°C) until tender, 3 to 4 minutes per side. Top each cap with provolone cheese, torn to fit, about 1 minute before removing from the grill. Toast the rolls, cut sides down, on the grill until toasted, about 1 minute.

# Moroccan Potato Cakes

## with harissa mayonnaise in pita

**Makes 6 sandwiches**

If you like falafel, you will love these spiced potato patties in pita (say that three times, fast). It is kind of amazing how plain potatoes can be transformed into something very special with the right spices, a little parsley, and an egg. This is a gateway recipe to the fascinating spices of Moroccan cooking.

### potato cakes

1½ pounds/680 g baking potatoes, scrubbed but unpeeled

2 tablespoons finely chopped fresh flat-leaf parsley

1 teaspoon ras el hanout (see Note)

1 teaspoon ground turmeric

½ teaspoon sweet paprika

½ teaspoon ground cumin

1½ teaspoons fine sea salt

½ teaspoon freshly ground black pepper

1 large egg, beaten

1 teaspoon baking powder

Canola oil for frying

½ cup/120 g all-purpose flour

6 pocket pita breads, warmed

About ¾ cup/180 ml Harissa Mayonnaise (page 219; see Note)

About 2 cups/150 g mixed spring greens

2 ripe plum tomatoes, seeded and cut into ¼-inch/6 cm dice

Pickled Red Onions (page 222)

Good-quality extra virgin olive oil for drizzling

**1) Make the potato cakes:** Put the potatoes in a large saucepan and add enough salted water to cover well. Cover with the lid and bring to a boil over high heat. Reduce the heat to low. Cook, with the lid ajar, until tender when pierced with a sharp knife, about 25 minutes, depending on the size of the potatoes. Drain well. Return to the saucepan, fill with cold water, let stand until easy to handle, and peel the potatoes. Using a potato ricer, rice the potatoes into a large bowl. (Or mash the potatoes well with a masher in the bowl.) Add the parsley, ras el hanout, turmeric, paprika, cumin, 1 teaspoon of the salt, and the pepper and mix well. Stir in the egg and baking powder. Shape into 12 equal balls (about ¼ cup/65 g each) and slightly flatten to make 2-inch/5 cm cakes.

**2)** Pour enough canola oil to reach about ¼ inch/6 mm up the sides of a very large skillet and heat over medium-high heat until the oil is shimmering. Mix the flour and the remaining ½ teaspoon salt in a shallow bowl. Coat the potato cakes in the flour, shaking off excess flour, and add to the hot oil without crowding. (If necessary, cook in two batches.) Do not skimp on the oil. Cook, turning once, until crisp and golden brown, 4 to 5 minutes. Transfer to a wire rack to drain. Blot with paper towels.

**3)** For each sandwich, cut the top ½ inch/1.25 cm from each pita and open into pockets. Spread the inside of each with about 2 tablespoons of the mayonnaise. Add 2 potato cakes, a handful of greens, a sprinkling of diced tomato, a few red onions, and a drizzle of olive oil. Serve immediately.

**note** Moroccan seasonings, in both their dry (ras el hanout) and paste (harissa) forms, are mainstreaming. They are now sold at many supermarkets, as well as Mediterranean markets, and are also available online. **Ras el hanout** is a dry Moroccan spice blend based on warm spices. It literally means "top of the shop," loosely translated to "top shelf," indicating its importance in North African cooking. If you can't find it, mix 1 teaspoon each ground cumin and ground ginger; ½ teaspoon each ground allspice, ground cinnamon, freshly ground black pepper, ground coriander, freshly grated nutmeg, and freshly ground white pepper; and ¼ teaspoon each ground hot red (cayenne) pepper and ground cloves. **Harissa** is a paste made from ground peppers and various spices. While ras el hanout can be thrown together with spices you may already have in the kitchen, it is more convenient to purchase harissa already made. It lasts forever in the fridge.

# Japanese Egg Sando

**Makes 2 sandwiches**

Egg salad sandwiches don't usually hold many surprises, but that is not the case with my version of this Japanese classic. The salad itself is based on the familiar hard-boiled eggs, but the sandwich also has whole boiled eggs that show their jammy, golden centers to make you extra-hungry to bite into this beauty. If egg salad can be a showstopper, this is it.

### soft- and hard-boiled eggs

8 high-quality large eggs, preferably organic

### egg salad

3 tablespoons mayonnaise, preferably Kewpie

1 tablespoon minced scallion, white and pale green parts only

2 teaspoons Dijon mustard

1 teaspoon unseasoned rice vinegar

Fine sea salt and freshly ground black pepper

4 slices Japanese-style milk bread or white sandwich bread, lightly toasted

3 tablespoons mayonnaise, preferably Kewpie, or softened butter

**1) Cook the eggs:** You are going to cook the eggs in one pot, but half will be timed to the jammy yolk stage and removed, and the remainder will simmer until hard-boiled. Place a bowl of ice water near the stove. Bring a medium saucepan of water to a full boil over high heat (be sure you have enough water to completely cover the eggs when they are added). The saucepan should be just large enough to hold the eggs in a single layer so they won't move too much. Using a slotted spoon, gently transfer the eggs to the water, being careful to avoid cracking. Adjust the heat so the water is boiling but isn't disrupting the eggs. Set a timer and cook for 7 minutes. Using the slotted spoon, transfer 4 of the eggs to the ice water. (These will be the eggs with soft and jammy yolks, the way I like them.) Keep the remaining eggs in the water and boil for 5 minutes more. Remove the jammy eggs from the ice water and set them aside. Using the slotted spoon, transfer the hard-boiled eggs to the ice water, adding more ice as needed. Let the hard-boiled eggs chill in the ice water for at least 5 minutes.

**2)** Rap the chilled first batch of (jammy) eggs all over on the work counter to crack the shells. Starting at the wide end, and working under a stream of cold running water, peel the eggs. Set these eggs aside.

**3) Make the egg salad:** Peel the chilled hard-boiled eggs (the second batch). Cut in half and transfer the egg yolks only to a medium bowl and mash well with a fork. Finely chop the egg whites and add to the mashed yolks. Mix in the mayonnaise, the scallion, mustard, and vinegar. Season with salt and pepper.

**4)** To make each sandwich, spread the toast with half the mayonnaise. Spread 1 slice with half of the egg salad in a mound. Nestle 2 soft-boiled eggs in the center of the egg salad, with the egg tips running vertically. Cap with the second toast slice, mayonnaise side down, and press gently to even out the salad. Place the sandwich on a dinner plate. Using a serrated knife, cut through the center of the sandwich horizontally, which will slice through the whole eggs to reveal the yolks.

**190**

# Toasted PBJ
## with grilled banana

**Makes 2 sandwiches**

A peanut butter and jelly sandwich does not have to be the same old, same old. Make it with homemade peanut butter and fruit jam from your kitchen and add a caramelized banana, and you are going to have a sandwich that will clearly prove why this combo has remained popular for over a century. I am always blown away at how easy it is to make these two pantry staples. I never buy peanut butter anymore and think twice before purchasing jam. I think the chocolate chips knock this out of the park, but omit them if you wish. If you are making this for kids, substitute orange or apple juice for the rum.

### three-berry jam

One 6-ounce/170 g container fresh blackberries (about 1⅓ cups)

One 6-ounce/170 g container fresh blueberries (about 1⅓ cups)

6 ounces (about one-third of a 16-ounce/455 g container) fresh strawberries, hulled and cut in half (about 1⅓ cups/170 g)

¾ cup/150 g sugar

2 tablespoons fresh lemon juice

### homemade peanut butter

1 pound/455 g roasted unsalted peanuts

2 tablespoons honey (optional but recommended)

Fine sea salt

### honey-rum grilled banana

1 tablespoon golden or dark rum

1 tablespoon honey

¼ teaspoon ground cinnamon

1 large firm-ripe banana, unpeeled and cut in half lengthwise

Vegetable or canola oil for brushing

4 slices sourdough bread, preferably without a lot of holes

2 tablespoons mini chocolate chips

2 tablespoons unsalted butter

**1) Make the three-berry jam:** Place a saucer in the freezer to chill. Place the blackberries, blueberries, and strawberries in a heavy medium saucepan and add the sugar and lemon juice. Coarsely mash the mixture with a potato masher or large fork to release some juices. Bring to a boil over medium heat, stirring often. Reduce the heat to medium-low and cook at a steady simmer, stirring often to avoid scorching, until the juices thicken, about 20 minutes. Drop a teaspoon of the jam onto the frozen plate. Run your finger through the jam, and if it cuts a swath, the jam is done and will set. If it's too loose, cook a few minutes longer until the jam tests done. Let cool completely. Transfer to a covered container and refrigerate until set, at least 2 hours or overnight. Makes about 2 cups/440 g. (The jam can be refrigerated for about 2 months.)

**192**

**2) Make the peanut butter:** Grind the peanuts in a food processor until smooth, 8 to 10 minutes (yes, it takes that long). It will go through stages of gritty, grainy, smooth, and buttery. Add the honey, if desired, and season with salt and pulse to incorporate. Transfer to a covered container. Makes about 2 cups/455 g. (The peanut butter can be stored in a covered container in a cool, dark place for up to 1 month, or refrigerate for up to 6 months. Bring refrigerated peanut butter to room temperature and stir well before using.)

**3) Grill the banana:** Mix the rum, honey, and cinnamon in a small bowl. Heat a large grill pan over medium-high heat. Lightly brush the cut sides of the banana halves with some of the rum mixture, then brush with oil. Place the banana halves, cut side down, in the pan. Cook until seared with brown marks, about 3 minutes. Flip the banana halves over, brush with the remaining rum mixture, and cook until heated through, about 3 minutes more. Transfer them to a chopping board and let cool slightly. Peel the banana halves and cut into ½-inch/1.25 cm slices.

**4)** For each sandwich, spread a bread slice with about 2 tablespoons peanut butter and sprinkle with 1 tablespoon of the chocolate chips. Top with half of the sliced banana. Spread a second bread slice with about 2 tablespoons jam and place over the first slice, jam side down.

**5)** Melt the butter in a large skillet over medium heat. Add the sandwiches and cook until the undersides are toasted and golden, about 2 minutes. Flip and cook to toast the other side. Cut in half and serve.

## celebrity couple: peanut butter and jelly

Many factors play into the love story of peanut butter and jelly. Many people believe George Washington Carver invented peanut butter. He didn't, although he was responsible for many improvements that made the plant an important crop in the southern states. Peanut butter was actually formulated to be a "health food" for people who could not chew. It was introduced to the general public at the Chicago World Fair in 1893, and from there, even Dr. John Harvey Kellogg (as in the corn flakes) got onboard and patented his version. It then became a staple of ladies' lunches, but paired with savory foods like pimiento, cheese, and celery. The first recipe for peanut butter and jelly was in the 1901 *Boston Cooking School Magazine*, but the recommended jellies were crab apple or red currant. (Good luck finding either of these easily today.) When Paul Welch invented his eponymous grape jelly in 1917, Americans discovered a match made in heaven. In World War II, both peanut butter and jelly were in soldiers' rations, and it wasn't a leap for the two to be turned into a familiar sandwich that reminded them of home. When the troops returned, they made the sandwich in stateside kitchens, especially as a quick and easy lunch for kids. It retains its position as an MVP of Team Sandwich.

# 8

# sweet

# Brick Toast "Sundae"

## with matcha cream

**Makes 4 servings**
**Special equipment: Small ice cream (cookie dough) scoop**

Brick toast is a favorite on tea shop menus in Asia but not so well known here. So, what is it? Unsliced bread is cut into a brick shape and oven-toasted, making a beautiful container for an extraordinary ice cream sundae, here layered with a green pastry cream, fruits, and other goodies. Be creative with your garnishes, buying them for shape and color as well as taste. You may need to order the unsliced bread ahead from a bakery because they tend to slice all loaves. Or make your own according to the recipe on page 237. Other unsliced enriched bread, such as challah, can also be used—don't worry too much about making a perfectly square shape. For ice cream portions that fit best in the bread toast, use a small (cookie dough) scoop with a capacity of a tablespoon or two.

### matcha pastry cream

- 1 cup/240 ml heavy cream
- 1 cup/240 ml whole milk
- ½ cup/100 g sugar
- 5 large egg yolks
- 1 tablespoon culinary grade matcha (green tea powder)
- 1 teaspoon vanilla bean paste or extract

---

### brick toast

- 1 loaf (at least 12 ounces/340 g) *unsliced* sandwich bread, such as Japanese Milk Bread (page 237), pain de mie, or challah
- 4 tablespoons/56 g (½ stick) unsalted butter, melted, as needed

---

- 1 pint/480 ml high-quality ice cream, gelato, or sorbet, preferably a tropical flavor such as mango or passion fruit
- About 2 cups/280 g assorted fresh fruit cut into bite-sized pieces as needed, in any combination (berries, mango, kiwi, bananas)
- Assorted cookies, such as Pocky sticks, tea cookies, or macarons
- Chopped pistachios for topping

**1) Make the matcha pastry cream:** Heat the cream, milk, and ¼ cup/50 g of the sugar in a medium saucepan over medium heat, whisking occasionally, until simmering. Whisk the yolks and the remaining ¼ cup/50 g sugar in a medium bowl until pale and thick. Gradually whisk in the hot milk mixture. Rinse out the saucepan. Return the custard to the saucepan and cook over medium-low heat, stirring constantly with a wooden spoon, until an instant-read thermometer reads 185°F/85°C and a finger run through the custard on the spoon cuts a swath, 3 to 5 minutes. Do not boil. Strain through a wire sieve into a medium bowl. Add the matcha and vanilla and whisk well. (For the most even color, mix with an immersion blender.) Place in a large bowl of ice water and let stand until cooled. Cover and refrigerate until

*Recipe continues*

S
T
A
C
K
E
D

completely chilled, at least 2 hours or overnight. (The cream can be refrigerated for up to 2 days.)

**2)** **Prepare the brick toast:** Preheat the oven to 350ºF/180ºC.

**3)** The idea here is to shape the bread into individual bricks or boxes. Using a serrated knife, cut the loaf crosswise into 4 slabs, each about 2½ inches/6 cm tall. Lightly trim off the brown crust from the slabs. Using a steak knife, cut a ½-inch/1.25 cm border around the inside of the bread. Pull out the crumbs to make a box, leaving a ½ inch/1.25 cm layer at the base and sides. Brush the boxes all over with the melted butter. Place the boxes on a half-sheet pan. Bake until the edges of the boxes are golden, about 15 minutes. Let the bread cool completely on the pan. (The bread bricks can be made an hour or two ahead of serving, stored uncovered at room temperature.)

**4)** Place each bread brick on a plate. Layer with ladles of matcha pastry cream, small scoops of ice cream, and fruit. Garnish with cookies and a sprinkle of pistachios. Spoon some of the remaining pastry cream around the "brick." Sprinkle the remaining fruit on the plate. Be generous—the filled toast should look abundant and irresistible. Serve immediately with forks, knifes, and spoons.

## the greatest thing since sliced bread

Of all the conveniences of modern life, in the sandwich world, one "given" is sliced bread. But that innovation is fairly recent and was even the subject of a wartime ban. Before 1928, consumers had to slice bread by hand. If you have done this yourself, you know that it is difficult to get consistently thin slices. A jewelry store owner by profession but a hobbyist inventor, Otto Frederick Rohwedder invented a machine that would slice an entire loaf at a time, but his prototype was destroyed in a fire in 1917. It took him a decade to replace it, and he sold it to a bakery in Missouri, where it became a sensation. Before long, all commercial bakeries were using his machine. During World War II, a ban on sliced bread (which was ostensibly to save waxed paper and steel) occurred, but it was as short lived as it was ill advised. Uniformly sliced bread also had a side benefit, leading to the popularity of the electric toaster. "The greatest thing since sliced bread" became a phrase to describe anything especially terrific.

# Chocolate-Dipped Oatmeal Ice Cream Sandwich

**Makes 15 sandwich cookies**

Oatmeal cookies, vanilla ice cream, chocolate coating . . . what is not to love about these frozen sandwiches? If you can only eat one, you are a stronger person than I am. This makes 15 "servings," so unless you are feeding a party, you will have plenty. Who cares? You will be very happy when you come across one of these hidden away in your freezer.

### cookies

1⅓ cups/185 g all-purpose flour

1 teaspoon ground cinnamon

1 teaspoon baking soda

1 teaspoon fine sea salt

1½ cups packed/330 g light brown sugar

¾ cup/145 g shortening

1 large egg, at room temperature

1 teaspoon vanilla extract

½ cup/120 ml whole milk

2 cups/180 g old-fashioned (rolled) oats

About 1½ quarts/1.4 L vanilla ice cream, slightly softened

### chocolate dip

¼ cup/60 ml coconut oil

1 cup/170 g semisweet chocolate chips

**1)** Position a rack in the center and top third of the oven and preheat to 375°F/190°C. Line 2 half-sheet pans with parchment paper.

**2) Make the cookies:** Whisk the flour, cinnamon, baking soda, and salt together in a large bowl. Using an electric mixer, beat the brown sugar and shortening until light in color and texture, about 3 minutes. Beat in the egg and vanilla. Using a wooden spoon, mix in the flour mixture, followed by the milk, and then the oats.

**3)** Using about 1 tablespoon for each, shape the dough into 30 equal balls. Arrange the balls about 2 inches/5 cm apart on the lined pans, allowing 15 cookies per pan, keeping in mind that the cookies will spread during baking. Bake, switching the positions of the pans from top to bottom and front to back halfway through baking, until the edges feel set and crisp, 10 to 12 minutes. Let cool on the pan for 5 minutes. Transfer to a wire cooling rack and let cool completely.

**4)** To avoid melting the ice cream, you must work quickly for this next step. Enlist a helper or freeze the filled sandwiches as you work. For each sandwich, place a scoop (about ¼ cup/60 ml) of ice cream

*Recipe continues*

**199**

onto the flat side of a cookie. Add another cookie and sandwich them together, pressing so the ice cream reaches the edges of the sandwich. Cover loosely with plastic wrap and freeze for at least 1 hour. The cookies must be very cold for the next step.

**5)** **Dip the cookies:** Melt the coconut oil in a small saucepan over medium heat. Remove from the heat. Add the chocolate chips and let stand for 2 to 3 minutes. Stir well (do not whisk, as it makes bubbles) until the chips are melted and the mixture is smooth. Let cool until tepid and slightly thickened but still liquid, about 15 minutes.

**6)** Line a baking sheet with parchment or waxed paper. Tilt the saucepan so the chocolate pools on one side. Working quickly, one at a time, dip half of a frozen sandwich into the chocolate and transfer to the prepared baking sheet. Freeze until the chocolate is set, about 30 minutes. Individually rewrap each sandwich cookie in plastic wrap and freeze until serving. (The cookies can be frozen for up to 2 months.)

# Brie Toast

## with strawberry-ginger jam

**Makes 2 sandwiches**

Do not reserve this for an after-dinner dessert, because it also excels as a sandwich for breakfast, brunch, or lunch ... whenever you crave a sweet/savory/spicy combination. If you have a griddle, you can knock out at least four of these babies at once in no time flat. The ginger and jalapeño in the jam shake up this simple pairing of fruit and cheese.

spicy strawberry-ginger jam

1 pound/455 g strawberries, hulled and quartered

2 tablespoons seeded and minced jalapeño chile, or more to taste

2 tablespoons peeled and minced ginger

¾ cup/150 g sugar

2 tablespoons fresh lemon juice

Pinch of fine sea salt

4 slices French or Italian bread

8 ounces/225 g Brie cheese, including rind, cut into long, thin slices

2 tablespoons unsalted butter

**1)** **Make the spicy strawberry-ginger jam:** Place a saucer in the freezer to chill. Combine the strawberries, jalapeño, and ginger in a heavy medium saucepan and add the sugar, lemon juice, and salt. Coarsely mash the mixture with a potato masher or large fork to release some juices. Bring to a boil over medium heat, stirring often. Reduce the heat to medium-low and cook at a steady simmer, stirring often to avoid scorching, until the juices thicken, about 20 minutes. Drop a teaspoon of the jam onto the frozen saucer. Run your finger through the jam, and if it cuts a swath, it is done and will set. If it is too loose, cook a few minutes longer until the jam tests done. Let cool completely. Cover and refrigerate until set, at least 2 hours or overnight. Makes about 1 cup/200 g. (Leftover jam can be refrigerated for about 2 months.)

**2)** For each sandwich, generously spread the jam over 2 bread slices. Top 1 slice with half of the cheese. Cap with the remaining slice, jam side down.

**3)** Melt the butter in a large skillet over medium heat. Add the sandwiches and cook, flipping once, until golden brown on both sides, about 5 minutes. Transfer to a chopping board, cut each in half, and serve with the remaining jam.

# Salted Brownie Ice Cream Bar

**Makes 9 large bars**

Homemade ice cream sandwiches from your freezer? Hell, yes! The brownie layers are amazingly easy to make. Allow plenty of time for the sandwiches to freeze, which is a real exercise in patience and resisting temptation. A little flaky salt really brings out the chocolate flavor. For the darkest brownies, use Dutch-processed cocoa, but American natural cocoa works fine, too.

### salted brownies

Nonstick cooking spray

1 cup/140 g all-purpose flour

⅔ cup/60 g unsweetened Dutch-processed or natural cocoa powder

¾ teaspoon baking powder

½ teaspoon fine sea salt

1 cup/230 g (2 sticks) unsalted butter

2 cups/400 g sugar

2 teaspoons vanilla extract

4 large eggs

About 1 teaspoon flaky salt, such as Maldon, for topping

About 1½ quarts/1.4 L high-quality dulce de leche ice cream or vanilla ice cream, slightly softened

Mini chocolate chips or your favorite sprinkles for decoration (optional)

1) **Make the salted brownies:** Preheat the oven to 350°F/180°C. Spray a 10 × 15-inch/25 × 38 cm jelly roll pan with nonstick spray. Line the bottom and sides of the pan with parchment paper. (To do this easily, cut a large sheet of the paper about 1 inch/2.5 cm larger than the pan on all sides. Cut a diagonal slit about 2 inches/5 cm long from each corner toward the center. Press the paper into the pan on the bottom and sides—the slits will overlap to fit the paper in the pan.)

2) Whisk the flour, cocoa, baking powder, and fine sea salt together in a large bowl. Melt the butter in a large saucepan over medium heat. Remove from the heat and whisk in the sugar and vanilla. Let cool slightly. One at a time, whisk in the eggs, whisking well after each addition. In three additions, stir in the flour mixture and mix until smooth. Scrape into the prepared pan. Using an offset metal spatula, spread the batter evenly. Sprinkle with the flaky sea salt.

3) Bake just until the brownie is set in the center and a wooden toothpick inserted in the center comes out clean, 18 to 20 minutes. Let cool completely in the pan on a wire cooling rack.

4) Invert and unmold the brownie over a large chopping board. Peel off the parchment paper. Using a sharp knife and a ruler, cut the brownie in half crosswise. Cut one half into 9 equal rectangles and set them aside, keeping track of their original sequence. Mash the ice cream in a large bowl with a silicone or rubber spatula until it is spreadable. Transfer the whole brownie half to a large sheet of plastic wrap. Scoop the ice cream onto the brownie half and spread as evenly as possible. Arrange the rectangles on the ice cream in their original sequence. Wrap the ice cream bars in the plastic wrap, using more as needed. Slip the wrapped bars onto a cookie sheet and freeze for at least 1 hour or overnight.

5) To serve, unwrap the brownie bars on a chopping board. Use a large knife rinsed briefly under hot water to cut between the brownies into individual bars. If using sprinkles, put them in a small bowl and press the exposed ice cream into the sprinkles to make them adhere. Serve immediately. (For longer storage, individually wrap each bar in plastic wrap and freeze for up to 3 weeks.)

# Japanese Fruit Sando

**Makes 2 sandwiches**

This Japanese-style fruit sandwich is so good-looking that you won't want to eat it. There are a few things to keep in mind when you make it. First, it is all about "the look." Imagine where you are going to cut the sandwich in half and line up the center of the fruits so the cut sandwich reveals a colorful cross-section. The sandwiches must be wrapped, weighted, and refrigerated for at least a couple of hours before slicing—don't rush them.

½ cup/120 ml heavy cream

2 tablespoons confectioners' sugar

Grated zest of 1 lemon or ½ orange

8 ounces/225 g mascarpone cheese, at room temperature

2 ripe kiwi fruits, peeled and cut crosswise in half

4 strawberries, hulled

½ ripe mango, peeled and cut into strips about ½ inch/1.25 cm wide

4 slices Japanese Milk Bread (page 237), pain de mie, or sandwich bread, cut about ¾ inch/2 cm thick

**1)** Whip the cream, confectioners' sugar, and zest in a chilled medium bowl with an electric mixer set on high speed until very stiff. With the mixer on low, beat in the mascarpone in two or three additions. Do not overmix, or it may separate. Set aside at room temperature.

**2)** Place the kiwi fruits, strawberries (hulled sides down), and mango slices on paper towels, cover with more paper towels, and let stand to soak up excess juices.

**3)** For each sandwich, place a bread slice on a work surface. The finished sandwich will be sliced on the diagonal into 2 triangles. Using one-quarter of the cream mixture, spread a thick layer onto the bread slice. Using a knife, score a diagonal line from corner to corner on the cheese. Keep the location of this line in mind when you cut the sandwich. Arrange 1 kiwi half, 1 strawberry, and 3 mango strips, centered on the diagonal line, with all the fruit running vertically. The location of the remaining fruit isn't essential for the look, so cut it to fit anywhere on the sandwich. Spread another one-quarter of the cream mixture on top to completely cover the fruit and smooth the top. Cover with a second bread slice. Wrap tightly in plastic wrap. To help find the line during cutting, use a marker on the plastic wrap to mirror the location of the diagonal line inside the sandwich. Place the sandwich on a half-sheet pan. Top the sandwiches with a second pan to weight it lightly. Refrigerate for at least 2 hours or overnight.

**4)** To serve, unwrap the sandwiches, noting the location of the diagonal line. Using a large sharp knife wiped clean between cuts, cut each sandwich in half diagonally into 2 triangles, revealing a cross-section of fruit. Stand the sandwich on a dinner plate to reveal the fruit and serve.

**206**

# Frozen Fruity Sherbet Bar

**Makes 6 large bars**

Fruit-flavored cereal is only on my shopping list when I make these incredible dessert sandwiches. They are fun all around: fun to make, fun to look at, and fun to eat. These will make kids very happy and bring out the inner kid in grown-ups. Use any fruit sherbet or sorbet that strikes your fancy, but the more colorful the better.

Nonstick cooking spray

4 tablespoons/56 g (½ stick) unsalted butter

One 10-ounce/280 g bag mini marshmallows (about 5 cups)

1 teaspoon vanilla extract

¼ teaspoon fine sea salt

One 7.9-ounce/223 g box fruit-flavored breakfast cereal (such as Froot Loops, about 7 cups)

1 quart/960 ml of your favorite fruit sherbet, slightly softened

1) Spray a 10 × 15-inch/25 × 38 cm jelly roll pan with nonstick spray. Line the bottom and sides of the pan with parchment or waxed paper. (To do this easily, cut a large sheet of the paper about 1 inch/2.5 cm larger than the pan on all sides. Cut a diagonal slit about 2 inches/5 cm long from each corner toward the center. Press the paper into the pan on the bottom and sides—the paper corners will overlap to fit the pan. Spray the paper with cooking spray.)

2) Melt the butter in a large, wide saucepan over medium heat. Add the marshmallows and cook, stirring often, until completely melted, about 5 minutes. Remove from the heat and stir in the vanilla and salt. Stir in the cereal and mix well. Using a silicone or rubber spatula sprayed with nonstick spray, scrape the cereal mixture into the pan. Spray another sheet of parchment paper with the oil, place it, oil side down, over the cereal mixture, and use the parchment to help press and spread the mixture in an even layer. Refrigerate until set, about 30 minutes.

3) Invert the cereal slab onto a chopping board and remove the paper. Using a sharp knife and a ruler, cut the slab in half vertically. Cut one half into 6 equal rectangles and set them aside, keeping track of their original sequence. Mash the sherbet in a large bowl with a silicone or rubber spatula until it is spreadable. Scoop the sherbet onto the uncut half and spread it in an even layer. Arrange the rectangles on the sherbet in their original sequence. Cover the bars with a large sheet of plastic wrap. Place a half-sheet pan or chopping board on the bars, hold together, and invert. Wrap the entire slab of bars in the plastic, using more wrap as needed. Slip onto a baking sheet and freeze for at least 1 hour or overnight.

4) To serve, unwrap and place on a chopping board. Using a large knife rinsed briefly under hot water, cut between the rectangles into individual bars. Serve immediately. (For longer storage, individually wrap each bar in plastic wrap and freeze for up to 1 week.)

STACKED

# Roasted Strawberry and Chocolate-Hazelnut Spread Sandwich

**Makes 4 sandwiches**

Nutella is Italy's version of peanut butter. All Italian kids love pane e Nutella, which is an iconic snack of a slice of white bread smeared with a thick layer of the spread. Because I prefer the not-easy-to-source imported Nutella to the US version, I have started making my own at home. For the smoothest results, use a heavy-duty blender, but there's nothing wrong with the bit of texture in the food processor version. The strawberries pick up some caramelization from roasting, adding another layer of flavor to this sandwich that is sure to please kids and grown-ups alike.

### chocolate-hazelnut spread

2 cups/200 g hazelnuts

⅓ cup/70 g unsweetened cocoa powder

⅓ cup/45 g confectioners' sugar

2 tablespoons coconut oil, melted

1 teaspoon vanilla extract

Pinch of fine sea salt

1 pound/455 g strawberries, hulled and halved

3 tablespoons granulated sugar

1 teaspoon vanilla extract

8 slices brioche loaf, challah, or white sandwich bread, toasted and warm

1) **Make the chocolate-hazelnut spread:** Preheat the oven to 350°F/180°C.

2) Spread the hazelnuts on a half-sheet pan. Bake, stirring occasionally, until the skins are cracked and the flesh is toasted to light brown, 10 to 15 minutes. Wrap the nuts in a kitchen towel and let cool for about 15 minutes. Rub the nuts in the towel to remove the skins. Let the nuts cool completely.

3) Transfer the nuts to a heavy-duty blender or food processor. Blend until very finely chopped. Add the cocoa powder, confectioners' sugar, coconut oil, vanilla, and salt and process until very smooth. This will take a couple of minutes, less time in the blender. Use immediately. Makes about 1 cup/310 g. (The spread can be transferred to a covered container and refrigerated for up to 2 months. It will get hard when chilled. To use, let stand overnight at room temperature or microwave on medium-low/30% power for about 1 minute and stir well until spreadable.)

4) Increase the oven temperature to 400°F/200°C.

210

5) Toss the strawberries and granulated sugar in a medium bowl and spread on a half-sheet pan. Bake, stirring occasionally, until the berries are tender and the juices are syrupy and turning brown, 20 to 25 minutes. Transfer to a bowl, stir in the vanilla, and let cool completely. (The berries can be refrigerated in a covered container for up to 2 weeks.)

6) For each sandwich, generously smear 2 toasted brioche slices with the spread. Top 1 slice with one-quarter of the roasted strawberries. Cap with the second slice, spread side down. Cut in half and serve immediately.

## italian taste: chocolate and hazelnuts

Nutella, the creamy chocolate-and-hazelnut spread, is beloved around the world, especially by kids. Like peanut butter, it has an interesting history. When chocolate and hazelnuts are married, Italians call the mixture *gianduja*, also the name of a character in the classic Italian commedia dell'arte plays that toured the countryside to entertain peasants. Gianduja, the confection, first appeared during the Napoleonic Wars, when an embargo on cacao beans left Italian chocolatiers strapped for their essential ingredient. An enterprising chocolatier from northern Italy, where hazelnuts were an important commodity, began mixing hazelnut paste with reduced amounts of chocolate to create a new product. For the next hundred years, gianduja was used exclusively as a filling for chocolate candies. Then another war, another shortage. Pietro Ferrero (also famous for his company's Rocher bonbons) took the gianduja concept and used cocoa and hazelnuts to make a nut paste that was originally a sliceable loaf. It took a few more years for Ferrero to develop the familiar spreadable consistency. The made-in-the-US version of Nutella, is, to my palate, sweeter and less nutty than the Italian OG.

# S'mores Toasties

**Makes 2 sandwiches**

Simple, yes . . . but also the ultimate definition of yummy. Do not overfill the sandwiches. Otherwise, the melted ingredients will ooze out of the closed sandwich, and this is a case of when too much of a good thing is not necessarily a good thing.

4 slices whole wheat bread
6 marshmallows, cut in half crosswise, to make 12 halves

3 ounces/100 g milk chocolate bars, coarsely broken

1) Position a broiler rack about 4 inches/10 cm from the source of heat and preheat the broiler on High.

2) Arrange the bread on a broiler rack and toast one side in the broiler. Remove from the oven. Turn the toast untoasted sides up.

3) For each sandwich, top 1 slice with 6 marshmallow halves and the other slice with the broken chocolate to mostly cover the surface. Return to the broiler and broil just until the marshmallow browns and the chocolate softens, about 30 seconds. Watch carefully to avoid burning.

4) Using a spatula as an aid, press the 2 slices together. Let cool slightly, cut in half, and serve.

# Pumpkin Whoopie Pie

## with ginger filling

**Makes about 18 whoopie pies**
**Special equipment: 1-tablespoon-capacity cookie scoop**

This sandwich is the epitome of autumn desserts. For a long time, whoopie pies were one of Maine's best-kept secrets, and now the secret is out. These tender and spicy cookies hold a creamy filling spiked with crystallized ginger. If you ask me if you can serve these at Thanksgiving, my answer is "Absolutely!"

### cookies

2½ cups/350 g all-purpose flour

1 teaspoon ground cinnamon

1 teaspoon ground ginger

1 teaspoon baking powder

1 teaspoon baking soda

½ teaspoon freshly grated nutmeg

½ teaspoon ground cloves

½ teaspoon fine sea salt

4 tablespoons/56 g (½ stick) unsalted butter, at room temperature

¼ cup/60 ml vegetable oil

¾ cup/150 g granulated sugar

¾ cup packed/165 g light brown sugar

1 cup/245 g canned solid-pack pumpkin

1 large egg, at room temperature

1 teaspoon vanilla extract

### filling

2 ounces/55 g cream cheese, at room temperature

4 tablespoons/56 g (½ stick) unsalted butter, at room temperature

2½ cups/290 g confectioners' sugar

1 teaspoon fresh lemon juice

½ teaspoon vanilla extract

¼ cup/65 g finely chopped crystallized ginger

**1)** **Make the cookies:** Preheat the oven to 350°F/180°C. Position racks in the center and top third of the oven. Line 2 half-sheet pans with parchment paper.

**2)** Whisk the flour, cinnamon, ground ginger, baking powder, baking soda, nutmeg, cloves, and salt together in a large bowl. Beat the butter and oil together with an electric mixer on medium-high speed until combined, about 1 minute. Add the granulated and brown sugars and beat until pale and light in texture, about 2 minutes more. Beat in the pumpkin, egg, and vanilla. With the mixer on low speed, beat in the flour mixture.

3) Using a cookie scoop (preferred) or a tablespoon for each cookie, drop the batter onto the prepared sheet pans, spacing the drops about 2 inches/5 cm apart. Flatten slightly with your fingertips. Bake, switching the pans from top to bottom halfway through baking, until the cookies feel set when the tops are gently pressed, about 17 minutes. Let cool on the pan for 5 minutes, then transfer to a wire cooling rack and let cool completely.

4) **Make the filling:** Beat the cream cheese and butter together in a medium bowl with an electric mixer on medium speed. On low speed, gradually beat in the confectioners' sugar, then the lemon juice and vanilla. Beat on high speed until fluffy, about 2 minutes. Mix in the crystallized ginger.

5) Preferably using the same cookie scoop, divide the filling (about 1 generous tablespoon each) on the flat sides of 18 cookies and spread with a small offset spatula. Sandwich with the remaining cookies. (The cookies can be stored in an airtight container for up to 3 days. Serve chilled or bring to room temperature.)

# 9

# essentials
## sauces, sides, and home-baked breads

# Mayonnaise and Friends

**Makes about 1 cup/240 ml**

I'm not saying that you have to make homemade mayonnaise for every sandwich in your life. But when you want that something extra to level up the dish, take a few minutes to whiz up some ultra-creamy homemade mayo. Mayonnaise is very friendly to riffing, and I have listed some of my favorite easy variations on the opposite page. All of them can be made with your favorite store-bought mayo.

---

1 large egg

1 tablespoon fresh lemon juice or white wine vinegar

1 teaspoon Dijon mustard

1 cup/240 ml canola or oil

Fine sea salt and freshly ground black pepper

**1)** Put the egg in a small bowl and add hot tap water to cover. Let stand for about 3 minutes to take the chill off the egg.

**2)** Crack the egg into a food processor. Add the lemon juice and mustard. With the machine running, gradually drizzle in the oil through the feed tube. (This should take about 1 minute—don't rush it.) Beat in 1 teaspoon water. Season with salt and pepper. The mayonnaise can also be made in a bowl with an immersion blender. Keep the bowl steady by placing it on a folded wet towel, which will act as a brake.

**3)** Transfer to a covered container. (The mayonnaise can be stored in the refrigerator for up to 5 days.)

**Aioli:** Whisk 1 cup/240 ml mayonnaise, 1 or 2 cloves garlic, minced or crushed through a garlic press, and 1 teaspoon Dijon mustard.

**Cajun Aioli:** Whisk ¾ cup/180 ml mayonnaise, 1 teaspoon Creole or spicy brown mustard, 1 teaspoon hot sauce (such as Tabasco), 1 teaspoon salt-free Cajun seasoning, 1 teaspoon fresh lemon juice, ½ teaspoon smoked paprika, and 1 large clove garlic, crushed through a press.

**Calabrian Mayonnaise:** Mix ½ cup/120 ml mayonnaise, 1 tablespoon crushed Calabrian chiles, and 1 teaspoon of the oil from the chiles.

**Caper-Dill Mayonnaise:** Mix ⅔ cup/165 ml mayonnaise, 2 tablespoons rinsed nonpareil capers, 2 tablespoons finely chopped fresh dill, 1 teaspoon caper brine, and freshly ground black pepper, to taste.

**Chipotle Mayonnaise:** Mix ½ cup/120 ml mayonnaise, 1 chipotle chile in adobo with its clinging sauce, minced, 2 teaspoons fresh lime juice, and a pinch of smoked paprika.

**Cilantro Mayonnaise:** Process ½ cup/120 ml mayonnaise, ½ cup packed/15 g fresh cilantro leaves (and their thin stems), and 2 tablespoons fresh lime juice in a food processor until the cilantro is minced and the mayonnaise is full of green flecks. Substitute Thai basil or coarsely chopped shiso leaves for the cilantro, if you wish.

**Dijon Mayonnaise:** Whisk ¼ cup/60 ml mayonnaise, 2 tablespoons Dijon mustard, and 1 teaspoon fresh lemon juice.

**Harissa Mayonnaise:** Whisk ⅔ cup/165 ml mayonnaise, 2 tablespoons harissa, and 2 teaspoons fresh lemon juice.

**Jalapeño Aioli:** Whisk ½ cup/120 ml Aioli (see variation at left), 2 tablespoons finely chopped fresh cilantro leaves, 1 teaspoon seeded and minced jalapeño chile, 2 teaspoons fresh lime juice, and ¼ teaspoon ground cumin.

**Kimchi Mayonnaise:** Pulse ⅓ cup/75 ml mayonnaise, ⅓ cup packed/45 g drained kimchi, and 1 teaspoon toasted sesame oil in a mini–food processor until the kimchi is minced. Or mince the kimchi by hand and mix with the other ingredients.

**Lemon-Herb Mayonnaise:** Whisk ½ cup/120 ml mayonnaise, 2 tablespoons finely chopped fresh basil (or chervil, chives, dill, chives, parsley, or tarragon, or a combination), the grated zest of 1 lemon, and 1 tablespoon fresh lemon juice.

**Old Bay Aioli:** Whisk ¼ cup/60 ml mayonnaise, 1 tablespoon fresh lemon juice, 2 teaspoons Old Bay Seasoning, and 1 clove garlic, crushed through a press.

**Russian Dressing:** Whisk ½ cup/120 ml mayonnaise, 2 tablespoons ketchup-style chili sauce, 2 tablespoons sweet pickle relish, ½ teaspoon Worcestershire sauce, and ¼ teaspoon hot red sauce.

**Spicy Asian Mayonnaise:** Whisk ½ cup/120 ml mayonnaise (preferably Kewpie; found at Asian markets and many supermarkets), 2 tablespoons gochujang, and 1 teaspoon toasted sesame oil.

**Sriracha Mayonnaise:** Whisk ⅔ cup/165 ml mayonnaise and 2 teaspoons sriracha.

*Pictured:* Roasted Tomatillo
Salsa variation

# Smoky Tomato Salsa

**Makes about 2 cups/430 g**

I will put this salsa up against anything you can get at a restaurant or certainly at the supermarket. It is on the thin side, so it clings nicely to your burrito, taco, tostada, or chimichanga. Broiling really brings out the flavor of the vegetables. For spicier salsa, add the reserved ribs and seeds from the prepped jalapeño.

4 plum tomatoes, halved lengthwise, about 1 pound/455 g

½ medium white onion, cut into ½-inch/1.25 cm half-moons

1 jalapeño chile, halved lengthwise, ribs and seeds removed and reserved

4 whole cloves garlic, peeled

3 tablespoons finely chopped fresh cilantro

2 tablespoons fresh lime juice

½ teaspoon ground cumin

½ teaspoon smoked paprika

Fine sea salt and freshly ground black pepper

**1)** Position a rack about 4 inches/10 cm from the source of heat and preheat the broiler on High. Line a half-sheet pan with aluminum foil.

**2)** Place the tomatoes, onion, and jalapeño halves, cut sides down, on the pan and add the garlic. Broil until blackened, removing the smaller items as they brown first, about 10 minutes. Cool slightly. Peel off and discard the blackened tomato and jalapeño skins.

**3)** Add the vegetables to a food processor with the cilantro, lime juice, cumin, and paprika. Pulse until very finely chopped. Transfer to a bowl and season with salt and pepper. (The salsa can be refrigerated in a covered container for up to 5 days.)

**Roasted Tomatillo Salsa:** I learned a trick from a Mexican cook that I share here—use chicken bouillon powder to balance the strong flavor of the tomatillos. Omit the cumin and paprika. Add 1 teaspoon dried oregano, preferably Mexican oregano. Substitute 1 pound/455 g tomatillos, husks discarded, for the tomatoes. Leave the tomatillos whole. Broil the tomatillos and turn them with tongs as the skins brown. The skins do not need to blacken, and do not peel the tomatillos before processing. Add 2 teaspoons/one 4-gram packet granulated chicken bouillon (or 2 teaspoons well-crushed bouillon cubes) during processing.

## Pickled Red Onions

**Makes 1 quart/960 ml**

Pickled red onions quickly elevate any sandwich with lots of flavor for little effort.

1 large red onion, about 12 ounces/340 g, cut into thin rings

1½ cups/360 ml distilled white or cider vinegar

1½ teaspoons sugar

1½ teaspoons fine sea salt

**1)** Pack the onion rings into a 1-quart/960 ml glass canning jar or covered container.

**2)** Bring the vinegar, 1½ cups/360 ml water, the sugar, and salt to a boil in a small saucepan, stirring to dissolve the sugar. Pour the hot liquid over the onions. Let cool to room temperature. Use immediately or cover and refrigerate for up to 3 months.

# Quick Pickles

You can make pickles at home without a huge canning pot and a mountain of jars. Prepare them in small batches, and they still last a long time in the fridge. Here are the ones that I like to make. In the case of the red onions and Asian pickles, you can't buy them at the store anyway.

# Quick Dill Pickles

**Makes 1 quart/960 ml**

Serve your own homemade dill pickles next to your sandwiches and sit back to hear the compliments roll in. Pre-salting helps them keep a crisp texture.

4 Kirby (pickling) cucumbers, cut into ¼-inch/6 mm rounds

1¾ teaspoons fine sea salt

¾ cup/180 ml distilled white or cider vinegar

1 teaspoon dill seeds

½ teaspoon yellow mustard seeds

¼ teaspoon coriander seeds

¾ teaspoon sugar

**1)** Place the cucumbers in a colander and sprinkle with 1 teaspoon of the salt. Let stand to drain on a plate or in the sink for 1 hour. Do not rinse. Pat dry with paper towels. Pack the cucumber slices into a 1-quart/960 ml glass canning jar or covered container.

**2)** Bring the vinegar, ¾ cup/180 ml water, the dill seeds, remaining ¾ teaspoon salt, the mustard seeds, coriander seeds, and sugar to a boil in a small saucepan, stirring to dissolve the sugar. Pour over the cucumbers and let cool. Cover and refrigerate overnight before serving. Refrigerate for up to 6 months.

# Pickled Jalapeños

**Makes 1 pint/480 ml**

Some people call these nacho jalapeños, but there's no reason you can't put them on tacos or burritos.

8 jalapeño chiles, sliced into rings about ⅛ inch/3 mm thick

¾ cup/180 ml distilled white or cider vinegar

¼ teaspoon dried oregano, preferably Mexican oregano

1 bay leaf, broken in half

¾ teaspoon sugar

¾ teaspoon fine sea salt

**1)** Pack the jalapeños into a clean 1-pint/480 ml canning jar or covered container.

**2)** Bring the vinegar, ¾ cup/180 ml water, the oregano, bay leaf, sugar, and salt to a boil in a small saucepan, stirring to dissolve the sugar. Pour over the jalapeños and let cool to room temperature. Use immediately or cover and refrigerate for up to 6 months.

*Pictured, left to right:* Asian Pickles for Banh Mi,
Quick Dill Pickles, and Pickled Red Onions

# Asian Pickles for Banh Mi

**Makes 1 pint/480 ml**
**Special equipment: Mandoline or plastic slicer**

These bicolored pickles are a must for Banh Mi (page 144).

1 small carrot, peeled

¼ small daikon (about 6 ounces/170 g), peeled and halved crosswise

¾ cup/180 ml unseasoned rice vinegar

2 tablespoons sugar

1½ teaspoons fine sea salt

**1)** Using a mandoline or plastic slicer, cut the carrot and daikon into strips about ⅛ inch/3 mm wide and 2 inches/5 cm long. You want about 1½ cups packed/160 g julienned vegetables. Put the vegetables in a 1-pint/480 ml jar or covered container.

**2)** Bring the vinegar, ¾ cup/180 ml water, the sugar, and salt to a boil in a small saucepan over high heat, stirring to dissolve the sugar. Pour over the vegetables and let cool. Use immediately or cover and refrigerate for up to 2 weeks.

# Spicy Cucumber Pickles

**Makes 1 pint/480 ml**

My friend and social media influencer H Woo Lee serves these with his Lobster Tempura Bao (page 98).

2 Kirby cucumbers (about 8 ounces/ 225 g), unpeeled but scrubbed

⅔ cup/165 ml unseasoned rice vinegar

¼ cup/50 g sugar

1 tablespoon fine sea salt

⅛ teaspoon Sichuan peppercorns

⅛ teaspoon crushed hot red pepper

**1)** Using a mandoline, plastic slicer, or large knife, cut the cucumbers into rounds about ⅛ inch/3 mm thick. Pack into a 1-pint/480 ml jar or covered container.

**2)** Bring the vinegar, ⅓ cup/80 ml water, the sugar, salt, Sichuan peppercorns, and hot red pepper to a boil in a small saucepan over high heat, stirring to dissolve the sugar. Pour over the cucumbers and let cool. Use immediately or cover and refrigerate for up to 5 days.

# My Hot Sauce

**Makes about 1 cup/240 ml**

It is fun and easy to make hot sauce. Chile fans will want to put this on everything. Experimenting with different chiles is part of the fun, and every batch will be a little different because of the variables. See the Notes for more details.

---

8 ounces/225 g assorted hot red chiles (such as red jalapeño, Fresno, or cayenne, singly or in combination)

1 cup/240 ml apple cider or white distilled vinegar, plus more as needed

2 cloves garlic, crushed and peeled

1 teaspoon sugar

½ teaspoon fine sea salt

**1)** Wearing protective gloves, stem and coarsely chop the chiles, seeds and all. (For a milder sauce, remove the ribs and seeds.) Transfer to a small saucepan (not unlined aluminum) and stir in the vinegar, garlic, sugar, and salt, adding enough vinegar to barely cover the chiles.

**2)** Bring to a boil over high heat. Reduce the heat to medium-low and cook at a low boil until the chiles are very tender, about 15 minutes. Stay clear of the fumes. Let cool completely.

**3)** Transfer the mixture (seeds and all) to a blender and blend until smooth. Pour into a clean 1-cup/240 ml glass canning jar (or use a funnel to fill a clean, small glass bottle) and cover. (The hot sauce can be refrigerated for up to 3 months. Shake well before using.)

## notes

- The level of heat will depend on the chiles and their ripeness. Fresno chiles (they look like pointed red jalapeños) are a good choice because they are spicy but not crazy-hot. Long, red cayenne chiles are spicier. Mix chiles as you wish to come up with your own "house hot sauce."

- If you are concerned that your sauce will be too spicy, substitute about half of the chiles with red bell pepper.

- Be sure to wear protective gloves when handling the chiles—blue rubber gloves have become common household items for me.

- Chile fumes are irritating, so don't breathe deeply near them when they are being cooked or ground in the blender.

- Don't mix green chiles with red chiles or the bright color will be dulled.

- After the sauce is pureed, taste a dab on a piece of bread or a cracker to gauge the heat. If it turned out too spicy, return to the blender and add a handful or so of chopped fruit (pineapple, peach, or mango are great) and puree. The fruit is a quick fix to balance the heat with sweetness.

- This makes a relatively thick hot sauce. For a thinner consistency, thin with a little more vinegar.

# Crispy Onion Rings

**Makes 2 to 4 servings**

Sometimes there is no substitute for good old onion rings. While they are famous as a side dish, they are good on sandwiches, too. Plus, onion rings are surprisingly easy to make.

1 large yellow onion, cut into ¼-inch/6 mm rings

1 cup/240 ml buttermilk

Fine sea salt and freshly ground black pepper

1 cup/140 g all-purpose flour

Vegetable or canola oil for deep-frying

**1)** Combine the onion rings, buttermilk, ½ teaspoon salt, and ¼ teaspoon pepper in a large bowl. Let stand for 10 to 15 minutes.

**2)** Put the flour in a shallow bowl. Pour enough oil to come about 3 inches/7.5 cm up the sides of a large heavy saucepan and heat over high heat until the oil reads 350°F/180°C on a deep-frying thermometer.

**3)** Place a wire cooling rack over a half-sheet pan. Preheat the oven to 200°F/95°C.

**4)** In batches, lift the onions from the buttermilk mixture and toss in the flour to coat well. A batter will form on the rings. Carefully add to the oil and fry until golden brown, about 3 minutes. Using a wire spider or slotted spoon, transfer to the rack and keep warm in the oven. Repeat with the remaining onions. Season with salt and pepper and serve hot.

# Frico Crisps

**Makes 4 to 5 crisps**

Friuli, a mountainous region in northern Italy, is the birthplace of the frico, a Parmigiano-Reggiano cheese crisp that adds crunch and cheese flavor to sandwiches. This is a good recipe to have in your repertoire when you need a quick appetizer to serve with wine. No matter what you use them for, they are fast, easy, and irresistible.

1 cup/100 g freshly grated Parmigiano-Reggiano cheese

Heat a medium nonstick skillet over medium heat. For each frico, sprinkle about 3 tablespoons of the cheese into the center of the skillet, making a 3- to 4-inch/7.5 to 10 cm round, spreading the cheese into shape with a fork. Cook until the cheese is bubbling, melted, and browning around the edges, about 1½ minutes. Using a spatula, loosen the edges of the frico all around, flip it over, and cook just to set the other side, about 10 seconds. Carefully transfer to paper towels to cool and set further. Repeat with the remaining cheese to make 4 or 5 crisps. Frico crisps are best used within an hour or so of making (humidity can cause them to soften).

# Oven French Fries

**Makes 4 to 6 servings**

While French fries are usually deep-fried, they are much easier to make when baked in the oven and every bit as good. Be as patient and precise as you can when cutting the potatoes for the most uniform slices. I advise against kitchen gadgets that do only one thing, but a French-fry cutter is useful if you make them a lot, or your mandoline or plastic slicer may have the right adjustment for cutting them. Always use starchy baking potatoes (russet or Idaho) for fries. Do not salt your fries until just before serving, or they will soften. Aside from that, you have many options—peeled, unpeeled, olive oil, canola oil . . . they all work.

2 large baking potatoes, about 1½ pounds/680 g, such as russet or Idaho, peeled (or unpeeled and scrubbed)

2 tablespoons olive, vegetable, or canola oil

Flaky sea salt and freshly ground black pepper

**1)** Preheat the oven to 400°F/200°C.

**2)** Using a large knife, trim the top and bottom of a potato so it will stand upright on a work surface. Cut the potato vertically into slabs about ¼ inch/6 mm to ½ inch/1.25 cm thick. Now stack a couple of slabs and cut lengthwise to make fries about the same width. Transfer the fries to a medium bowl. Repeat with the remaining potato. Drizzle with the oil and toss well to coat. Spread in a single layer on a half-sheet pan.

**3)** Bake for 30 minutes. Using a metal pancake turner, scrape the potatoes to loosen them from the pan and turn them over. If they are sticking, bake a few minutes more. Once turned, bake until golden brown, crisp, and tender, about 10 minutes. Transfer to paper towels or a brown paper bag to drain quickly. Season with salt and pepper, transfer to a serving dish, and serve hot.

# Roasted Garlic

# Deli-Style Coleslaw

**Makes about 2 tablespoons mashed garlic**

**Makes 6 to 8 servings**

Roasted garlic is now one of the most popular American flavors. Roasting mellows garlic's bite and lets it pair well with other ingredients. Get in the habit of roasting batches so you always have it on hand in the fridge to add a smear to your favorite sandwiches whenever the mood strikes you.

This is an all-purpose coleslaw that you can serve as a side, but it is versatile enough to be a topper, especially on fried chicken sandwiches. Crisp, creamy, and cool, it pushes all the buttons for this delicatessen classic. Honey gives the dressing a "just right" sweetness.

---

2 large firm heads garlic

Olive oil for drizzling

Fine sea salt and freshly ground black pepper

**1)** Preheat the oven to 400°F/200°C.

**2)** Using a large knife, cut each garlic head about ½ inch/1.25 cm from the top to make "lids," keeping the lids intact. Drizzle the garlic bottoms with oil and sprinkle with salt and pepper. Replace the lids in their original positions. Put the heads on a sheet of aluminum foil and wrap tightly. Put the garlic on a baking sheet.

**3)** Bake until the garlic flesh is golden and tender (open the foil to check), about 45 minutes, depending on the size of the garlic. Unwrap and let cool.

**4)** Squeeze the garlic flesh out of the hulls into a small bowl, discarding the hulls. Mash the flesh with a fork. (The roasted garlic can be refrigerated in a covered container, with a thin layer of olive oil poured on top, for up to 2 weeks.)

---

⅔ cup/80 ml mayonnaise

2 tablespoons cider vinegar

2 tablespoons honey

1 teaspoon Dijon mustard

½ teaspoon celery seeds

Fine sea salt and freshly ground black pepper

½ medium head green cabbage, cored and cut into thin shreds (about 6 cups/600 g)

1 large carrot, shredded

½ small red onion, thinly sliced

2 scallions, white and green parts, finely chopped

3 tablespoons finely chopped fresh flat-leaf parsley

Whisk the mayonnaise, vinegar, honey, mustard, celery seeds, 1 teaspoon salt, and ¼ teaspoon pepper in a large bowl. Add the cabbage, carrot, red onion, scallions, and parsley and mix well. Season with additional salt and pepper. Cover and refrigerate for at least 1 hour and up to 3 days. Stir well and serve chilled.

# Picnic Potato Salad

**Makes 6 to 8 servings**

My goal here is to provide you with an old-fashioned potato salad that pushes all the right buttons and will play nicely with any sandwich. Some people like a little sweetness to their potato salad, and if you fall into that category, swap sweet pickles and their brine for the dill. Starchy salads (like potato and pasta salads) change flavor as they stand, so always re-season them with salt and pepper, and maybe a splash of vinegar, before serving.

2 pounds/910 g red-skinned potatoes (about 6 potatoes), scrubbed

2 tablespoons dill or sweet pickle brine, plus more for seasoning

⅓ cup/80 ml mayonnaise

⅓ cup/80 ml sour cream

2 teaspoons Dijon mustard

2 hard-boiled eggs (see Note), cut into ½-inch/1.25 cm dice

2 celery ribs, cut into ¼-inch/6 mm dice

2 scallions, white and green parts, finely chopped

¼ cup/35 g finely chopped dill or sweet pickles

2 tablespoons finely chopped fresh flat-leaf parsley

Fine sea salt and freshly ground black pepper

**1)** Put the potatoes in a large saucepan and add enough cold salted water to cover them by 1 inch/2.5 cm. Cover the saucepan and bring to a boil over high heat. Reduce the heat to medium and set the lid ajar. Cook the potatoes at a steady simmer until tender when pierced with the tip of a small, sharp knife, 20 to 30 minutes. Drain and rinse under cold running water. Return the potatoes to the pot and fill it with cold water. Let stand until the potatoes are still warm but easy to handle, about 5 minutes.

**2)** Slice the potatoes into ½-inch/1.25 cm cubes, peeling them if you wish, and put them in a large bowl. Drizzle the brine over the warm potatoes and toss.

**3)** Whisk the mayonnaise, sour cream, and mustard in a large bowl. Stir into the potatoes. Add the eggs, celery, scallions, pickles, and parsley. Season with ½ teaspoon salt and ¼ teaspoon pepper. Cover and refrigerate until the salad is chilled, at least 2 hours or up to 3 days. Just before serving, taste and re-season the salad with additional salt, pepper, and brine. Serve chilled.

**note** To hard-boil eggs, bring a small saucepan of water to a boil over high heat. Using a slotted spoon, gently transfer the eggs to the water, being careful to avoid cracking the shells. Adjust the heat so the water is just boiling but isn't moving the eggs. Set a timer and cook for 13 minutes. Using the slotted spoon, transfer the eggs to a bowl of ice water. Let stand until the eggs are chilled, at least 5 minutes and up to 15 minutes.

# Buttermilk Sandwich Biscuits

**Makes 4 large biscuits**

This recipe makes large, tall, and fluffy biscuits perfect for your sandwich needs. For smaller biscuits to serve with a meal, cut the dough into 6 equal squares. I'm sharing all the tips I've learned about making beautiful Instagram-ready biscuits. These tricks include using a combination of buttermilk and heavy cream, folding the dough to create layers, trimming the edges for a clean lift, cutting into squares for heartier portions (thereby avoiding the scraps from stamping out round biscuits), and baking the biscuits with their sides touching for support to rise to loftier heights. I highly recommend baking a double batch and freezing some to always have on hand.

2 cups/280 g unbleached all-purpose flour, plus more for rolling

1 tablespoon baking powder

¼ teaspoon baking soda

2 teaspoons sugar

½ teaspoon fine sea salt

6 tablespoons/90 g (¾ stick) cold unsalted butter, cut into ½-inch/1.25 cm cubes

½ cup/120 ml buttermilk (see Note), or as needed

½ cup/120 ml heavy cream, or as needed

1) Preheat the oven to 400°F/200°C.

2) Whisk the flour, baking powder, baking soda, sugar, and salt together in a medium bowl. Add the butter and toss to separate and coat the cubes. Using a pastry blender or two knives, cut in the butter until the mixture resembles coarse breadcrumbs with some pea-sized bits. Mix the buttermilk and heavy cream together in a small bowl. Gradually stir in the liquid to make a shaggy dough, adding more or less as needed, being sure all dry bits are incorporated. Gather the dough together in the bowl.

3) On a lightly floured work surface, roll or pat out the dough into a 12 × 6-inch/30.5 × 15 cm rectangle. Brushing off excess flour, fold the dough in thirds, like a business letter. Turn the dough so the open seam faces the bottom. Flour again, pat or roll out the dough again into the same size rectangle, and fold as before. Turn so the open seam faces the bottom, and pat or roll into a 6¼-inch/15.25 cm square about 1 inch/2.5 cm thick. Using a sharp knife cutting down without dragging the knife, narrowly trim ¼ inch/6 mm from the rough sides to give the dough clean edges and end up with a neat 6-inch/15 cm square. Discard the scraps. (Or press the scraps together to make a single smaller biscuit and make it next to the others for a baker's treat.) Cut the dough in half horizontally and then vertically to make four 3-inch/7.5 cm squares. Transfer to an ungreased half-sheet pan with the sides of the biscuits barely touching each other.

4) Bake the biscuits until golden brown and risen, 20 to 25 minutes. Let cool on the pan for 10 minutes because piping-hot biscuits are very crumbly. Cut the biscuits apart, and then split with a serrated knife, if desired. (The completely cooled biscuits can be individually wrapped in plastic wrap and frozen in a plastic freezer bag for up to 3 months. Thaw at room temperature overnight. If you are in a hurry, microwave the unwrapped biscuit at Medium/50% power at 15-second intervals until thawed.)

**note** Serious bakers keep buttermilk on hand. It is used in many baking recipes, plus it can be a marinade base for fried chicken (Nashville Hot Fried Chicken Sandwich, page 62) or turned into ranch dressing (see page 141). Shake it well before using. Because buttermilk is cultured, it keeps a couple of months and sometimes even beyond its stamped expiration date. Powdered buttermilk is not recommended, as it is too thin when reconstituted.

5½ cups/805 g bread flour

1 tablespoon instant yeast (also called quick-rising or bread-machine yeast)

2 tablespoons extra virgin olive oil, plus more for the bowl, baking sheet, and drizzling

2¼ teaspoons fine sea salt

Flaky sea salt, such as Maldon (optional)

# Overnight Schiacciata

I fulfilled a bucket-list desire when I got to shoot a video at the New York outpost of the beloved Italian sandwich shop All'Antico Vinaio (At the Old Winemaker), which I already knew from their shop in Florence. I learned a lot about panini from them and one game-changer was their bread, called *schiacciata* ("smashed" in Italian, for the dimpling of the dough), the Tuscan version of focaccia. I make an easy, no-knead dough that bakes up thick and fluffy, ready for splitting into layers to hold your favorite cold cuts. This is a very wet dough, and the high moisture allows you to skip kneading, and the long fermentation creates a very light and airy flatbread. Because the dough needs to rise at least overnight, you can have it ready in the morning to bake for lunch. Leftovers freeze well.

**1)** At least one day before baking, stir the flour, 2¾ cups/660 ml water, the yeast, oil, and fine sea salt together in a large bowl to make a wet, sticky dough without any dry bits. Scrape down the sides of the bowl. Be sure to use a bowl large enough to hold the doubled dough. Cover with plastic wrap or a wet kitchen towel and let stand for 10 minutes.

**2)** Using a hand rinsed in cold water, grab the dough at the 12 o'clock position and stretch it above the rest of the dough by about 8 inches/20 cm. Fold the stretched dough over to the center of the remaining dough in the bowl. Working around the bowl at the 3, 6, and 9 o'clock positions, repeat the stretching process. The dough will get slightly firmer after each stretching. Cover with plastic wrap or a wet kitchen towel and let rest for 10 to 15 minutes. Repeat the process around the bowl for a total of four times, covering and resting for 10 to 15 minutes after each, for a total of four stretching processes over about an hour's time. After the last stretching, tightly cover the bowl with plastic wrap. Refrigerate the dough for at least 12 hours and up to 3 days (really, the longer the better, but don't obsess over it).

**3)** Generously grease the bottom and sides of a half-sheet pan with oil. Line the bottom of the baking sheet with parchment paper, then flip the paper over so the oiled side is up.

*Recipe continues*

**4)** Scrape the moist and sticky dough into the prepared pan. Using oiled hands, pat and stretch the dough to fit the pan as much as you can. Brush or drizzle the top of the dough with oil and loosely cover with plastic wrap. Let rest for 5 to 10 minutes to relax the gluten in the dough. Continue patting and stretching the dough under the plastic into an even layer, being sure it fills the corners of the pan. (If the dough still retracts, give it another few minutes' rest and try again.) Let it stand in a warm place (such as a turned-off oven with the door ajar so only the light is on; the ideal temperature is 75° to 80°F/24° to 26°C) until the dough doubles and reaches the top edge of the baking sheet, 1½ to 2 hours.

**5)** Position a rack in the center of the oven and preheat the oven to 400°F/200°C. (If the schiacciata is rising in the oven, don't forget to remove it first!)

**6)** Using your fingertips, stipple with ¼-inch (6 mm) deep "dimples" all over the top of the dough. Drizzle with olive oil to pool a little in the dimples. Sprinkle the top with flaky salt, if using. Bake until the schiacciata is golden brown, about 30 minutes. Let it cool for 10 minutes. Slip the dough on its paper out of the pan onto a chopping board and discard the paper. Let cool completely. Cut the schiacciata into six 6 × 5-inch/15 × 12.5 cm rectangles. (For smaller panini, cut into 8 portions.) The schiacciata is best the day of baking. (Or double wrap each portion in plastic wrap and freeze for up to 3 months. Thaw at room temperature before using.)

# Japanese Milk Bread

**Makes one 9 × 5-inch/23 × 12.5 cm loaf**

Fans of white sandwich bread can do no better than this tender and fluffy bread that is also called Hokkaido bread (after its origin, the Japanese island) or *shokupan* (or "eating bread," as it is perfect for toast, too). It is helpful to have this recipe if you have a craving for brick toast (page 197), which calls for an unsliced loaf, as it can be hard to locate in the US. The tangzhong roux method is used a lot by Asian bakers because the cooking gelatinizes the flour, leading to a very soft loaf that keeps well. One loaf will make four servings of brick toast.

### tangzhong

¼ cup/60 ml whole milk

2 tablespoons bread flour

———

### dough

2½ cups/350 g bread flour, plus more for the work surface

¼ cup/50 g sugar

One ¼-ounce/7 g packet instant yeast (also called quick-rising or bread-machine yeast; about 2¼ teaspoons)

1 teaspoon fine sea salt

½ cup/120 ml whole milk, plus more for brushing

1 large egg

4 tablespoons/56 g (½ stick) unsalted butter, softened well, plus more for the bowl, pan, and crust

**1) Make the tangzhong:** Whisk the milk, ¼ cup/60 ml water, and the flour in a small saucepan until smooth. Whisking often, bring to a boil over medium heat. Reduce the heat to low and cook for 30 seconds, or until very thick. Scrape into the bowl of a heavy-duty stand mixer and let cool until tepid, stirring often. (This happens quickly.)

**2) Make the dough:** Combine the flour, sugar, yeast, and salt in the bowl of a heavy-duty stand mixer. Whisk the milk and egg together and add to the bowl. Mix with the paddle attachment on low speed until a sticky and shaggy dough forms. Remove the paddle, scrape down the bowl, and cover the bowl with a kitchen towel. Let stand for 10 to 15 minutes. Affix the dough hook and knead on medium speed until the dough is smoother but sticks to the bottom of the bowl, about 3 minutes. One tablespoon at a time, add the butter, letting each addition be absorbed before adding more. From this point, knead until the dough is smooth but still sticking to the bottom of the bowl, about 3 minutes more. Do not add more flour, as this dough is supposed to be sticky and will become easier to handle as it rests and rises. Test the dough with the windowpane test (see page 239).

To make the dough by hand, stir all the ingredients together in a large bowl. Using a plastic bowl scraper, lift and slap the dough in the bowl to knead it for 3 minutes. One tablespoon at a time, work in the butter. Work the dough in the bowl until it is very smooth and passes the windowpane test (see page 239), about 5 minutes more.

**3)** Butter a medium bowl. Scrape the dough out onto a lightly floured work surface and shape into a ball. Place in the bowl smooth side down, turn to coat with butter, and leave smooth side up. Cover with plastic wrap and let stand in a warm place (such as an oven with the door ajar and its light on) until the dough doubles in volume (if you poke a hole in the dough with a finger, the hole will slowly fill in), about 1 hour.

*Recipe continues*

**237**

**4)** Lightly butter a 9 × 5-inch/23 × 12.5 cm loaf pan. Turn out the dough onto a lightly floured work surface and knead briefly to expel the air. Divide the dough into three equal pieces. Pat and stretch one piece into an oval about 12 inches/30.5 cm long and 4 inches/10 cm wide. Fold in the right and left sides to overlap slightly in the center, then tightly roll up the dough from the bottom. Pinch the seams closed to make a roll about 5 inches/12.5 cm long. Fit the roll at one end of the loaf pan, running across the pan's width. Repeat with the remaining two portions of dough, placing them side by side, to fill the pan. Cover loosely with plastic wrap. Let stand in a warm place until the dough rises almost 1 inch/2.5 cm over the top of the pan, about 1 hour. The loaf should look quite puffy.

**5)** While the dough is rising, position a rack in the center of the oven and preheat the oven to 350°F/180°C.

**6)** Brush the top of the dough lightly with milk. Bake until the loaf is golden brown, about 25 minutes. (An instant-read thermometer inserted into the center will read about 200°F/95°C.) Brush the top of the bread with some softened butter. Let cool completely in the pan on a wire cooling rack. (Wrapped in plastic, the bread will keep for about 5 days at room temperature.)

## the windowpane test

The windowpane test is a surefire method for checking that your dough has been sufficiently kneaded. With well-floured fingers, pull off a walnut-sized ball of dough. Press into a flat disk. Gently pull and stretch the dough from all sides. If it easily stretches into a membrane without breaking (a "windowpane," if you will), showing that you have created a nice gluten structure in the dough, then the kneading is done. If the dough tears easily, continue kneading for another couple of minutes and try again.

# Acknowledgments

I am deeply grateful to all those who made this journey with me, from social media to cookbook author, offering their support, wisdom, and encouragement along the way.

First and foremost, I'd like to extend my sincerest thanks to my coauthor Rick Rodgers. This collaborative endeavor wouldn't have been possible without his expertise and commitment to our shared vision.

Thank you to my manager, Noah Swimmer. You're the man—and I wouldn't be where I am now without your hard work. I love working with the people at align Public Relations. Here is a shout-out to Megan Smith, Madison Stewart, Taylor Rodriguez, and Megan Dunn for all you do for me. My literary agents, Mia Vitale and Sarah Passick, believed in this project from the start. Sarah Pelz, my editor at Harper Harvest, and her assistant, Emma Effinger, helped shape and refine this manuscript. Also, my gratitude goes out to designer and art director Melissa Lotfy, who established the book's vibrant look.

To my exceptional cookbook photographer, Ren Fuller, and her team of Ashli Buts and Ty Ferguson (photo assistants), Carrie Purcell (food stylist), Daniela Swamp and April Rankin (food styling assistants), Jaclyn Kershek (prop stylist), and Haylie Harwood and Hina Mistry (prop styling assistants): Thank you all for capturing each moment with your positive energy, making the entire photo process incredibly smooth and enjoyable.

To my close friends and fellow social media creators, and our followers—your unwavering support and shared passion have been a driving force for me. There are many people whom I could thank, but I need to call out two people in particular. First, Salt Hank, my sandwich "adversary." You may not know it, but you have pushed me to be better, and I cherish the friendship we've built. And to my dear friend H Woo Lee, from our days of cooking for USC students to your dedicated encouragement, pushing me onto social media, you've always had my back. I genuinely believe that I wouldn't be where I am today if I had never met you. Your friendship and support have been immeasurable, and I'm beyond grateful for your influence.

And last, but certainly not least, thank you to my incredible family for always being my support system. To my grandmothers, Nonna and Ma, whose heritage-inspired dishes fed my soul and ignited my love for cooking, and to my mom and dad, who showed me how to savor the world's flavors, often right in their original settings, and opened my eyes to the beauty of global cuisine. To my siblings, Olimpia, Oliver, and Octavien (aka Bam), who shared countless meals, laughs, and learning moments by my side. (Sorry for always stealing your food, Bam!) Your influence is at the heart of this book.

# Index

Note: Page references in *italics* indicate photographs.